BOB DYLAN

Celebrities series

Series editor: Anthony Elliott

Published:

Dennis Altman: *Gore Vidal's America*
Ellis Cashmore: *Beckham* 2nd edition
Ellis Cashmore: *Tyson*
Charles Lemert: *Muhammad Ali*
Chris Rojek: *Frank Sinatra*
Nick Stevenson: *David Bowie*

Lee Marshall is a lecturer in Sociology at the University of Bristol where he specialises in popular music. His first book, *Bootlegging: Romanticism and Copyright in the Music Industry* (2005) was awarded the Socio-Legal Studies Association's Hart Early Career Prize.

BOB DYLAN

THE NEVER ENDING STAR

LEE MARSHALL

polity

First published in 2007 by Polity Press

Polity Press
65 Bridge Street
Cambridge CB2 1UR, UK

Polity Press
350 Main Street
Malden, MA 02148, USA

ISBN-13: 978-07456-3641-2
ISBN-13: 978-07456-3642-9 (pb)

A catalogue record for this book is available from the British Library.

Typeset in 10.75 on 14 pt Adobe Janson
by Servis Filmsetting Ltd, Manchester
Printed and bound in Great Britain by
MPG Printers Ltd, Bodmin, Cornwall

The publisher has used its best endeavours to ensure that the URLs for
external websites referred to in this book are correct and active at the time
of going to press. However, the publisher has no responsibility for the
websites and can make no guarantee that a site will remain live or that the
content is or will remain appropriate.

For further information on Polity, visit our website: www.polity.co.uk

For Catherine,
my fairest critic

CONTENTS

Dylan's sixties stardom
Dylan's emergence in the folk revival and the contra-
dictions of being a 'folk star'. His move into rock, polit-
ical individualism and the tensions between culture and
commerce. Dylan's withdrawal from the scene in the

late sixties. His attempts to reclaim his stardom and their effect on the rest of his career.

Dylan's later stardom
Changing social values and Dylan's problems in the 1980s. Dylan's attempt to reconstruct the relationship with his audience. An overview of the Never Ending Tour and its key features. Debates about Dylan's later work. Time Out Of Mind *and the changes in Dylan's stardom since 1997.*

ACKNOWLEDGEMENTS

I guess that the first mention should go to my dad, as it was through his scratched LPs that I first heard the music that has held me enthralled for so long (even if I was resistant at first). Thanks should also be offered to the other members of my family, who are always wonderfully supportive, and to Catherine, who really does have to put up with far too much and attends more Dylan shows than necessary without complaint. On that subject, thanks to all those I have passed time with at gigs – Mike, Elaine, Pauline, Les, Step and Steve to name just a few. It is a remarkable feeling to arrive at a show alone in the safe knowledge that I'll soon bump into someone I know. Following Dylan has given me some of my longest-lasting friends, even if (or is it because?) we only see each other a couple of times a year

It was series editor Anthony Elliot who first asked me to write a book on Dylan. It was something I said I would never do, but in the end I'm glad I did, and so I am grateful for his request. Andrea Drugan at Polity has been very helpful and, unusually for a publisher in my experience, has actually shown an interest in the work. Several people have read draft chapters of this book, so my thanks go to: Catherine Dodds, Simon Frith, Dai Griffiths, Dave Hesmondhalgh, Gregor McLennan and Graham Stephenson. All of you offered very useful advice, most of which I was sensible enough to take. A particular mention should go to Keith Negus, who offered me engaged comments on many parts of the book and encouragement to persist with my ideas.

A NOTE ON REFERENCING

'Song Titles' are written in quotation marks; *Albums* in italics. Any substantive footnote is marked with an asterisk and given on the bottom of the page; endnotes, which are numbered, merely provide reference to academic sources.

1

INTRODUCTION

I have experienced many spellbinding moments at Bob Dylan's concerts, but one stands out: Bournemouth, 1 October 1997. Dylan's new album, *Time Out Of Mind*, had been released at the start of the week and many of us congregating on the front few rows were hoping to hear some songs from it. All through the main set, however, there was nothing new and by its end I had resigned myself to the fact that the new songs would have to wait, consoled that it had been a very good show regardless. Then, as he returned for the encores, the opening bars of 'Love Sick' creaked through the air, and Dylan stepped up to the mike and began the song. The moment was electric. The reason I remember it so clearly, however, is not just the excitement of hearing a live debut but, rather, a realisation I had during it. Towards the end of the song, Dylan sang:

I'm sick of love, I wish I'd never met you
I'm sick of love, I'm trying to forget you

I felt at that moment that Dylan was singing directly to us, the audience in front of him. That 'you' for which he expressed so much contempt was actually us. The love he was so sick of was that given to him by the thousands of fans around the world. There is a sting in this tale, though, for in the song's final lines, the singer himself capitulates:

Just don't know what to do
I'd give anything to be with you

Whether or not I'm right in this reading of 'Love Sick', it is certainly true that Dylan's relationship with his audience has always been marked by this kind of ambivalence. Around the same time as the Bournemouth show, he said in an interview that:

A lot of people don't like the road but it's as natural to me as breathing. I do it because I'm driven to do it, and I either hate it or love it. I'm mortified to be on the stage but, then again, it's the only place where I'm happy. It's the only place you can be who you want to be. You can't be who you want to be in daily life. (Jon Pareles interview, 1997)

This ambivalence has been a defining feature of Dylan's career since he emerged as a star in 1962. Since then he has been involved in what at times seems like a constant battle with fans and media over what he should perform, how he should relate to others, how he should act, and more. Such ambivalence inhabits his songs:

People see me all the time, and they just can't
      remember how to act
Their minds are filled with big ideas, images and
      distorted facts

                                        ('Idiot Wind')

In short, Dylan has been in a battle about what the concept 'Bob Dylan' means. This book is about that battle. It is not, however, a biography detailing a poor, misunderstood singer harassed from all sides, constantly misinterpreted by the media. It is instead a sociological account of Dylan's stardom. Dylan is a singer, a songwriter, a live performer, but, more than anything else, Dylan is a star. His stardom is an essential feature of his existence. It is the lens through which everything in his life is understood, not just his creative achievements but inherently personal things like fatherhood and divorce. Because Dylan is a star, his life has public meaning. This means that what 'Bob Dylan' stands for is open to social determination and not under the control of Dylan himself.

This project differs from existing work on Dylan in that it seeks to present a sociological account of his stardom rather than either a biography or a textual analysis of his lyrics (though both of these provide material for a sociological analysis). Conventional biographies take a 'subjectivist' approach to their topic, concentrating on the life of the star by looking solely at biographical detail. Such an approach tends to portray the star's stardom as a series of discrete, visible, relationships (such as that between star and record label). These relationships are used to construct a coherent story of a life that is, to a greater or lesser extent, orchestrated by the star. This is problematic in a number of ways. Most significantly, it places too much power in the hands of the star – the star's career is seen as the result of decisions and actions taken by the star or her representatives. This is understandable because it tends to be how we view everyday life too – we see ourselves as the 'author' of our own lives. However, we are not the authors of our own lives, at least not totally. The chances of obtaining a high level of education, or good health, or a living wage, depend on a variety of factors such as class, race, nationality and gender which are beyond our control. Similarly, even though stars may be extremely powerful agents, what a particular star means or achieves depends on factors outside of their control, and may well happen 'behind their back' (including those just mentioned: think of the ten 'greatest' rock stars, and count how many of them are black and/or female). To take an obvious example, how a particular star is portrayed and understood depends on a relationship between media and audiences that is completely independent of the star's control. This is a clearly observable phenomenon, but there are less observable factors too: how does Dylan's stardom relate to the rise of consumerism, for example? Whatever we may like to think, Dylan is not famous just because of the quality of his work. Wider social factors have enabled his stardom to develop in certain ways and closed off other possibilities. In this way, he is no different from any other star.

This leads me to the second weakness of the subjectivist approach: it presumes that the star's success is the direct result of skill or charisma. This is not true. Neither of these is a necessary or sufficient condition of stardom. Many untalented people become stars, while many charismatic people do not. It is not inevitable that Dylan would be a success because he was talented; it was not inevitable that he would have such a long career in popular music. Charisma is not a natural trait, it is a social effect. This is not to imply that stars are not viewed as charismatic – some obviously are, and this is important – but a range of social conditions must be in place that enable an individual's talents and personality to become recognised as skilful and charismatic. Concepts such as 'revolutionary', 'groundbreaking', 'skill' and 'charisma' are socially organised, defined and valued differently in different times and places. We need, therefore, to investigate the social circumstances in which Dylan emerged and has continued to exist as a star.

An overall criticism of the biographical approach would be to say that it seeks an explanation for the stardom of an individual solely within the life story of that individual. However, I think it is more effective to follow Pierre Bourdieu's suggestion: 'We must . . . ask, not how a writer comes to be what he is . . . but rather how the position or "post" he occupies – that of a writer of a particular type – became constituted.'[1] Too often, biographies show an unwillingness to investigate important contextual factors, or to consider the similarities between their particular star and other stars. This conformity is also something that fans rarely consider. A star is assumed to be unique. Yet, actually, the life stories of stars share many things in common. Consider the following:

> For the essence of his art has always derived from the tension between his impulse to truth and his instinct to hide.[2]

This will surely ring true to Dylan fans; it could have been pulled from any Dylan biography. It is, however, from Richard Schickel's description of Marlon Brando and I could find similar quotes in biographies of Robbie Williams, Kurt Cobain and hundreds of others. Despite the emphasis on uniqueness, stars' stories are never unique. Complaints about misrepresentation, invasion of privacy, and conflicts with management are features of most stars' lives. Stardom is something more than just the life stories of a bunch of famous people and this means that *we need to consider stardom as a system*, one with distinctive characteristics and effects. To do so gives us a much richer understanding of the star in question.

Dylan fans may have noticed that I haven't talked much about Dylan yet. This is out of necessity, as this chapter outlines the theoretical map for how I'll discuss Dylan later. At this juncture, it is probably useful to clarify some of the concepts I'm bandying about. You may think it odd to be considering Bob Dylan in a book series called 'Celebrities' because you don't consider Dylan to be a celebrity. In contemporary culture, 'celebrity' often refers to people such as reality TV participants, quickly popular and quickly forgotten. Dylan, on the other hand, has had a career of over forty-five years and, you may reasonably think, deserves his success because of the work he has produced. That is why I have concentrated on Dylan's stardom rather than celebrity. Evans suggests that 'star' is often used to describe an individual famous for their achievements in a particular field,[3] so we tend to talk of 'film stars' and 'pop stars' rather than 'film celebrities' or 'pop celebrities'. To this I would add that a star is someone who produces a body of work that has some existence outside of the individual celebrity's person (unlike, say, a reality TV participant). Dylan is thus a star rather than a celebrity in the conventional sense. His public existence shares things in common with celebrities but there are distinctive elements too, characteristic of a certain type of celebrity – stardom.

Dylan is not just a star, however, but a particular kind of star – a rock star. The first sustained academic work into famous media figures concentrated on film stars. This is mainly the result of film emerging as the first audio-visual mass media with an established 'star-system'. It is surprising, however, given their significance over the last fifty years, that so little subsequent work has been conducted on popular music stars. Only one or two books have dealt with the specific phenomenon of popular music stardom, so while the literature on stardom is useful for this study, there are particularities of popular music that need to be considered. Popular music stars seem to me to fall somewhere in between film stars and television personalities (such as Michael Parkinson and David Letterman). Unlike film stars,

TV personalities are generally assumed to be 'being them-selves' on screen (Turner suggests that, for this reason, TV personalities are more characteristic of modern celebrity than film stars).[4] This is useful for considering rock stars because they too are often assumed to be 'being themselves' rather than playing a specific character – this is the subject of the next chapter.

There is one final distinction I would like to make here, between 'stardom' and 'star-image', as I am using them to mean slightly different things. Star-image is relatively straightforward: it refers to all of the specific things we know or think we know about a particular star. The star-image is the 'what is' of a star. This does not necessarily mean the actual 'this is what really happened' biography of the star, because it can include inaccuracies, urban legends, malicious lies, images and distorted facts. A star's star-image refers to everything – true and false – that is publicly known about that specific star. In this way, the star-image is similar to how Stephen Scobie defines Bob Dylan as 'a text – made up of all the formal biographies, newspaper stories, internet statistics and just plain gossip that has entered into public circulation'.[5] The star-image is thus an observable phenomenon which can be uncovered through empirical research (Clinton Heylin's work, for example, adds to Dylan's star-image by increasing the amount of biographical information we know).

While 'star-image' concerns the empirical, verifiable, on-the-ground elements of a particular star, 'stardom' is less easily recognised as it exists mainly at an ideological level.*

---

* The notion of ideology is extremely complex, and contested, but, briefly, I would define it as the ideas and beliefs through which we, individually and socially, make sense of the world. Depending on one's perspective, this can be an entirely neutral thing or it can be the way through which power-ful social groups impose their own belief systems upon less powerful groups.

With its intrinsic relationship to ideas such as individualism, meritocracy, democracy and personality, stardom plays
a significant role in reproducing the ideological structures
of contemporary society. The fact that ideology is taken for
granted, and the fact that it is not immediately visible to us
makes it more problematic for studying it in relation to a
particular star. Whereas 'star-image' is all about the individual star, stardom is (in one sense) not 'about' the star at
all. It is, however, impossible to fully understand the star
without understanding the ideology of stardom. Dylan's
star-image is structured (enabled and constrained) by his
stardom, by the ideological elements of stardom more generally. We need an understanding of stardom's ideology in
order to understand how Dylan's career has turned out as it
has.

In order to gain a deeper understanding of Bob Dylan, we
therefore need to draw on the insights of the literature on
both stardom and celebrity, as well as the wider literature on
popular music. I do not intend to provide an exhaustive
overview of this work here, but I do want to emphasise the
key elements as it provides the intellectual framework for the
rest of this book. The following points are generally applicable to both stardom and celebrity, but they explain the overall system rather than describing specific individuals. To be a
star, or a celebrity, it is not necessary to tick all of these boxes
(some stars do, but it's not an entrance requirement), but
most stars will cover most of these points, which reflect the
most important characteristics of celebrity and stardom in
general.

Stardom is an inherently modern phenomenon Although 'fame'
existed in pre-modern times, this was mainly associated
with either royalty or as posthumous recognition for great
achievements. The contemporary ideas of celebrity are a

product of mass society and the emergence of a leisure culture since the eighteenth century, the result of deep-rooted ideological factors and technological advancement that accelerated in the twentieth century. The key characteristic of modern celebrity is what Schickel refers to as the 'illusion of intimacy',[6] the idea that we 'really know' those who are famous, even though we have (in the main) never met them.

Stardom fulfils ideological functions As a modern phenomenon, stardom is intricately bound up with two key ideological pillars of modern society: individualism and democracy. Stars are the ultimate individuals who supposedly become famous because of their unique individuality (their 'personality', a word which gains its modern meaning from stardom). At the same time, however, they also highlight the meritocracy of modern society because fame is no longer dependent upon being born into the right family. Anyone can be a star if they work hard enough, are talented enough, or lucky enough.

Stardom fulfils industrial functions Rojek describes modern celebrity as a marriage of democracy and capitalism.[7] One of the reasons that stardom exists is that it provides a means to transform unique personalities into commodities. In all of the media industries, stardom plays a crucial role in their organisational structure as they help control the inherent instability of media markets. Failure rates in media industries are high – around 90 per cent of released records fail to make a profit – and creating stars is one way in which the industries can create a guaranteed audience. I'll buy Bob Dylan's next album without knowing what it sounds like because I am a fan. The central activity of a record label is not making records, but creating stars.[8]

Stars have a representative function By their very existence, stars always represent the ideals of individualism and democracy, but stars also tend to stand for, or symbolise, something more. It could be that they represent a cultural stereotype – the tortured artist starving in a garret, for example – and therefore serve to reinforce that stereotype. But a star could also represent something more tangible, like Black Power, or a particular geographical region, such as Liverpool. But in all cases, a star 'always represents something more than him- or herself'.[9]

Stars unite subjectivities Because of their representative function, stars bring people together – sometimes literally (for example, Martin Luther King), more often emotionally, uniting people through belonging to a particular group, a particular audience. Some writers see this as a positive thing (for example: Rojek suggests that Sinatra 'articulate[d] a basis for identification and recognition [that is] the basis for developing collective consciousness').[10] Others see it as potentially dangerous, with Marshall suggesting that 'the emergence of the celebrity is connected to . . . the strategies employed by various institutions to contain the threat and irrationality of the mass [audience]'.[11]

These issues will receive further elaboration during the course of this book.

Recognising the systemic nature of stardom raises questions over the best way to study it. The biographical approach may pay inadequate attention to sociological factors, but we must be attuned to the individual circumstances as well. Stardom is not just structural, it is also the result of actions by individuals and social groups.[12] It does matter what individuals do. Social structures such as meritocracy and consumerism do not just reproduce themselves but are reproduced through the actions of individuals and groups. We therefore need to consider how stardom is reproduced through micro-social interactions (for example, how a particular manager talks to a particular magazine editor), while keeping in mind that stardom is produced within a specific social environment that constrains the ways in which the manager and the magazine editor can act (for example, whether interviewing a particular star could cause controversy and lead to revenue shortfalls).

If a charge can be laid against me in this book, it is that I have not paid enough attention to this type of micro-interaction. There is very little discussion of the strategies employed by Albert Grossman, Dylan's first manager, in amplifying Dylan's early stardom, nor in how Dylan himself manipulated the media in his early days (Robert Shelton's biography is good on this kind of detail). There is no doubt that Dylan would not have become as big a star as he did without Grossman, so his absence will be notable to some. Similarly, there is little direct discussion about how Dylan's later stardom has been strategically managed, for example, by Jeff Rosen in determining what recordings are released as part of *The Bootleg Series*. The lack of emphasis on these issues does not indicate that I think they are unimportant. On the contrary, they are very important, and one of the problems of studying stardom is that, if such management strategies are well executed, then we see only their effects and not their implementation. However, they are not my focus in this book. This project is targeted slightly differently, in that I am looking at how the social meaning of Dylan's star-image has developed and changed over his career. I am therefore approaching Dylan's stardom in relatively broad terms. My goal is to provide an overall framework for how Dylan has been understood and interpreted throughout his career, based on ongoing documentary analysis (through my role as

a fan) and the broader contextualisation of an academic sociologist. Dylan is a popular text and, as such, is open to many
different 'readings'. Such readings are not random, however,
but structured and I want to map out that structure. Social
relations are not just micro-social, they are macro-social too.
My argument may seem exaggerated at times, but I would
hope that most fans would agree with the general drift of my
framework.

This book therefore looks at Dylan's stardom in more
holistic terms. Dylan has been a star for a very long time,
and the meaning of his stardom has changed over that
period. What affected his emergence and these changes?
How was the meaning of his stardom facilitated by particular
historical circumstances, and constrained by others? Why
did a 'Bob Dylan' emerge in the sixties? What impact did his
emergence have on others, or on his later stardom? At the
same time, however, I have no intention of writing Bob
Dylan out of Bob Dylan's story, of turning him into a powerless individual at the whim of social forces, powerless to prevent the misinterpretation of what he represents. It is
certainly true that I will concentrate on the details of Dylan's
life less than conventional biographies of him – this is a necessary counterbalance to accounts that give him too much
power – but Dylan has actively negotiated his star-image; in
song, in public appearances and performances, in interviews
and, recently, in autobiography. This question of Dylan's
agency, of his power to shape his image, is important and
features particularly heavily in two chapters which look at
times when Dylan has deliberately attempted to reconstruct
his star-image – the late sixties and the late eighties.

My overall argument is that Dylan's stardom has been
closely tied to the idea of 'rock'. If stars always represent
something other than themselves, the marker 'Bob Dylan'
has often symbolised rock and the restless ideals of sixties

youth. How rock itself is conceptualised therefore impacts on Dylan's own star-image. After the more theoretical introduction (this chapter and chapter 2), the book follows a broadly chronological structure. There are three chapters that deal with the emergence of rock in the sixties and Dylan's starring role within it. The third of these chapters (chapter 5) is a pivotal one; it discusses how Dylan's stardom became firmly associated with the ideals of rock even as he attempted to move away from it. Dylan dropping out of the scene at the very moment that rock critics were canonising him as the most important figure in rock had a defining impact on Dylan's later stardom. The final part of the book (chapters 6–8) concentrates on his later career. Dylan's career beyond the sixties has received woefully inadequate coverage (for example, Howard Sounes' biography has 300 pages on the sixties, 107 pages on the seventies, and 98 pages on the eighties and nineties combined). Some of the material in chapter 5 explains this imbalance, but I intend this book to partially rectify it. In particular, I look at how Dylan's stardom was constructed in such a way that made it difficult for him to shake off his mythical history. This problem was most acute in the 1980s, when Dylan seemed out of place in the remodelled music industry. His way of managing this problem was to begin the 'Never Ending Tour', an extraordinary project that successfully redefined his stardom, resulting in a remarkable return to the limelight which began in 1997.

2

STARDOM, AUTHORSHIP AND THE MEANING OF SONGS

On 31 October 1964, Bob Dylan played a concert at the Philharmonic Hall in New York. He began to play the song 'If You Gotta Go, Go Now (Or Else You Got To Stay All Night)' with a shrill blast of his harmonica but stopped as his guitar was out of tune. 'Don't let that scare ya', Dylan assured his audience, 'it's just Halloween. [pause] I have my Bob Dylan mask on.' After another short pause he exclaimed, 'I am mask-erading!' and giggled, evidently pleased with his pun. Fast forward eleven years to another Halloween concert, the second night of his first *Rolling Thunder Revue* tour. Without warning, Dylan appeared on stage wearing a plastic Richard Nixon mask, and wore it through the entire first song, 'When I Paint My Masterpiece'. Two years later, this performance would feature as the opening to Dylan's movie *Renaldo and Clara* in which Dylan played the role of Renaldo while actor Ronnie Hawkins played 'Bob Dylan'. Dylan's estranged wife, Sara, played the role of Clara while another actress, Ronnee Blakeley, played 'Sara Dylan'.

Dylan evidently likes playing around with the idea of Bob Dylan. This is perhaps unsurprising given his life as a public figure, as a celebrity. One of the major ways that we think about celebrities is through a discrepancy between the 'public' celebrity and the 'private' individual. Many celebrities have commented that they play up to their celebrity image, acting out that persona – becoming 'Keith Richards' – for the public sphere. Still more celebrities have bemoaned the lack of privacy afforded them. Indeed, we may perhaps consider whether celebrities are prohibited from having a 'private life' at all. Dylan seemingly understands his own public status this way. In 1986 he stated that 'I'm only Bob Dylan when I have to be' and when asked who he was the rest of the time, replied 'myself'.[1] There is much written on Dylan that takes this kind of approach. Heylin, for example, argues that the goal of his book is 'to establish the relationship between [the] artist and the man'[2] while Larry David Smith goes further, arguing that 'Bob Dylan' is a consistent persona controlled by its creator Robert Zimmerman.[3] These books offer evidence for Frith's contention that the main role of pop biographies is to expose the 'real' individual that cannot be heard in their music.[4] Frith's comment, however, points to a further issue – the fact that there is not only the 'private individual' and 'public figure' to consider, but also a third, external, factor: the work. I said in the first chapter that we must consider Dylan as a star rather than merely a celebrity because he has produced a body of work that in some ways stands apart from him. So how does this work relate to Dylan's stardom, and vice versa? Discussing film stars, Dyer states that, in general, 'films have a distinct and privileged place in a star's image'.[5] This is generally true for rock stars also (their music has a privileged place), but things are complicated by the fact that rock stars commonly perform 'as themselves'. Dyer argues that, in analysing film stars,

we must distinguish between authorship of films and authorship of star-image,[6] but such a distinction is more problematic when analysing rock stars. Dylan is a star because of his
songs just as Jack Nicholson is famous because of his films,
but those two uses of 'his' mean different things: the actor
may add considerable qualities to a film but, in most cases, he
does not write the script and, while the actor's presence in a
film is never completely subsumed by the character he is
playing, the actor is famous for pretending to be other
people. Dylan, on the other hand, became famous for performing songs he had written and the impression is that
when he performs these songs he performs as himself. We are
thus left with an entanglement of various concepts – private
self, artist, singer, writer, star, work – that all coalesce in the
figure of a 5 feet 8 inches tall, 65-year-old, Jewish American
man. I don't think these things can ever be disentangled, but
in this chapter I want to pull them apart a little, not in order
to uncover the 'real' Bob Dylan, but to better understand
how we think about him, and stars and artists more generally.

AUTHORSHIP AND SONG MEANING

Let me begin by raising some familiar issues concerning
Dylan as the writer of his own songs. Consider the following
lines:

> I'll tell it and think it and speak it and breathe it
> And reflect from the mountains so all souls can see it
> ('A Hard Rain's A-Gonna Fall')

> In fourteen months I've only smiled once and I didn't
>   do it consciously
> Somebody's got to find your trail, I guess it must be up
>   to me
> ('Up To Me')

I used to care, but things have changed
('Things Have Changed')

Can we ever assume that the 'I' is the person Bob Dylan? Do the words offer a glimpse into Bob Dylan's personality? There are very few songs by Dylan in which he explicitly adopts the voice of a specific character (for example, in 'North Country Blues' he takes on the voice of a miner's widow, while he adopts the character of a dispossessed worker in 'Workingman's Blues #2'). The majority of his songs feature an 'I' (one even features an 'I and I'), that could be interpreted as the singer. So who is the I in these songs? Is it the songwriter himself?

There is certainly a common-sense way in which we take songs as an index of the writer's innermost self. For example, in Howard Sounes' biography, he states that Dylan 'would occasionally open up to girlfriends. But it was in his songs that he really revealed himself',[7] while Paul Williams states that 'Dylan's true autobiography, as with any artist, is his work, in which he consciously and unconsciously shares everything that occurs in his inner and outer life'.[8] Such an idea is part of the legacy of Romanticism, an ideology of art that emerged in the late eighteenth and nineteenth centuries that was developed most by poets.* M. H. Abrams' detailed account of these ideas explains how the determination of a poem's value shifted fundamentally during this period.[9] In pre-Romantic times, art was understood as a mirror reflecting society. A poem was therefore deemed successful if it reflected the world around it. During the latter half of the

---

* Romanticism was also a highly influential ideology within classical music. As the least representational of the arts, music was often assumed to be the most personally expressive. Today, we still tend to consider poetry and song as more personally expressive than either novels or plays, and this had a considerable impact on the development of rock.

eighteenth century this radically altered so that poetry came to be understand not as a 'mirror' but as a 'lamp', illuminating the deepest, most profound emotions of the author. What mattered now was not whether the work was an accurate portrayal of the world but whether it was an honest representation of its creator. These assumptions often colour how we perceive songs; if we assume that the song offers an insight into the real Bob Dylan, it is only a small jump to assuming that the 'I' of a Bob Dylan song must therefore *be* Dylan. Two albums in particular are prone to this sort of analysis: *Blood On The Tracks* (1975), which is widely considered to document the disintegration of Dylan's marriage; and *Time Out Of Mind* (1997), which is conventionally understood as Dylan reflecting on his 'brush with death' earlier that year.* This kind of response, one that uses the author as the frame of reference for the work's meaning, is criticised by many literary critics. In 1954, W. K. Wimsatt and Monroe Beardsley published an article called 'The Intentional Fallacy', in which they argued that we can never assume a text means what the author says it means – the text must stand alone. The intentional fallacy is part of a 'new criticism' that developed in literary studies from the 1920s and was most influential during the 1950s and 1960s. The central tenet of new criticism is that the only way to understand the meaning of a work is through close textual analysis of the work itself. The work says what it says; the meaning of a work is embedded in the words on the page and thus the new critics rejected any form of interpretation that relied on sources other than the work itself, and they were especially critical of any use of biography to explain what a text meant. Even if we can obtain detailed diary entries, or interview

---

* Dylan did not really have a brush with death; the episode is discussed in the last chapter.

comments (for example, Dylan undertook many interviews in 1977 to try to explain what he was attempting in *Renaldo And Clara*), we cannot use them to infer any meaning in the text. According to this approach, only the text can show us what it means and we can only find this out through forensic scholarship.

The ideas of the new critics bear some similarity to those outlined by Roland Barthes in his famous 1968 essay 'The Death of the Author', which also argues that the intentions of the author should not be used as a way of determining the meaning of a work. However, whereas 'The Intentional Fallacy' argues that the meaning of a work is inherent in the work itself, 'The Death of the Author' argues that the meaning of a text is generated by the act of reading. Rather than persist in close textual analysis, we need to see how readers create meaning by interpreting the work in relation to other cultural texts, ideas, beliefs, values and so on. This approach has the advantage of highlighting the social nature of how cultural meaning is reproduced and circulated. By concentrating on how the reader generates meaning, issues such as how, when and where the text is used become important.

As an example of how 'reading' generates meaning, consider the line 'Even the president of the United States sometimes must have to stand naked' from the song 'It's Alright Ma (I'm Only Bleeding)'. The song was written in 1964, performed at concerts that year and the next and, in 1965, was released on the album *Bringing It All Back Home*. The line was not held up for special scrutiny and did not receive any special audience response. When he returned to touring in 1974, Dylan performed the song regularly. This time, however, the line elicited a specific response: a spontaneous cheer from the crowd because of the ongoing Watergate scandal, during which President Nixon was incriminated in a burglary of Democratic Party offices. Concerts from this tour were recorded and released as a live album, *Before The Flood*. This meant that a much wider audience became aware of the crowd's reaction at these shows and for the next twenty years or so, the 'spontaneous' cheer became a standard response to the line whenever Dylan performed the song. In the late 1990s, to my ears at least, the meaning of the cheer changed once more, this time to irony, as then president Bill Clinton faced allegations of sexual impropriety. In more recent years, the cheer has perhaps gained a new political significance as a response to George W. Bush's presidency and the invasion of Iraq. This one particular line has thus had several different meanings in its lifetime: from generalised philosophical comment, to contemporary political statement, to rock cliché, to ironic joke, to contemporary political statement once more. It would be impossible to claim that all of these meanings were embedded in the words themselves, and nonsense to suggest that these later meanings could have been in any way intended by Dylan when he wrote the song in 1964 (though we could argue that he has chosen to play the song in concert at particular times for a reason). The meaning of the text changes because of its social circulation, because of how we as listeners have created meaning (we might also add here that because of this social circulation it is impossible for the line to mean in 2005 what it meant in 1964). In recognising this fact, Barthes' exaggerated argument is that we can only 'liberate' the reader by 'killing' the author, by dismissing the 'author-God' as the originator of meaning.

During the course of the twentieth century, then, the author as the keystone of meaning within a work has been accosted on both sides – trumped by either the text itself or its readers. This has certainly had an impact on Dylan scholarship, and key principles of writers such as Day, Ricks and Scobie are not only that we can never assume the 'I' of a Bob

Dylan song to be Dylan himself, but also that any biographical reading of a song is necessarily restrictive and inferior:[10]

> What purpose has been served by determining a biographical reference? Does it really contribute anything worthwhile to our critical understanding and appreciation of the songs themselves?[11]

Dylan himself has criticized those who offer biographical readings of his songs:

> I read that this ['You're A Big Girl Now'] was supposed to be about my wife. I wish somebody would ask me first before they go and print stuff like that. I mean, it couldn't be about anyone else but my wife, right? Stupid and misleading jerks sometimes these interpreters are . . . Fools, they limit you to their own unimaginative mentality. (Cameron Crowe interview, 1985)

> People say the record [*Time Out Of Mind*] deals with mortality – my mortality for some reason! Well, it doesn't deal with my mortality. It maybe just deals with mortality in general . . . I found this condescending attitude toward that record revealed in the press quite frequently. (Mikal Gilmore interview, 2001) *

Dylan's songs often seem constructed in ways that work against an author-centred reading. Firstly, he regularly inserts fictional detail into seemingly autobiographical songs.[12] Scobie uses the line 'They say I shot a man named

---

* I appreciate that using Dylan's words in the form of interviews may be considered as going against the spirit of the approaches outlined in this section. My reasons for utilising them should become clearer below.

Gray and took his wife to Italy' (from 'Idiot Wind') as an example of this. One further example would be 'Boots Of Spanish Leather', in which the singer's loved one leaves for Spain, whereas the song was surely prompted by Dylan's girlfriend leaving for Italy. Secondly, Dylan 'refuses the role of omniscient narrator'.[13] As Romantic thought developed in the eighteenth century, the work of art became conceptualised as a 'heterocosm', its own world subject to its own internal laws. The poet, as creator of this world, was obviously its all-seeing God.[14] However, Dylan often subverts such an idea by emphasising that he never knows everything about the tale he is telling, that the view he can offer is always partial and can only be incomplete. For example, in 'John Wesley Harding', he sings:

> John Wesley Harding
> Was a friend to the poor,
> He trav'led with a gun in ev'ry hand.
> All along this countryside,
> He opened a many a door,
> But he was never known
> To hurt an honest man.

This begins by sounding authoritative – Dylan is telling us what is, not what he thinks – but by the last lines, the narrator's authority is undermined. He cannot definitively say that the outlaw never hurt anyone, only that he was never known to. This fragmentary knowledge is a convention in much folk music. As songs were passed down, and moved around, pieces of information were lost, misheard and so on. Knowledge in folk music is often uncertain and the narrator of a folk song often makes clear what is known and unknown. The difference here, however, is that Dylan wrote the song and is famous for writing his own songs. By adopting this convention, Dylan adds an inherent irony to the work, playing with the generic conventions and undermining the Romantic assumptions about works revealing things about their authors. For example, in 'Lily, Rosemary And The Jack Of Hearts', the narrator tells us:

> No one knew the circumstance but they say that it
>   happened pretty quick
> The door to the dressing room burst open and a Colt
>   revolver clicked.

No one? Come on, Bob, you wrote the song – surely you can tell us!

HOW WE HEAR MUSIC: RECORDINGS, WORDS AND VOICE

Some Dylan critics thus argue that Bob Dylan's life should not be considered the final arbiter of the meaning of a song. I would not want to argue strongly against this but it fails to consider the effects that stardom has on the production and interpretation of songs. The criticisms of author-centred analysis have, in the main, emerged within literary criticism and it is notable that the three critiques I provided as examples (Day, Ricks and Scobie) are written by scholars of literature. Dylan is a particularly literary songwriter; from his earliest years, he was being described as a poet. I will discuss this in a later chapter but the question it raises for our current purpose is this: what should we be thinking about when discussing a Bob Dylan song? Is it only the words that matter? Is the meaning of the song to be found only in the meaning of the words?

This is certainly the way it seems to some people, both fans and critics. However, this literary approach produces a kind of disassociation of Dylan and the song that to me, as a fan, seems intuitively wrong. Let me try to explain by analogy. A poem written by William Wordsworth was intended to be read by an individual. Following the principles of new criticism, we could consider the poem to have some existence independent from that of its author – as words on a page. When the reader picks up the book containing the poem, their direct engagement is with a text and not with an author. In this instance, the literary argument about whether the words contain meaning intended by the poet, whether it is the words themselves that create meaning, or whether meaning is generated by the act of reading, seems to me a reasonable one in which to engage.

We may even be able to engage in a similar discussion regarding classical music. The development of written musical notation generated an idea of the musical 'work' outside of its performance. The musical score therefore exists independently of its creator. However, the idea of 'the work' in popular music (broadly conceived as a commercialisation of folk music facilitated by the invention of recording technology) is founded on the recorded performance. As an example, think of 'Like A Rolling Stone'. I'd be willing to bet that the overwhelming majority of readers have just thought of the recorded version, maybe even heard the recorded song in their head – the opening snare drum, the swirling organ, the rolling piano, the confident voice.* There are certain elements of that performance – a performance that most people would think of as 'the work' – that cannot be adequately expressed in written form. In popular music the distinction between performance and score is unsustainable.[15] We cannot fruitfully say that the song has any existence outside

---

* I will discuss the relationship between records and live performances more in chapter 7.

of its particular performance. Instead, the song is only instantiated, made real, by that particular performance. As such, it is inseparable from the singer.

In differentiating between songs and poems, I am not just pointing out that songs provide a 'different system of punctuation' for words than poems,[16] important though that may be. More important is how the words are mediated through the voice (in this instance, the voice of a star) and the effects that this mediation has on our interpretations of authorship. We do not hear the words in isolation (unlike the Wordsworth poem), but only through Bob Dylan. This is crucial for understanding the meaning of Dylan's songs, but is yet to be adequately addressed in Dylan literature. Writers such as Gray pay lip service to the idea that Dylan's words are performed rather than read but still essentially treat the songs as poems, with the meaning of the song resulting from the words. It is notable that in the index to Gray's 900-page analysis of Dylan,[17] there is no reference for singing, vocals, voice or performance. Yet, as Allan Moore argues, if the meaning of a song can be reduced to its words, why bother to sing it?[18] *

In trying to work out how songs create meaning, Simon Frith suggests that rather than treating songs 'as poems, literary objects which can be analysed entirely separately from music', we need to consider them 'as speech acts, words to be analysed in performance'.[19] Words are important to songs – there are few instrumental hit records – but research conducted on listeners suggests that what the words say – their

---

* This is not to suggest that there has been no discussion of performance within studies of Dylan. In fact, prompted by Paul Williams' work, this has become one of the key motifs of writing on Dylan in recent years, but generally in fanzines rather than published books, and it has yet to develop an adequate critical vocabulary to discuss *how* Dylan's performances create meaning.

'meaning' – is actually an insignificant reason for liking a song.[20]* What matters is not the content of the words, but their expression, their presentation.[21] This is something Dylan has repeatedly iterated:

> When I do whatever it is I'm doing, if there's rhythm involved and phrasing involved then that's where it all balances out – in the rhythm of it and the phrasing of it. It's not in the lyrics. People think it's in the lyrics – maybe on the records it's in the lyrics y'know, but in a live show it's not all in the lyrics. It's in the phrasing and the dynamics of the rhythm. It's got nothing whatsoever to do with the lyrics. I mean, it does . . . it does have something to do with the lyrics – the lyrics have to be there, sure they do, but . . .
> (Bruce Kleinman interview, 1984)

If the meaning of a song was purely 'in the lyrics' then we would surely become tired of the song quickly and not replay it. Yet even songs with 'mundane' lyrics can be a joy to rehear if the joy is transmitted through the singing and/or the music (*Nashville Skyline*, for example), while songs with interesting and skilful words can fall flat and not be amenable to repeated listening (the fate of most political pop).**

Let me approach this argument from another direction; I'm sure I can't be alone among Dylan fans in saying that

---

* This was from a study of general pop fans; it would be interesting to see if the results were repeated in a study of Dylan fans. My guess is that the meaning of words is more important for Dylan fans but that it is the fact that the words mean something (rather than being meaningless) that is most important to them.

** I would venture to suggest that people are more likely to give a recording repeated plays than they are to reread a poem. They are, however, more likely to reread a poem than reread a novel, which suggests that a poem has a certain type of 'musicality' in creating meaning – the form of the words' presentation matters.

there are songs I listened to for years without actually concentrating on the meaning of the words. I knew the words, sure, and could sing along with them, but had never thought about what they actually 'meant' until, one day, my ears picked up on certain words and I paid particular attention to them ('I Want You' is an example that springs to mind). Perhaps new critics would dismiss my behaviour as absent-minded listening but I would say that I knew what the song meant before I paid attention to those words. I would also contend that this is how most people listen to Dylan, even dedicated fans (for example, Paul Williams notes how it was years before he recognised that 'Chimes Of Freedom' involved the singer being caught in a storm).[22]

Lyrics need to be considered as a form of rhetoric. In order to understand how songs 'work' for us, how they mean something,

> we have to treat them in terms of the persuasive relationship set up between the singer and the listener. From this perspective, a song doesn't exist to convey the meaning of the words; rather, the words exist to convey the meaning of the song.[23]

What matters in many cases is not the logical development of an entire narrative, but rather how specific lyrical phrases become invested with force through the music and performance. Frith suggests Public Enemy's 'Don't Believe The Hype' and Springsteen's 'Born In The USA' as good examples.[24] In Dylan's catalogue, 'Rainy Day Women Nos 12 & 35' would be a good example. It is not the most sophisticated of lyrics, but it works as a song because the chorus line 'But I would not feel so all alone / Everybody must get stoned!' is joyous and brilliantly matches the collective, Salvation Army band-style performance of the musicians. And what does 'I Want You' 'mean' other than the singer's insistent claim 'I want you . . . so bad'? Another example from the same album is 'Stuck Inside Of Mobile With The Memphis Blues Again'. The song is clearly 'about' displacement and alienation but the meaning is not really in the words. The series of experiences recounted offer glimpses but nothing like a coherent explanation of the feeling. The alienation is clear, however, in the way that the singer tells Ruthie 'Aw, c'mon now!' and in the repeated chorus line that invests these particular words with force:

> Ah, mama, can this really be the end?
> To be stuck inside of Mobile with the Memphis blues
>   again.

This kind of approach is encapsulated by Paul Williams in his argument that Dylan songs evoke feeling rather than meaning.[25]* This is not to say that songs are *meaningless*, however, which Williams' insistence upon the impossibility of explaining the meaning of the song sometimes suggests. 'Sad Eyed Lady Of The Lowlands' is obviously not meaningless, even if the meaning of the song is not exactly clear from the mysterious build up of images in the verses.

One of the ways in which words are given emphasis, or the meaning of the song is conveyed is, obviously, through music:

> A lot of times people will take the music out of my lyrics and just read them as lyrics. That's not really fair because the music and the lyrics I've always felt are pretty closely wrapped up. You can't separate one from the other that simply. (Toby Cresswell interview, 1986)

---

* I think this was what Dylan was reaching towards when he said 'I never try to figure out what [the songs are] about. If you have to think about it, then it's not there' (Joe Dolen interview, 1995).

Allan Moore has been critical of the lack of consideration given to music's role in the construction of meaning, arguing that accounts of songs often relegate music to the role of pleasant back-drop to the words. He concludes that 'by failing to take into account the attitude set up by the music, so many other analyses of song lyrics are not only incomplete, but lead to erroneous conclusions'.[26] It is certainly the case that the music in my two previous examples is extremely important for establishing meaning. The music to 'Sad Eyed Lady Of The Lowlands' is sensuous and luxuriant. It is essential to projecting the meaning of the song and envelops the listener like a lover's limbs. If the accompaniment was different, then the song would have a different meaning. In 'Stuck Inside Of Mobile With The Memphis Blues Again', the distinctive musical changes at the chorus – the staccato beat, the falling bassline – definitely serve to invest those lines with particular meaning.

The music works by creating a structure for Dylan's voice to impart meaning through his emphasis – 'OH, mama can this REAlly BE the END?' – and, although music is important for creating meaning in itself, what I am particularly interested in here is how the voice works to convey meaning, because

> in songs, words are the sign of a voice. A song is always a performance and song words are always spoken out, heard in someone's accent. Songs are more like plays than poems; song words work as speech and speech acts, bearing meaning not just semantically, but also as structures of sound that are direct signs of emotion and marks of character.[27]

This is why the distinction between poems and songs is important: whereas poems can exist independently, it makes no sense to think of a song as existing outside of its performed voice. And the voice is, obviously, a mark of the singer. It's *that* voice. When you hear the song, you know who is singing.

Dylan's voice is distinctive and has been the subject of much discussion. Philip Larkin described it as 'cawing, derisive' while it was characterised by Robyn Hitchcock as 'a corrosive voice, restless, inconsolable, eating through the excuses that humanity feeds itself'.[28] Dylan has a remarkable voice. John Bauldie's description of 'I'm Not There (1956)' offers some indication of how Dylan's voice creates meaning separately from the words it utters. This song, still officially unreleased, was recorded in Woodstock during the summer of 1967. Bauldie states:

> 'I'm Not There' is remarkable . . . Dylan improvises only vaguely realised lyrics against a hauntingly beautiful melody. The remarkable thing about it is that even though, for the most part, the lyrics are not lyrics at all, but sounds, the performance is moving, emotionally overflowing. It is Dylan's saddest song, and one of his greatest vocal performances, for he catches feeling without words.[29]

I consider Dylan a great singer and writing this book has forced me to address why I think this. In the end, the word I have been led to is 'authority'. It seems to me that the great singers have 'authoritative voices', by which I mean that they demonstrate a total control over the song, to the point of domination or ownership. This is not merely a technical mastery (though that is significant) but a quality of personality that the voice contains. Think of truly great performances, such as Sinatra singing 'My Way' or Johnny Rotten singing 'Anarchy In The UK', and you hear a singer claiming 'this is MY song, and it will do what I want it to'.

Dylan regularly displays this kind of authority: there is a confidence, a certitude in the voice. The great singers are those that can consistently 'take over' the song they are singing, their personality shines through the song rather than being subsumed within it. Dylan almost always achieves this. This quality of great singers, this vocal authority, is the reason that I suggested earlier that it makes no sense to consider a popular music 'text' as having any existence outside of its performance. You cannot take the singer out of the song.*

VOICE, CHARACTER AND PERSONALITY

The inextricable link between voice and song returns us to questions of authorship, only this time concerning the relationship between the singer and the lead character of the song. If songs are a form of rhetoric, then they contain a central character who demonstrates a particular attitude. So how do we conceptualise the relationship between the singer and the song's lead character?

One answer is that it depends on the conventions of the genre. There are many different streams of influence on Dylan's songwriting and performing styles but, given their significance to the development of rock, folk and blues are particularly notable. Though this obviously over-generalises, the two traditions offer different ways of placing the singer

---

* This is the case even if the song may have alternative existences, for example through cover versions. It may be the case with particular authoritative performers, however, that any alternative existences may still be shadowed by the 'original' performance (which is why CBS could run an advertising campaign claiming 'no one sings Dylan like Dylan' – most covers of Dylan songs do not have the same quality of vocal ownership, always being 'covers of Bob Dylan songs' rather than great songs in their own right though some, most notably Jimi Hendrix's 'All Along The Watchtower', do manage it).

within the song. In the folk tradition, the singer's personal character is often absent from the story being told in the song. The songs 'Stack A Lee' and 'Jack A Roe' from *World Gone Wrong* are examples of this. In this type of song, the singer clearly exists as a narrator of a story rather than as a participant within that story. Folk music thus offers a kind of 'third person' approach to singing, and the status of the singer as a narrator is often explicitly noted within the structure of the song, either by drawing an audience together to listen at the start of the song (Dylan utilised this most famously in singing 'Come gather round, people, wherever you roam') or by using their narrator position to cast judgement on the protagonists of the song (for example, in the last verse of 'Seven Curses', Dylan casts seven curses on the wicked judge).

In contrast, the blues singer is not singing 'to' anybody, and does not explicitly acknowledge an audience. Instead, the singer is a character in the narrative being described. To continue using songs on *World Gone Wrong* as examples, 'Blood In My Eyes' and 'Broke Down Engine' would illustrate this kind of format. Because the singer's character is placed within the story of the song (as in 'Blood In My Eyes', 'Woke up this morning, feeling blue / Seen a good-looking girl, can I make love with you?'), this means that the blues is often interpreted as a very self-expressive genre and blues songs are supposed to offer a representation of the singer's actual experience.* This interpretation of the blues means there is a greater likelihood of assuming the 'I' of the song is actually the singer representing his own real-life experiences. Even in this supposedly self-expressive genre, however,

---

* I know this is all too neat and tidy, and that 'folk singers' sang blues songs and vice versa, but there does seem to me a distinction of type that's worth highlighting.

things are not straightforward, for the essence of blues songwriting lies in irony: 'For obvious historical reasons, [blues] . . . has always been metaphorical, has always been dependent on double meanings, on allusion, indirection, and puns, on symbolism'.[30] If this is the case, can we ever be sure what we hear is true or honest? Can we rely on a blues song to provide a reliable barometer of the singer's personality? The theoretical answer has to be that we cannot, but, as with the discussion of authorship, I am more interested in the ways that we think we can.

The way to consider this still, I think, lies in discussing how the voice itself creates meaning. There are two things to consider here: firstly, how the voice is linked to the body and, secondly, how the voice is assumed to reflect a pure subjectivity. Although the voice more often than not reaches us in a disembodied form (on recordings), we strive to re-embody it, either imagining its bodily production – picturing Dylan with his guitar at the microphone singing these words – or going to see its bodily production at concerts (surely one of the major reasons for seeing someone in concert is to *see* them singing). Though the voice may seem easy to disembody, in reality it is clearly tied to the body. Commenting on Dylan's voice, Robyn Hitchcock states that 'he keeps you company. You put on a Dylan record and, by God, *you know someone else is there with you*'.[31] This is an idea that Roland Barthes has pursued, utilising two phrases – 'the grain of the voice' and 'writing aloud' – that insist upon the physicality of the voice. Barthes argues that the singing voice has its own texture, which offers a 'materiality of language' that 'signifies' (provides meaning) separately from what the words being sung may themselves be signifying. For Barthes, the grain of the voice exists in the 'friction between the music and . . . language'[32] and 'forms a signifying play having nothing to do with communication, representation (of feelings), expression; it is that apex (or that depth) of production where the melody really works at the language – not what it says, but the voluptuousness of its sound-signifiers'.[33]

What is significant for Barthes is not how the grain of the voice may put across the meaning of words especially well but simply that it offers us evidence of its bodily production. It is not the 'subjectivity' of the singer that is embedded in the voice, but the erotic body:

> Due allowance being made for the sounds of the language, *writing aloud* is not phonological but phonetic; its aim is not the clarity of messages, the theatre of emotions; what it searches for (in a perspective of bliss) are the pulsional incidents, the language lined with flesh, a text where we can hear the grain of the throat, the patina of consonants, the voluptuousness of vowels, a whole carnal stereophony: the articulation of the body, of the tongue, not that of meaning, of language.[34]

Barthes is thus interested in the bodily nature of the singing voice and one of his aims is to move away from the idea that the voice expresses a pure spirit, a pure, individual subjectivity. Despite Barthes' arguments, however, this is exactly how the voice is generally considered. Perhaps more than anything else, the voice is understood as representing the true essence of a person, as offering an unmediated self. One important development in this regard was the invention of the microphone in the mid-1920s. This meant that singers could utilise a variety of new singing techniques more subtle than the previous practice of singing as loudly as possible to reach the back of the theatre. This new style of singing (crooning) created a supposed intimacy that made it seem like the singer was revealing their innermost emotions to a trusted confidante, the listener.* This intimacy means that we tend to think that we in some way know the singer because we 'connect' with her voice[35] – her voice is assumed to tell us something about her personality. The voice in pop is thus interpreted as personally expressive (in contrast to classical music where the sound of the voice is more structured by the score).[36] The voice seemingly proves to us the existence of a real individual with real emotions behind the front, behind the performance (though in reality this works in reverse: socially, we already fervently believe in the reality of the private individual and this leads us to believe the voice offers evidence of this). Like the eyes acting as the 'window of the soul', the voice is assumed to tell us things about its owner, perhaps deeper things than they would otherwise choose to reveal. The voice seemingly offers us a glimpse of the authentic individual behind the star, but the listener's relationship to it is one of tension, bound up in the possibility of knowing that individual (through the voice) and the impossibility of knowing them (because you only have a record).[37]

Concerning Dylan, this tension – between knowing and not knowing – is often presented in a literary way, as being embedded in the lyrics. For example, Brown states that 'Dylan's lyrics construct an author-reader relation posited on the model of an irresolvable enigma which is both the incitement to and the perpetual frustration of readerly desire'.[38] However, the 'illusion of intimacy'[39] is actually a property of Dylan's stardom, particularly in the way his stardom is made flesh through his voice. The way that the voice suggests something going on beneath the surface is very similar to how stardom works, and we have thus returned to the starting

---

* There are some similarities here to the development of the close-up in cinema. Both processes are crucial in the emergence of modern stardom.

point of this chapter – the relationship between public figure and private individual.

STARDOM, PERSONALITY AND THE 'ILLUSION OF INTIMACY'

I do not mean to suggest that there is nothing in Dylan's 'texts' that deals with issues of self, naming, privacy and stardom. Dylan has obviously addressed such issues in his work, and there are examples throughout this book. I do think that in many ways they are secondary, however, to the way that Dylan *himself* has been interpreted by critics. In particular, he has consistently been portrayed as chameleon-like, continually picking up and casting off new identities – protest Bob, hipster Bob, country Bob, Vegas Bob, born again Bob . . . The interesting feature of Dylan's reinventions, however, is how they are often seen as a representation of the 'authentic' Bob Dylan. There is a reluctance to see Dylan's transformations as a form of acting and they are instead portrayed as reflective of his own essential self. Heylin, for example, refers to Dylan's 'perennial reinventions of himself',[40] while Roe states that 'a wardrobe of identities is stock-in-trade for many popular musicians . . . In Dylan's case, by contrast, multiple aliases are conditions of being'.[41] In one sense this is odd because, as music fans, we are generally aware that star personae are a performance (Madonna fans are aware of this, for example, in their appreciation of Madonna). Generally, audiences are aware of the constructed nature of stardom and celebrity (we know the effort that goes into producing an image, and the army of workers in the publicity industry). At the same time, however, we authenticate certain individuals as being the 'real thing', as somehow being untainted by all the artifice. The essential paradox is that a star-image (for that is all we can know) is being authenticated as something more real than an image. Dyer suggests that this is possible because stardom is embodied in physical persons, so there is always a promise of something 'real' behind the celebrity mask. However, he also points out the infinite regress to this logic – an individual authenticated by their stardom is then used to authenticate that very stardom![42]

One of the key facts that contributes to popular conceptions of Dylan is his change of name. As a teenager, Robert Allen Zimmerman adopted various pseudonyms before settling on Bob Dylan, to which he legally changed his name in August 1962. Various reasons have been offered for this particular choice, most persistently the idea that it was a homage to the Welsh poet Dylan Thomas. Such an argument is almost undoubtedly incorrect.* There are a number of possible inspirations for the name: Dylan suggested it was after an uncle called Dillon, while there is a Dillon Road in Hibbing where he grew up, and young Bob was a fan of sheriff Matt Dillon in the TV series *Gunsmoke*. I think it unlikely that Dylan chose the name in reference to any one particular thing and that the actual sound of the words was the most significant reason for his choice – remember that his first names were Bob Allen (Dylan reportedly initially spelt the name as Dillon rather than Dylan, and my hunch is that he changed the spelling when he practised signing autographs and preferred its look, but that's pure speculation). One of his earlier pseudonyms, Elston Gunnn, shares a similar rhythmic feel, and the names of his children also have comparable looks or sounds (Jesse Byron Dylan, Anna Lee

---

* Dylan stated 'Get that straight. I didn't change my name in honour of Dylan Thomas. That's just a story. I've done more for Dylan Thomas than he's ever done for me' (Jules Siegel interview, 1966). When a friend asked him if Dylan was spelt 'as in Dylan Thomas', he replied, 'No, as in Bob DYLAN!' (in Scaduto, 1996:69).

Dylan, Samuel Abram and Jakob Luke). One reason, which I have never seen given serious consideration, is that Dylan would not have had the success he did if he had kept his family name, Zimmerman. I think there are cultural (racist) reasons for this which can be pithily summed up by suggesting that the name lacks 'star quality' and that Dylan was aware of this. Reasons for this particular name are less significant than the act of changing, however, and how that change has been interpreted. Scobie argues for acknowledging 'the importance of the adoption of a pseudonym as the foundational moment of Bob Dylan's career. For him, this was more than a matter of convenience. It was a far-reaching gesture of self-definition, rooting his identity and signature in an archetypal trickster's move of self-disguise'.[43] This once again emphasises changes in persona as something more than mere surface, as a fundamental defining of the self. What we see regularly repeated in accounts of Dylan is that these changes of the self are of more personal significance than merely putting on a new act: this is an expression of the genuine Bob Dylan. Ultimately, I do not think this position is sustainable because it relies on the idea that there is an authentic self behind the public performance of stardom. My argument is that we can rely on no such idea. We should not assume that there is anything behind the celebrity screen – what you see is what there is and, while what we see may suggests to us a reality to which we do not have access, and while we may like to believe that there is something there, in the end, what we see is all there is.

Let me again try to explain by way of literary analogy. Samuel Clemens, following the convention of the time, adopted the pen name Mark Twain when he began writing. Maybe Clemens could have remained a private figure had he restricted himself to being a pseudonymous literary author. Rather than merely being a literary author, however,

Twain gave lecture tours and became a significant public figure. The distinction between Twain and Clemens thus becomes more difficult to sustain. The performances were given by 'Mark Twain' not 'Samuel Clemens as Mark Twain'. How can we possibly distinguish between the two? As Moran argues, 'The symbiotic relationship between promotion and self-promotion in the public construction of authors like Twain makes any attempt to distinguish between the "public" author and the "private" self a deeply problematic exercise'.[44] Twain himself made great play of his double-self, as has Dylan, who has regularly drawn attention to his dividedness. 'I don't think of myself as Bob Dylan' he told Cameron Crowe, 'It's like Rimbaud said, "I is another".'

In her discussion of Twain, Susan Gillman develops the notion of imposture for dealing with how the duality is understood. She argues against analysing Twain in terms of a simple division between the private individual and the public author because the two are so closely entwined as to actually be one: 'Whereas twinning or doubling suggests merely mathematical division, imposture leads to a kind of logical vicious circle. Since "posture" already implies posing or faking, "imposture" is the pose of a pose, the fake of a fake: the word implies no possible return to any point of origin.'[45] This is, I think, a useful way of considering Dylan – the impossibility of a return to any point of origin. Scobie has made similar points about Dylan. By interpreting 'Bob Dylan' as a 'text', Scobie correctly asserts that we cannot know a real Bob Dylan, only all of the different meanings and values attached to him through his work, interviews, star performances, criticism, fan discussion and so on. I would go further than this and suggest that there is no 'real Bob Dylan' for us to know because the idea that there is a private Bob Dylan implies that there is such a thing as human personality that exists independently of its social circumstances. Consider the following statement, however:

> People react to famous people, you know? . . . Say you're passing a little pub or a little inn, and you look through the window and you see all the people eating, talking and carrying on. You watch outside the window and you can see them all be very real with each other, as real as they're gonna be. Because when you walk into the room, it's over! You won't see them being real any more. (Christopher Sykes interview, 1986)

I think it is implausible that a major star could ever escape this situation. Even when alone, having the knowledge that people 'stop being real' in your presence affects everything you think or do. There is no time when Bob Dylan isn't 'Bob Dylan'. Given that, how can there be a 'real person' behind the image?

This may seem like quite a radical position but it is not something unique to stars but, rather, is a characteristic of us all. The idea of a pre-social self is not a defensible proposition. For one thing, it does not consider the recent historical emergence of ideas such as 'privacy' and 'personality'. 'Privacy' first became a significant concept during the late seventeenth century, most notably manifested in changes to domestic architecture that moved sleeping quarters upstairs and increasingly subdivided large communal areas into smaller, more private rooms.[46] 'Personality', with its current meaning of a set of personal characteristics or traits, is an even more recent development, intimately linked with the twinned discourses of stardom and consumerism in the first decades of the twentieth century.[47] What both concepts have in common, therefore, is that they both emerge in a particular social formation – modernity – that is more public than ever before, and both emerge as something that is constantly under threat. Privacy is something which you can never find in the modern world, while personality is how you try to distinguish yourself when you are already a part of an anonymous mass. We are never pure essence but are always socially mediated, even when we are alone. This is one of the conditions of modern individuality. Our belief in a 'constant self, distinct from the social roles we have to play and how we represent ourselves to others'[48] is a crucial way of making sense of the world in which we find ourselves (it is, in other words, ideological). At the same time, however, there is anxiety over whether, in the end, all we really are *is* how we perform for others. Stardom is a key way in which such ideologies are perpetuated and stars, as exemplars of individualism, experience the dilemma in a particularly intense form. In a sense, stars have more privacy to be invaded than ordinary people. So, when Dylan said in 1994 that, on becoming a star, 'a person ceases to become a person' (Ellen Futterman interview, 1994), he is not quite right: they actually become a super-person, aware of their privacy more intently than ordinary people.

Stars serve as a cultural form on which we can project our beliefs about privacy and individuality: as fans and critics, we spend a lot of time and energy searching for the 'real' Bob Dylan. We already know the real Bob Dylan, however: it is the one that we hear on record, see on stage, read in interviews. Whatever we think, know or believe about Dylan, we think, know or believe *from what we see in front of us*, not from anything backstage. And, while it may seem ironic that this ideology is developed most fully in an institution – the media – which is most closely associated with the invasion of privacy, it is actually the condition of its existence: 'privacy' emerges only in a society that was more public than ever before.

STARDOM, THE VOICE AND
THE MEANING OF SONGS

My argument in the previous section reads a bit like those of the literary theorists who argue that we cannot use the author as the source of literary meaning. I need to backtrack a little, for what I want to discuss is not 'what's real and what is not' but, rather, how people relate to stars. My approach is descriptive and not normative – I'm interested in how Dylan's stardom works, not whether this is right or wrong. Stars may be merely a surface form but stardom always promises something more. Because stars have a real world referent – a physical person – they are different from characters in a novel or play. There is more to a star than a purely academic interest in how their image has been constructed. So, while I have spent time arguing that there is no such thing as an authentic Bob Dylan hidden behind the celebrity smokescreen, it is important to acknowledge that this is actually the key way that we understand stars and artists. We believe that there is a real, unmediated person behind it all and, in popular music, we believe that it is the work that provides us with access to that unmediated self. The following quote from Paul Williams exemplifies what I have been discussing in this chapter; showing how he responds to the singer's voice as a way of getting to know the 'real person' to whom it belongs:

> It [Dylan's work] is a story that matters not because of what it contains but because of the way it is told: with anger, love, honesty, passion, wit, humility, arrogance and heart. With integrity and spirit. With enthusiasm, pain, curiosity and doubt. Human qualities. Even as we stand in awe of his gifts, it is the humanity of the storyteller that endears him to us.[49]

This returns me to the opening question of this chapter – how we hear the relationship between Dylan and his songs. Those who criticise utilising Dylan as the source of a song's meaning make use of a literary perspective. Such an approach has provided valuable insights into Dylan's work, but it overlooks the crucial way that stardom itself generates meaning. This is demonstrated by a general lack of concern in literary analyses for how Dylan's voice works as a carrier of meaning. The meaning of Dylan's songs is not 'in the words' but 'in the voice'. While we could conceivably remove the authorial figure from our understanding of the songs, we cannot remove the star. 'The meaning of pop is the meaning of pop stars, performers with bodies and personalities; central to the pleasure of pop is pleasure in a voice, sound as body, sound as person.'[50] Ultimately, it is the star that shapes the meaning of the song, not the words (of course, this is made more complicated in a case when one of the main reasons for a star's fame is his particularly good use of words). Thus, when Williams writes 'if we found out tomorrow that Bob Dylan was a 64-year-old woman who'd changed her sex, and a proven Communist agent, we might be surprised, but the words to "Mr Tambourine Man" would not change in the slightest. It would still be the same song',[51] he is wrong. Well, he's right that the words would not change, but the meaning of the song would be altered irrevocably. Whenever we heard the song we would automatically think of Dylan's sex change and so on. That information would have become an inescapable part of the song's meaning just as, whenever I hear 'Idiot Wind', I am forever aware that it was written and recorded at a time when Dylan was experiencing a traumatic marital breakdown.

To illustrate this point, I want to use an example from a book by John Berger.[52] It consists of a painting by Van Gogh (see next page).

On the next page is the legend 'this is the last picture Van Gogh painted before he killed himself'.* Berger then explains 'it is hard to define exactly how the words have changed the image but undoubtedly they have. The image now illustrates the sentence.' His point is to show that our understanding of works of art is shaped by a range of contextual factors and that we can never approach a work in a purely abstract manner. My argument here is that we *have* to consider Bob Dylan's stardom in order to understand how his songs work for his fans. In many ways, Dylan's performances of songs, written by himself and others, illustrate his star-image. We do not hear the songs in an unmediated form but only *through* his stardom, and through our understandings of that stardom. The meaning of Dylan's stardom is not stable or fixed. His stardom has changed over time, and so the meaning of his songs has changed even though the recordings haven't altered. Similarly, his stardom means different things to different people – very committed fans know more about Dylan's personal life than casual fans, and

* Subsequent research has suggested that it is not in fact the last painting, but that two further paintings were completed. This piece of information does not, however, weaken Berger's argument.

so will garner different, perhaps more nuanced, meanings out of the same songs. But what 'Bob Dylan' means structures what the songs mean. For example, in 'Beyond The Horizon', Dylan sings:

You think I'm over the hill,
Think I'm past my prime,
Let me see what you got,
We can have a whopping good time.

They don't have to be about Bob Dylan but, when considering how they are received, they clearly are. Every time Dylan plays this song in concert, these lines generate a cheer from the audience, who are undoubtedly linking their meaning to the meaning of the star singing them (similarly, almost every review of *Modern Times* made reference to these lines).

The fact that stardom shapes song meaning does not mean we can merely reproduce biographical explanations of songs. We need to be aware, however, that biography (with its emphasis on the individual self) is an important way that stardom signifies and, therefore, is important in how songs acquire meaning. The reliance on biography is used to 'validate' the cultural belief that works of art express an artist's inner experiences. What we need to consider, therefore, is not whether a particular biographical detail is 'wrong' (though this can sometimes be useful) but, rather, how a particular star-image (of which biography is a part) works to give a song meaning. For example, Ricks explicitly criticises a biographical reading of 'Not Dark Yet' that associates the song with Dylan's 'heart trouble' of that year.[53] Now, in biographical terms, Ricks is correct – the song was written and recorded months before Dylan's illness. But the song was released after his much publicised stint in hospital and the album's melancholic sound became inextricably linked with his 'brush with death' – his stardom influenced the meaning given to the song. However good the song, and whatever its author's intentions, it is given meaning through stardom, and stardom as a mediator of meaning does not depend upon biographical accuracy. Dylan certainly knows this, as illustrated by his construction of several fictitious biographies when trying to become a star.

Stardom as the mediator of meaning thus does not depend on authorial intention – Dylan's stardom provides a source of meaning for songs on *Time Out Of Mind* even if not intended by Dylan. This is, however, not to say that Dylan is ignorant of the effect that his stardom has on his songs. There are times when he has dealt with it directly (such as in 'Brownsville Girl', discussed in chapter 6).* There are also times when he strategically employs this effect in songs not explicitly 'about' stardom. For example, when, in 1963, Dylan opens a song with the lines:

> Oh my name it ain't nothin'
> My age it means less
> ('With God On Our Side')

he is doing three things simultaneously. Firstly, and least consequentially, he is pastiching a folk song ('The Patriot's Game') which begins 'My name is O'Hanlon, I've just

---

* Ironically, Dylan has perhaps most explicitly addressed the issue in film. In *Pat Garrett and Billy The Kid* (1973), in which Dylan plays a character called Alias, the fact that audiences know that Alias is being played by Bob Dylan is a crucial part of the film. The complexities of *Renaldo and Clara*, which Scobie (2003:245) describes as dealing with the 'staging of Dylan's private life as public spectacle' have already been mentioned while in 1986, Dylan played a lead role in the film *Hearts of Fire* about a disillusioned rock singer. Finally, in *Masked and Anonymous* (2003), a film written by Dylan, he plays Jack Fate, an old star bearing a striking resemblance to the Dylan of the Never Ending Tour.

turned sixteen'. Secondly, he is constructing the narrator as a democratic, everyman figure, the importance of which will be discussed in the next chapter. Thirdly, however, he makes an ironic acknowledgement of his stardom for by this point the name 'Bob Dylan' was not nothing but the name of a figurehead, the name of a star. This song is so important not because it is sung by a nobody but because it is sung by Bob Dylan. And he further exaggerates the irony by suggesting that his age is even less important – even though at this point his star image symbolises politicised youth (as, for example, when he sings 'Come mothers and fathers throughout the land / And don't criticise what you can't understand').

These lyrics (from 'The Times They Are A-Changin') lead me to one final point. Dylan's star image influences our understandings of his songs, but the songs also influence our understanding of his star image. Discussing film stars, Richard Dyer suggests that we need to consider the importance of a film as a 'vehicle' for an actor whereby a film is deliberately utilised to construct a particular star image.[54] Not all films are vehicles, but once a star image is constructed, analysing films this way is a useful strategy as we can see which films help construct and maintain an image, which may offer a subversion of it, and so on. This idea has some use for contemplating Dylan. For example, songs such as 'The Times They Are A-Changin' and 'Like A Rolling Stone' play a particular role constructing Dylan's star-image in the 1960s, while the album *Self Portrait* can be read as an attempt to subvert, or deconstruct that particular star-image. More recently, the albums *Time Out Of Mind* and *Love And Theft* have been significant in constructing Dylan's current star-image. If we define stars as people who are famous because they have produced a body of work, then it makes sense that the body of work plays a prominent role in the creation, maintenance and revision of the star's wider meaning. The relationship between stardom and work is a two-way process, however: the songs and concerts affect how we interpret Dylan while how we interpret Dylan affects how we 'read' the songs and performances. But the songs can never be innocent; stardom always impinges on musical meaning.

Snapshot: The man of the people

Bob Dylan was born Robert Allen Zimmerman in May 1941, in Duluth, Minnesota. When he was six, his family moved 100 miles north to Hibbing, a small mining town. He experienced a conventional childhood. As a teenager, he was passionate about both rock and roll and the movies. He became interested in folk music around the age of eighteen, an interest that intensified when he started attending the university of Minneapolis. He soon dropped out of university and hitchhiked to New York City, partly to visit his hero Woody Guthrie in hospital and partly to make it in the folk scene in Greenwich Village. As a performer, he adopted a variety of pseudonyms, including Blind Boy Grunt and Elston Gunnn. By the time of his arrival at university, he had settled on the name Bob Dylan. He legally changed his name in August 1962.

Dylan joined a flourishing folk scene with a number of young and talented musicians. He very quickly rose to prominence, however, because of his mature performing style. He also began writing his own songs, many of which were very highly regarded. In September 1961, Robert Shelton, the esteemed folk critic of the *New York Times*, wrote a career-opening review and one month later, Dylan was signed by John Hammond to Columbia Records, becoming the first of the new folk singers to be signed to a major label. His first album was recorded in November and released in March 1962. This album contained ten traditional covers and two original songs. By the time of its release, however, Dylan had progressed and was writing songs with astonishing rapidity. He began writing more politically aware 'protest songs', early in 1962 and in April wrote 'Blowin' In The Wind', the song that made him famous and became the anthem of the folk movement. This brought him to the attention of businessman Albert Grossman, who became Dylan's manager. Another of Grossman's acts, Peter, Paul and Mary, recorded 'Blowin' In The Wind' and it reached number one on the US charts.

In the years either side of 1960, folk music was undergoing a revival in popularity in the US. The success of 'Blowin' In The Wind', and the quality of Dylan's other songs, quickly resulted in him becoming the figurehead of this new revival. Songs such as 'A Hard Rain's A-Gonna Fall' and 'The Times They Are A-Changin'' were interpreted as reflecting the feelings of a discontented youth and earned him the title 'spokesman for a generation'. It was a label and a role with which he was distinctly uncomfortable.

Albums* and major events

January 1961	Arrives in New York. On his first full day in the city, he visits Woody Guthrie in hospital
April 1961	Spends two weeks as opening act for John Lee Hooker
November 1961	First solo concert is held at the Carnegie Recital Hall
March 1962	*Bob Dylan*
May 1962	Albert Grossman becomes Dylan's manager
May 1963	*The Freewheelin' Bob Dylan*
June 1963	Peter, Paul and Mary's 'Blowin' In The Wind' sells a million copies
July 1963	Newport Folk Festival
August 1963	Dylan performs at the 'March on Washington' in front of 250,000 people. Later that day, Martin Luther King gives his famous speech
January 1964	*The Times They Are A-Changin'*

* Listings in these snapshots include only albums of original material – greatest hits collections and live albums are not included.

3

FOLK STARDOM: STAR AS ORDINARY, STAR AS SPECIAL

It is important to not allow the one label, 'stardom', obscure the differences between the experiences of celebrity in different areas of cultural life. The expectations and limitations of, say, film stars differ from those associated with television personalities. Similarly, even though popular music stars share some elements of stardom in common, there can still be widely divergent expectations within different genres. Take, for example, the issue of wealth. Conspicuous consumption on clothes, or yachts, by pop stars such as Elton John is not questioned; pop is about glamour and wealth. Hip hop, in a parody of American consumerism, is also a genre where extravagant consumption is endorsed. Such consumer extravagances have to be justified or downplayed by rock stars such as Bruce Springsteen, however, as they are seen to undermine the artistic credentials of the artist involved.[1]

Allowing for such generic differences, there are ways in which popular music stars are distinctive from other types of celebrity and star. One example is the link between popular music stars and the particular 'community' from which they emerge.[2] Stars are often seen as representing and reflecting the attitudes of the social group from which they emerge and of speaking for that group; the young, the working class, the urban, and so on. This fact is emphasised when one considers that many of the significant popular genres have emerged from dispossessed social groups; so, for example, soul stars spoke for the black experience, country music the southern white experience, and so on. It is hard for bands like Keane, who are clearly not dispossessed, to gain cultural legitimacy.

What is particularly important, however, is how popular music stars from a range of genres are seen as representing a particular *generational* experience. More than an association with a particular locality or social group, popular music is primarily interpreted as an expression of youth experience. Rojek offers one example of this:

> Pop icons differ from other celebrities in appearing to speak for their generation. They provide a sexual focus and a populist articulation of generational beliefs and values which lifts them from the confines of popular entertainment and bestows upon them general cultural and political significance.[3]

Rojek goes on to suggest that, during the 1940s, Frank Sinatra represented the youth that America lost because of the war. While this may be true, it is different from the way that stars came to be understood as the spokespeople of youth during the 1960s. Sinatra may have been a *representation* of a generation, but he was in no way a *representative* of that generation. Rojek points out that Sinatra never approached his audience as an equal and made no claims to be speaking on behalf of a particular group. Neither was he primarily a young person's singer, his audience comprising both adults and young people, reflecting the general listening patterns of the 1940s and early 1950s. However, the emergence of rock and roll, particularly Elvis Presley, gave young people a distinctive music that could be claimed as their own. Elvis also demonstrated the emerging market power (and hence social power) of young people,[4] which brings me to the second way that popular music stars are distinctive: they have a *political* significance. By political, I do not necessarily mean conventional politics. Elvis was not a political radical. He was, however, political in the way he energised a social group with radical potential. He signified a particular group that was portrayed as threatening and out of control. Elvis thus symbolised the potential for change and this explains his social significance and that of subsequent popular music stars. 'Popular music, in its constant reformulation into new songs . . . represents change itself and the chaos that change can potentially produce. The popular music celebrity, then, is often the public representation of change.'[5]

The idea that pop stars reflect and represent a generational experience, and that this experience is politically significant, emerged during the 1950s. It is in the 1960s, however, that these characteristics developed into a more explicit creed. During this decade a new generation was portrayed as exhibiting a new and radical social consciousness and popular music stars came to be seen as embodying that radical consciousness. Particularly significant in this regard is the emergence of a new genre of music – rock – and the integration of ideals from the earlier folk revival into mainstream popular music. In these transformations, Bob Dylan's stardom is a crucial factor. Dylan is portrayed as virtually single-handedly providing popular music with a political awareness. Wayne Hampton suggests that he was 'the first truly popular artist in America to exhibit a social consciousness'.[6] Such hyperbole is clearly unsupportable. Whatever Dylan's achievements at this time, they depend on a variety of factors beyond his control and a social and musical context that structured his musical development and star persona. Stardom, however, is different from sociological or biographical fact. One of the chief functions of stardom is to individualise complicated social processes, to 'stand for' and represent particular historical moments. In this instance, both at the time and in subsequent portrayal, the symbol 'Dylan' represents a radical youth, a politicised sixties and (together with The Beatles) the symbiotic relationship of rock music and social experience. 'More than any other popular artist in America, Bob Dylan came to embody the essence of the 1960s counterculture.'[7] However, star representations are always simplifications, and Dylan's relationship to the politics of the decade, and to the folk revival more generally, is more ambivalent than symbiotic. Chapter 5 will discuss how Dylan's star-image became more thoroughly entwined with the politics of the sixties counterculture even as he tried to distance himself from it. In this chapter, I want to discuss the initial development of Dylan's stardom by looking at his emergence into the folk music scene of the early sixties and discuss the political and musical tensions in his relationship with the folk revival. I will then explain how these tensions reflect the emergence of a new type of political consciousness within popular music and how the inherent contradictions in the idea of a 'folk star' reflects the commercial origins of the folk revival.

FOLK MUSIC AND THE FOLK REVIVAL

The American 'folk revival' is generally presented as beginning with the release of 'Tom Dooley' by The Kingston Trio in 1958. With smooth harmonies and well-produced sound, neither the song nor the band could really be considered 'authentic folk', but the song was an old folk tune and featured an understated presentation and acoustic instrumentation. It heralded an interest in songs that told stories and were presented without the usual trappings of mainstream commercial music. The revival's commercial and cultural apex occurred in 1963 and it fizzled out soon afterwards, with a final ending date generally given as the 1965 Newport Folk Festival when Dylan was backed by an electric band. In all likelihood, the American folk revival would warrant a small paragraph as another short-lived fad in a historical survey of popular music, were it not for two things: its historical congruence with the American civil rights movement; and the fact that it produced the most influential figure in popular music history and, as such, is foundational in the emergence of rock music.

The folk revival of the late fifties and early sixties had its roots in earlier folk movements. These maintained explicit links to organised working-class politics. In America, this historical link goes back to the 1900s and the International Workers of the World union (IWW, also known as the Wobblies). The principle of the union was that all members of the working class, whatever their profession or nationality, should join together in one union. It favoured direct political action to advance working-class rights and one of its notable features was its use of song to unite members on picket lines and marches. From its inception in 1905, the IWW published *The Little Red Songbook*, a regularly updated collection of labour songs. One individual dominated the songbook, however: Joe Hill, a prolific songwriter who often parodied hymns to incite political awareness. Hill was convicted for murder, and executed, thus becoming a martyr to the Wobblies' cause. His execution can be seen as part of the violent government repression of the IWW and, by the end of the

1910s, many of its leaders had been killed or imprisoned. By the mid-1920s, IWW membership was in terminal decline. This was far from the end of the link between folk music and working-class politics, however. The 1930s, containing the depression, Roosevelt's New Deal and the rise of European fascism, was the only time in which communism made an impression on mainstream American political consciousness. Indeed, during this time, communism was promoted by its supporters as the only system true to American ideals and, once again, folk music was seen by left-wing intellectuals and folklorists as a way of raising political consciousness. From around 1935, folk music and radical politics became thoroughly intertwined. In 1945, a number of singers, 'led' by Pete Seeger, formed People's Songs, dedicated to the dissemination of folk songs that 'talk about life as it really is'. In 1948, Henry Wallace of the Progressive Party ran for president on a radical platform – against the Cold War and in favour of giving full voting rights to Black Americans – and folk music played a significant role in his campaign. Wallace was unsuccessful, however and, by the end of the 1940s, this folk revival ran out of steam, beset by disillusionment and McCarthyism. Many of the folksingers active in this period, including Pete Seeger, Josh White, Theo Bikel and Oscar Brand, were still important figures in folk music during the later revival that occurred around 1960.

Although figures from folk's past were still active in this later folk revival, the folk boom of the early sixties became clearly associated with young people. Cold War politics and 'the ever present danger of nuclear holocaust'[8] seems to have produced a change in generational consciousness and partly explains why the new revival took on a specifically youthful dimension. The existential experience of potential annihilation seems to have weighed particularly heavily on the newer generation's shoulders and played a significant role in the emergence of a critical, but specifically youthful, consciousness. The folk revival became, for a time, the chosen mode of expression for a new generation who saw it as their historical role to change society for the better, to force post-war society to live up to its ideals and promises. During this period, youth became the touchstone for critical consciousness, as 'a conception formed, more taste than ideology, more style than discourse, more interpersonal than historical, that the world had been gravely mismanaged by the parent generation'.[9] At this particular moment, the idea emerged that it was up to the young to take matters into their own hands if things were to be recovered. The demographic coincidence generated by the end of the Second World War produced a generation of young people who saw it as their destiny to put right the errors of their predecessors. It was also the first cohort to generate a distinctive politicised youth culture, and, initially, the channel through which it spoke was folk music. Rock would come later and be seen as the most significant form of youth culture, but rock would not have developed as it did without the folk revival and its associated understandings of the political role of youth. And, more than anybody else, Bob Dylan came to stand for, embody and define, this new generational understanding:

> As the revivalists knew, the meaning of their movement was thus most mysteriously and powerfully embodied in Joan Baez and Bob Dylan. In them youthful sexuality vivified the cultural forms to which certain ideals of American democracy had been aligned – innocence and freedom, independence, piety and duty, equality, conscience, and revolt; and at the same time those forms lent the kind of articulation, almost of poetry, to their considerable personal beauty, interest, and force.[10]

As Dylan's stardom developed, it came to signify a politically impatient generation with a willingness to speak out against society's ills. Dylan came to be seen not only as a representation of this particular social group, as a symbol that 'stood for' the group, but also as a representative of that group, someone speaking on their behalf. He was famously labelled as the 'Spokesman of a Generation', and this begs the question 'why?'. Why is it Bob Dylan who emerges as the embodiment of the movement and, beyond that, of politicised youth? Why, given that Dylan repeatedly said he was speaking for no one but himself, did he become defined as a spokesman? The conventional way of explaining this is to argue that it was the strength of his songs and his personality that led him to the top. His songs were much better than others, his personality more charismatic. This is the success myth of stardom in a meritocracy; that talent and hard work will be rewarded. It is also the myth of art, that there is absolute aesthetic quality which shines out. Neither myth is true – talented and charismatic people are overlooked; tastes and values in art change – and neither offers an adequate explanation for why Dylan and why that moment. We cannot rely on a purely individualistic or artistic explanation; instead we need to examine the relationship between Dylan and that particular moment.

The French sociologist of literature Lucien Goldmann attempted to develop a method for providing an analytical basis for aesthetic value. Rather than assuming aesthetic value to be based on subjective experience, Goldmann tried to explain why some works and writers were better than others. His approach was to look at the relationship between the work and the social environment in which it was produced because, for Goldmann, 'no important work can ever be the expression of a purely individual experience'.[11] Instead, Goldmann suggests the idea of 'the collective subject', the collective consciousness of a particular social group.

This collective consciousness is not separate from individuals – it can only exist through the consciousness of each individual – but it is also something more than merely individual consciousness; it is a shared mental structure which shapes the actions and thoughts of those in the social group. These mental structures 'simultaneously organise the empirical consciousness of a particular social group and the imaginative world created by the writer'.[12] Goldmann then distinguishes between the actual, empirical, consciousness of a group (what it actually thinks and acts in daily life, including its contradictions and inconsistencies) and its potential collective consciousness (the logical, coherent and unified expression of the social group). Goldmann calls this potential collective consciousness the group's 'world view' and argues that great works of art are those that best encapsulate a world view – thus the great work does not merely reproduce the empirical 'what is' of the social group but actually encompasses its wider coherence.

I do not agree entirely with Goldmann's approach as it tends towards overly sociological explanations of artistic works.* However, he is correct to argue that we can never explain the greatness of works merely by analysing their internal, aesthetic logic. This is because 'explanation always refers to a structure that contains and surpasses the structure being studied'[13] – we always have to bring social factors into our analysis. Furthermore, I think his concept of a 'world view' is useful for considering the relationship between Dylan and the folk revival. My argument is that Dylan's work best expresses the world view of the generation who initially used the folk revival as a means of voicing political disquiet.

---

* Goldmann denies this is his intention, accepting that only 'certain exceptional individuals' could create great works of art and stating that 'nobody would dream of denying that literary and philosophical productions are the works of their authors' (1975:43).

However, Dylan's relationship to the folk revival was not straightforward and at times the relationship was quite strained. This is because of the fact that, although on the surface there appears to be continuity between the sixties folk revival and earlier revivals, there is actually a significant rupture, and the political sensibility of the new generation had a different edge to the older folkies. This tension between the old and new illustrates how the content of a particular cultural object – in this case, a song – always contains social and political dimensions.

DYLAN AND THE FOLK REVIVAL

Dylan's initial musical interest was in rock and roll rather than folk music. Just before he enrolled at the University of Minnesota, however, he developed an interest in folk, mostly in the figure of Woody Guthrie. The link between folk music and radical politics during the 1930s and 1940s was mainly the product of middle-class activity – intellectuals, activists and folklorists like Pete Seeger and Alan Lomax. Woody, however, was a notable outsider; a folksinger from Oklahoma who had experienced family trauma (his older sister died in a fire, his dad was crippled, his mother institutionalised because of Huntington's Chorea) and social misfortune (the area in which he was born was devastated by the dust bowl storms that destroyed the farming industry in Oklahoma, pushing thousands into poverty). With his family destroyed, Guthrie, aged fourteen, began travelling, singing and writing songs. Guthrie's politics were inherently left-leaning but he was not the type to be allied to a dogmatic party political line, instead singing about the experiences of ordinary people and the trials they have to endure because of governments and corporations. When he arrived in New York in 1940, however, he was immediately welcomed by the politically minded folk community and he became the emblem of the inherent creativity and nobility of ordinary Americans. Guthrie became understood not as a representative speaking on behalf of the people, but a representation of 'the people', an embodiment of 'the folk'.

Dylan became enchanted by the figure of Guthrie, especially the romanticised portrayal in his autobiography, *Bound for Glory*.* Guthrie became a totem for the folk movement and an idol for Dylan. The image of the free-spirited traveller became a key motif of Dylan's early years and, arguably, throughout his career. Dylan soon dropped out of university and, ostensibly to meet Woody, hitchhiked to Greenwich Village in New York, home of the flourishing folk revival. He arrived in New York in December 1961, aged twenty. It might be expected that such a promising talent would be warmly welcomed on the scene but this was not so. His welcome would be best described as ambivalent: some people were drawn to the charismatic kid with a Woody Guthrie obsession, while others thought him phoney and contrived. In his first recorded original song, Dylan lampoons the response to his arrival, and immediately positions himself as an outsider by mispronouncing 'Green-witch Village':

I walked down there and ended up
On one of them coffee-houses on the block
Got on the stage to sing and play
Man there said 'Come back some other day,
You sound like a Hillbilly,
We want folk singers here'.

('Talkin' New York')

---

* In a scripted interview in 1965, Dylan was asked whether Guthrie was his greatest influence. He replied 'I don't know that I'd say that but, for a spell, the idea of him affected me quite much' (Jack Goddard interview).

This ambivalence inhabits the entirety of Dylan's relationship with the folk movement. Although he became elevated as the figurehead of the movement, he was never totally integrated into it. Many participants in the folk revival were cynical of Dylan's motives. Dylan was certainly sceptical of many in the movement and repeatedly tried to distance himself from the folk revival: 'They call anybody a folk singer [when] they don't know what to call him. I sing some blues, some country music, some songs I write myself' (Edwin Miller interview, June or July 1962).

Hampton describes Dylan as the first anti-hero of the folk movement.[14] One of the reasons for such mutual distrust was the eclecticism that Dylan describes in the above quote, but the ideological underpinnings of folk music meant that such stylistic differences also reflected different political outlooks. These differences, and Dylan's subsequent lack of engagement in direct political action, led to suspicions that he was merely using the popularity of the folk revival to become famous. His irreverence and eclecticism towards folk music could therefore be taken as evidence of his lack of commitment. Dylan's attitude to folk music, however, needs to be contextualised both within the history of folk music generally and in the specific context of the late 1950s and early 1960s.

An interest in folk culture, including folk songs, was a feature of the Romantic movement. Concerned at the effect of industrialisation and the rationalisation of daily life, artists looked to folk culture for examples of a more organic humanity that existed before the encroachment of dark satanic mills. 'Folk culture', therefore, is a product of modernity (in pre-modernity, it didn't have a special label) and has always been presented and packaged from a particular social perspective – one that looks down from a loftier social or cultural position. This does not necessarily mean 'looking down' in a dismissive or critical way; it is actually the reverse, with the view of folk culture characteristic of a particular kind of nineteenth-century middle-class paternalism towards the uneducated (although in America it was actually more of a maternalism).[15] This has ramifications for how 'folk music' becomes understood, however. For example, around 1900 there was a folk song revival in the UK, led by Cecil Sharp, a Cambridge graduate concerned that folk culture was dying out because of the migratory shift from the country to cities. Sharp undertook the task of documenting folk song before it disappeared. Rather than discovering what 'the folk' were singing, however, Sharp took to the project a clear definition of what could be considered a 'folk song': no songs from towns of any size, no songs from factory workers and no songs from music halls were permitted.[16] This obviously covered only a fraction of what people were actually singing but, more significantly, Sharp's rigid rules resulted in a 'fetishisation' (objectification) of the 'folk song', which became an artefact, cast in stone. The folk song ceased to be a living thing, part of an ongoing dynamic culture, and became a museum piece. A similar process occurred in America, as those from a high cultural background sought to elevate ordinary culture to a level comparable to traditional high culture. This reached its apex in 1938 with John Hammond's 'Spirituals to Swing' concerts held at the high cultural temple, Carnegie Hall in New York. While the motives of those, like Hammond and Alan Lomax, who sought to make a claim for folk culture were noble (and politically radical) one of the unfortunate by-products of their efforts was a 'freezing' of the folk process into 'culture'. Even when folk song revivalists made great efforts to 'reclaim' folk music's working-class origins (such as the British folk song revival in the 1950s, led by Bert Lloyd and Ewan MacColl), the rigid definition of what could be considered a 'folk song' remained in place.

It does not take too much awareness of Dylan's work to imagine why this attitude would not appeal to Bob Dylan, nor why Bob Dylan would not appeal to someone who holds these ideals dear (MacColl in particular was dismissive of Dylan, describing him as 'a youth of mediocre talent'). Dylan has never treated folk songs as too precious to touch. For example, he subverts the stately Scottish ballad 'Pretty Peggy-O' on his first album by exclaiming 'I bin round this whole country, but I never yet found Fennario'[17] while, in 'Talkin' Hava Nageilah Blues', he parodies the folk world by saying 'here's a foreign song I learned in Utah'. Dylan's irreverence and eclecticism are not merely a clash of styles, nor are they evidence of his lack of commitment to folk music. Rather, they reflect a different ideological attitude that makes Dylan's work consistent with the sensibilities of the new generation of folk aficionados, particularly with regard to the relationship between individuals and collectivities.

An interest in folk culture has always contained an element of political criticism. The Romantics, critical of the destruction of avarice caused by industrial capitalism, sought lost times and places where humans could exist with each other and nature unaware of the needs of profit and instrumentalism. Folk culture was used as an emblem for everything capitalism was not – honest, pure, community-minded, natural, organic, human. Even contemporary interest in folk culture retains some of this ideology. Folk music is assumed to be inherently good because it is produced by 'the people', for themselves, to keep themselves entertained rather than for profit. However, just as the folk song became a frozen object, this approach to 'the folk' produces a similar fetishisation. 'The folk' are not real people but symbols, an idealisation of a certain way of life, an innocent at-one-with-nature way of life that never existed. We can see at this point how the objectification of the folk song actually reflected a similarly frozen idea of 'the folk'. As Boyes claims, 'thanks to folksong collectors' preconceptions and judicious selectivity, artwork and life were found to be identical'.[18] Folk songs were understood as a distillation of the lives of ordinary people but what results is a breakdown of the relationship between art and life; rather than folk music being a form of popular art, a certain kind of life *becomes* art: 'the poor are art because they sing their lives without mediation and without reflection, without the false consciousness of capitalism and the false desires of advertising'.[19] There was thus a parallel objectification of the rural and the working classes. Great classes of people were put on a pedestal, assumed to be inherently good and noble merely because of their place in the social structure. Marcus characterises the values of such an understanding as 'the country over the city, labour over capital, sincerity over education, the unspoiled nobility of the common man and woman over the businessman and the politician'.[20] The fetishised (authentic) folk song thus represented a fetishised people.

One outcome of this is an emphasis upon the collectivity rather than the individual, and there is little room for individual subjectivity within this conception of the folk song. While named characters clearly exist within folk songs, they often serve as representative characters, intended to reflect a particular social type (the errant daughter, the evil judge) rather than being treated as individual human beings. Continuing his critique, Marcus states: 'whether one hears them ringing true or false, they were pageants of righteousness, and while within these pageants there were armies and generations, heroes and villains, nightmares and dreams, there were almost no individuals'.[21] The folk movement was founded upon the importance of a particular kind of people

– the 'folk', the 'people' – rather than the individual. If a certain type of life replaced art in the folk movement, then that life was understood only structurally, as poverty, as oppression. The individual experiences of those in poverty, or those suffering racial discrimination, were not the most important thing. Instead, it was their representative role that mattered.

In his early career Dylan buys into at least some of this ideology, locating goodness in the wild West and corruption in the urban East (for example, in 'Let Me Die In My Footsteps' the glory of America is to be found in 'Nevada, New Mexico, Arizona, Idaho'). In general, however, Dylan's work sits uneasily with this representation of folk and folk music because of the emphasis given to individual experience, feelings and subjectivity. In Dylan's work individual experiences have always been the most important thing; the first songs that he wrote were not 'pageants of righteousness' but were, rather, stories of individual people caught in the machinations of everyday life – songs such as 'Man On The Street', 'Talking Bear Mountain Picnic Massacre Blues' or 'Ballad Of Donald White'. These early considerations of social justice occur through an evocation of individual experience. In this way, Dylan reflected the changing sensibilities of the folk revival, although they would only become apparent as the sixties developed.

THE BABY-BOOMERS, FOLK MUSIC AND INDIVIDUALISM

It is commonly overlooked that Dylan is actually a child of the 1950s and not the 1960s. Whatever his influence on the latter decade, he was a couple of years older than his musical contemporaries and his formative development occurred in the earlier one. This has significant repercussions:

if you were born between roughly 1941 and 1948 or 1950 –
born, that is, into the new postwar middle class but on the
upward slope, not the crest, of the baby boom – you grew
up in a reality perplexingly divided by the intermingling of
an emerging mass society and a decaying industrial culture
. . . At the same time, you had been born soon enough to
take the lingering traces of an earlier way of life into your
own imagination.[22]

This biological coincidence of being born on the cusp of the
old and the new had implications for the folk movement
and, in particular, brought about a subtle but dramatic
change in ethos of the folk revivals of the 1930s–1940s
and the 1950s–1960s. Two momentous breaches separated
the revivals: Elvis Presley and Senator Joseph McCarthy. I
will discuss the emergence of rock and roll in the next section; this section deals with McCarthyism, its effect on the
folk revival, and how this can be seen in Dylan's early work.

Folk music's links to political organisation is not merely
coincidence but the result of its form; folk's 'emphasis on the
words and on simple instrumentation make it both adaptable
and hospitable to politics'.[23] Without the need for electrical
power for its instruments, folk music can move to where
people are; the easily repeatable, singalong choruses enable
the audience to participate, increasing the authority of its
sentiments and reinforcing the strength of the song's
union.[24] This historical union of folk and politics meant that
folk practitioners were also expected to be political activists
and many of the leading figures of folk music, including Pete
Seeger and Woody Guthrie, were members of the Communist Party. This ideological position was generally wedded
to a 'social patriotism' that promoted America as 'one big
union' in which all workers needed to unite to harness the
potential of their country. Such a perspective was a viable

political position during the 1930s and early 1940s. Though not exactly mainstream in American political life, it sided with the victims of the great depression, linked with FDR's New Deal policies to rebuild America for the common man, and was anti-fascist, with the Soviet Union being seen as a key bulwark against the rise of Nazism. Following the end of the Second World War, however, the Soviet Union became defined as America's chief opponent and a paranoid environment existed in which the American government sought to counter 'Communist subversion'. Individuals from all walks of life were accused of being Communist supporters, often on flimsy evidence. Once accused, it became almost impossible for people to exonerate themselves and being labelled a Communist meant there was little chance of obtaining work. One particular field that was decried as awash with Reds was the entertainment industry, particular Hollywood, and a number of actors, directors and other professional entertainers were 'blacklisted', which meant that they could not be employed in the entertainment sector.

Many in the folk movement were victims of McCarthyism but none more so than Pete Seeger. As part of the witch-hunt, Seeger was called to appear before the House Un-American Activities Committee in 1955. He refused to declare any personal or political links and was therefore charged with contempt and blacklisted.* Ironically, however, one of the indirect effects of Seeger's blacklisting was the increasing popularity of folk music by the end of the fifties. Unable to play at the majority of professional venues, Seeger engaged in 'cultural guerrilla warfare', playing at school summer camps and college campuses. These performances engaged a new generation with the sounds of folk

---

* He was found guilty in 1961 and sentenced to twelve months' imprisonment, though this was overturned on appeal.

music. According to Cantwell, however, the experience of McCarthyism stripped the songs of their ideological roots and the new revivalists therefore approached folk song in a different way, without an explicitly class-based ideology.[25] Rather than being entwined with working-class activism, the new generation heard folk songs as an aesthetic representation of particular types of life. This change can be demonstrated in the pages of *Sing Out!*, a folk magazine established in 1950. Whereas its first issue had lavished praise on the Soviet Union and its folk culture, it gradually dissociated itself from working-class politics until its mission statement fully explained the purpose of folk music in the new revival: 'We are, first of all, interested in folk and traditional music, as a living heritage – a link to the past – as an aesthetic experience, and as a vehicle for contemporary music.'[26] In the summer of 1959, John Cohen wrote in the magazine 'the emphasis is no longer on social reform or on world-wide reform. The effort is focused more on the search for real and human values'.[27] The purpose of folk music was thus seen as recreating lived experience, giving its listeners 'first hand' understanding of others' lives. The emphasis on individual experience within Dylan's work can be seen as reflecting this emerging ideology. In 1963, he wrote an open letter to his old friend Tony Glover explaining why he had to sing his own songs rather than traditional songs such as 'Red Apple Juice' and 'Little Maggie'. He made clear his debt to his folk heritage, however, for 'the folk songs showed me . . . that songs can say somethin' human'.[28] At the same time, however, the fact that Dylan was defending his need to sing songs such as 'Masters Of War' and 'Seven Curses' indicates that the shift in consciousness does not mean that folk song necessarily became depoliticised. Many from the earlier folk movements certainly saw it this way but the new generation of folk music aficionados reoriented folk's politics away from the collective politics of labour unions and towards the politics of individual experience. The songs dispersed by Seeger's guerrilla warfare, and those heard on Harry Smith's *Folkways Anthology Of American Folk Music* 'introduc[ed] into the cultural stream, folk images and sounds, dehistoricisized and yet replete with the past, deideologized but inherently political'.[29] *

I do not mean to suggest a simple binary split between the old folkies and the new generation engaged in the folk revival. Many younger members of the folk revival clearly did have simplistic political views with goodies and baddies, black and white (of the kind Dylan would later criticise in 'My Back Pages'). Neither do I want to suggest a clear time period for these changes. Real life is messy and things not necessarily clear. In fact, I would argue that the political differences between the old and new ways of interpreting folk music only become clear in the mid-sixties, once rock replaces folk as the voice of student protest. The relationship between folk music and collective politics was reoriented around this time, but it did not disappear entirely. Indeed, as it is intimately associated with the nascent civil rights movement, the fifties and sixties folk revival was highly politicised. The historical link between the revival and the civil rights movement can, I think, be explained by the fact that the advancement of black people in the US was a cause that could be placed into the interpretative framework of both the old left and the newly developing sensibility: racism could be addressed both in socio-structural terms and in terms of individual experiences of racist brutality. Nowhere is the tension between these two ways of seeing the same issue better expressed than in Dylan's 'The Lonesome Death Of Hattie Carroll', a song that offers 'a supreme understanding of the

---

* Marqusee suggests that Dylan's politics came 'largely from records' (2003:50).

difference between writing a political song and writing a song politically'.[30] It tells the story of the murder of a barmaid by William Zanzinger, the son of wealthy tobacco farmers. The first verse details the murder, the second verse describes Zanzinger. The third verse describes Hattie and her experience as a mother and waitress. After each of these verses the same refrain is repeated:

Ah, but you who philosophise disgrace
And criticise all fears
Take the rag away from your face
Now ain't the time for your tears.

The final verse details the courtroom scene, where Zanzinger is given a six-month sentence for murder. The refrain then changes to:

Ah, but you who philosophise disgrace
And criticise all fears
Bury the rag most deep in your face
Now's the time for your tears.

Here Dylan recognises that the real tragedy is in the death of a real woman and not the injustice of the courts. What matters is not the representative role that Hattie plays, but the fact that some real children have lost their mother. The final refrain chastises those who cry crocodile tears over the woman when they are really crying over the judge's trivial sentence.[31] Another way the song achieves this is through the absence of any mention of race: there is no telling from the song that Hattie Carroll is black and Zanzinger white. To those crying crocodile tears it is the crucial factor but to Dylan it misses the point. As he once rebuked a journalist, 'you have no respect for me, sir, if you think I could write about Negroes as Negroes instead of as people' (Sydney press conference, 1966).

The different political approaches can also be illustrated by looking at the use of pronouns in folk music. In the songs of the union era, 'the protest singer . . . presented his utopian visions in the second person plural (we)'.[32] 'We Shall Overcome' and 'We Shall Not Be Moved' are perhaps the most obvious examples. In some of his early work, Dylan follows this pattern. For example, in an early protest song, 'The Death Of Emmett Till', Dylan concludes:

> But if all of us folks that thinks alike, if we gave all we
>   could give,
> We could make this great land of ours a greater place
>   to live.

More typically, however, Dylan utilised singular pronouns (I and, particularly, you) in his work, as exemplified in his two most famous protest songs. Ricks suggests that 'Blowin' In The Wind' conveys 'a certain political loneliness . . . by continually playing plurals against singulars'[33] and points out that there is no 'we' in 'The Times They Are A-Changin' ' – 'it is another of the great Dylan *you* songs'.[34] The reference to a plural in this song ('they') refers only to the times and not to the people.

Hampton suggests that the use of singulars becomes a central feature of folk music beyond the 1950s[35] and this implies that sensitivity to subjective experience was not unique to Dylan. Indeed, it echoes the work of the earlier folk idol, Woody Guthrie (and was, presumably, a reason for Dylan's own admiration of Guthrie). However, Guthrie became politically radicalised by his engagement with the New York folk scene of the 1940s and, perhaps more attuned to the collective ethos of his contemporaries, strove to weld his championing of the underdog with a union-driven social patriotism.[36] Dylan's work makes no such concession and this explains why a change in musical form – the shift in pronouns – is actually a political shift that is both a symptom and a cause of Dylan's strained relationship with the folk revivalists.

This approach also offers one way of explaining the reason for Dylan's prominence within the revival. Dylan's work, more than anyone else's, gave expression to the shift in political consciousness that characterises the folk revival, from union collectivism to empathetic individualism. In Goldmann's terms, Dylan's work expresses the new revivalists' 'world view'. This quality of Dylan's work fundamentally links him to the folk revival:

> Dylan's early songs appeared so promptly as to seem absolutely contemporary with the civil rights movement. There was no time lag. He wasn't a songwriter who came into an established political mood, he seemed to be a part of it and his songs seemed informative to the Movement as the Movement seemed informative to the song writer. This cross-fertilization was absolutely critical in Dylan's relationship to the Movement and the Movement's relationship to Dylan. He gave character to the sensibilities of the Movement.[37]

This symbiotic relationship between Dylan's songs and 'the movement' is emphasised in a recent analysis by Mike Marqusee:

> the music Bob Dylan made in the sixties has long outgrown its national origins, just as it has outlived its era, but to understand it, to make best use of it, you need to trace its roots in both time and place. However you measure Dylan's

subsequent achievements (and they are substantial), they do not enjoy the same umbilical relation to the turmoil of the times as the work of the sixties.[38]

This is the fundamental element of Dylan's stardom. However much he has attempted to shake off the label, to change roles, to be an anti-leader, Dylan's stardom since he 'left the folk movement' over forty years ago, has been shaped by this image as a political leader. His politics, however, and his work, emerge from a change in consciousness of the folk revival, in particular the emergence of a new cohort of young revivalists at the start of the sixties. This changing generational consciousness explains why a Bob Dylan-shaped space should emerge at the beginning of the 1960s. The Goldmannesque explanation offered here provides only a partial explanation for why it was this particular Bob Dylan, and not any of the other emerging folk singers, that filled the space. It may explain why Dylan became seen as the greatest songwriter within the folk movement but it does not fully explain why he should emerge as a star in a way that Woody Guthrie, for example, never was. One explanation is in Dylan's shift from folk music and his role in the emergence of rock, discussed in the next chapter. What is also significant, however, is the way in which the folk revival was, unlike earlier folk music, intrinsically part of the mass media.

STARDOM, FOLK MUSIC AND MASS CULTURE

I have already mentioned that the interest in folk culture was part of a much wider cultural critique, as the Romantics sought times and places that had not been colonised by the ills of capitalism. An interest in folk music, even today, maintains an element of that critical consciousness. This is most clear in relationship to the music industry, as folk music is considered as more authentic and real than the music produced by record labels. Folk revivals are, therefore, their own form of cultural critique (one of the dominant discourses of the fifties folk revival in Britain, for example, was in opposition to the Americanisation of British music caused by the emergence of rock and roll). These assumptions (about 'real' and 'mass produced' music) can be seen in the conventions of folk music, in the seating arrangements in folk clubs and – notably for Dylan's story – in the absence of electrical amplification, both of which serve to minimise the distance between singer and audience. In folk music, the relationship between singer and audience should be 'natural' rather than 'mediated'. An interest in folk culture is in some ways, therefore, a form of criticism of mass culture. Folk music is supposed to be thoroughly anti-commercial because otherwise the capitalist music industry would sanitise and drain the emotion and/or politics from it. Folk music is 'our' music, the music of the people and not 'their' (the capitalists') music imposed upon us, providing us with a false consciousness and satisfying desires we didn't know we had. In an early critique of mass culture, Dwight MacDonald outlines the dichotomy:

> Folk Art grew from below. It was a spontaneous, autochthonous expression of the people, shaped by themselves, pretty much without the benefit of High Culture, to suit their own needs. Mass Culture is imposed from above. It is fabricated by technicians hired by businessmen; its audiences are passive consumers, their participation limited to the choice between buying and not buying.[39]

Whether these ideas are true or merely part of the same ideological process that defined folk music in the first place is not the point here: what matters is that, when looking at the folk revival around 1960 it becomes harder to maintain such distinctions. To a certain extent, the folk revival was commercially driven, filling in a gap left by the decline of rock and roll. It is certainly true that those young people attracted to folk music during the revival could not be considered representative of 'the folk', generally being white, middle class, well educated and from the Eastern Seaboard. More than anything, they were an audience defined by shared taste.

Serge Denisoff argues that this resulted in a major shift within the sensibilities of the folk revival because the new generation of folkies 'did not reject, as did the "working-class intellectuals" of the 1940s, the offerings of mass media as obscurantist ploys. Nor did they necessarily desire the creation of a "people's music". For them folk music was *already* part of popular music, subject to the structural nuances of the industry.'[40] In empirical terms, I think this is a little blunt. It would be incorrect to suggest that the music industry was no longer a subject of criticism by the new folkies. What the music industry was producing was being criticised and 'folk music' was still supposed to stand for the pure, the incorruptible and the uncommodifiable, in contrast to the commercial pop songs of the day. At a more ideological level, however, Denisoff is correct because the major change was that, for the younger folk-revivalists, the mass culture critique was no longer absolute. It was no longer assumed to be the case that *all* mass culture was necessarily drivel. Perhaps because some of them had experienced the radical potential of Elvis and James Dean, the new folkies were more optimistic, believing that the cultural industries could produce *some* aesthetically interesting and politically challenging work even if most of what it produced was pap. The belief was that, despite the industry's best intentions, good work could still sneak out.

The folk revival was thus built on a contradiction; it was a mass-mediated revival of a form of music that was against the mass media. It was a form of stylistic rebellion which borrowed from urban, bohemian, subcultures.[41] This is not to suggest that it was a fake, or that its participants were insincere. On the contrary, many of them were rather too sincere, and over-earnestness was a feature of the folk revival that Dylan most disliked. But it is to say that it was authentically inauthentic, a mediated presentation of unmediated folk music. It also means that the most prominent players in the folk revival – Dylan in particular – were subject to pressures of commerce and fashion the likes of which Pete Seeger never had to manage.[42] Because the folk revival happened in a mass-mediated environment, Dylan became a folk music star in a manner inconceivable to someone of Seeger's generation and this caused concern for that older generation. This is not merely because of the contradiction inherent in an individual representing a collective movement: as Hampton points out, the heroic singer-songwriter has always played an important role in the folk protest movement, most notably in the figures of Joe Hill and Woody Guthrie.[43] In those earlier instances, however, the individual had been an embodiment of the people – not a representative of, but a representation of the folk. While Woody Guthrie embodied the spirit of the folk, a personification of the multitudes, stardom offers something different. It utilises stars as embodiments of social groups and types, but it also valorises the specific individuality of the star.

If we go right back to the start of Dylan's career, we can see this tension. Dylan's early years as a performer were characterised by the elaborate tales he spun to create a fictional biography that mimicked the hard travelling undertaken by Guthrie. The specific details of his stories varied with each telling, but there are some consistencies in his overall projection. He acknowledged that he grew up in Hibbing, but told stories of how he had run away several times as a child and had travelled throughout the southwestern states. Dylan's vehicle for rationalising his travelling past was that he worked on carnivals. He would tell stories of carnival folk and the people he had met while travelling, frequently prefacing songs with details of fictitious characters from which he had supposedly learned the song. This fictional biography went on for a surprisingly long time, and also featured in some of his work. In 'My Life In A Stolen Moment', a poem included in the programme for his April 1963 concert at New York Town Hall, he wrote:

Hibbing's a good old town
I ran away from it when I was 10, 12, 13, 15, 15½, 17
    an' 18
I been caught an' brought back all but once.

Gibbens argues that Dylan's tall tales, 'did not really amount to an alternative, fictitious biography so much as an evasion of biography. The important thing was not that he should be from somewhere other than where he came from, but that he should be from nowhere in particular . . . that he should be a kind of Everyman.'[44]

There is some merit in this; the everyman figure – an individual like Guthrie that embodies the essence of the people – has played an important part in American culture. But Dylan's play-acting also opens up perhaps the most extreme contradiction of stardom – the tension between the star-as-ordinary and the star-as-special. The emergence of stardom is intricately linked to the emergence of democracy and meritocracy, 'only becom[ing] a phenomenon in the age of the common man'.[45] One feature of the transition from traditional to modern societies is the way that religion, monarchy and ascribed social roles that automatically commanded respect through birth were usurped by the idea that any individual could become a person of wealth and influence by virtue of hard work and talent. Stardom only emerges within this modern context. Stars function as public proof that success is open to all. So, ideas that stars come from a humble background, that everyone has a unique personality and that, yes, even you could be discovered as a star, are key elements of the ideology of stardom. This is apparent in the rags-to-riches Hollywood tales and has perhaps reached its ultimate end with reality TV shows. It is clear that the discourse of ordinariness played a key role in Woody Guthrie's celebrity. Dylan, in adopting a Guthrie-esque persona, follows that tradition.*

It is also clear, however, that something more is going on. Guthrie's experiences, and the portrayal in his autobiography make him out to be not just ordinary, but extraordinary. Guthrie's abundance of ordinary experience makes him an extraordinary character and Dylan, through deceit, tries to play a similar sleight of hand: presenting himself as a mundane, no high-flyer, regular kind of guy while at the same time offering a biography that clearly marks himself off as very different from other would-be folk singers. This contra-

---

* Most of Dylan's influences clearly come from the 1950s, and it has been noted in many biographies that the young Dylan was interested in movies. In his historical account of film stardom, Richard Schickel suggests that the 1930s–1950s era of Hollywood history can generally be described as an era of 'normality' in which, rather than scandal or excess, stars seemed to be normal, just like you and me, only richer. Acting was seen as a noble trade (2000:65–87). This idea runs deep in Dylan's conception of his own work and has become a notable element of his explanations for the Never Ending Tour – presenting himself merely as a craftsman doing his work and providing for his family.

diction, between ordinariness and specialness, is a central
element of stardom. As Dyer states:

> Particularly as developed in the star system, the success
> myth tries to orchestrate several contradictory elements:
> that ordinariness is the hallmark of the star; that the system
> rewards talent and 'specialness'; that luck, 'breaks', which
> may happen to anyone, typify the career of the star; and
> that hard work and professionalism are necessary for star-
> dom. Some stars reconcile all four elements, while with
> others only some aspects are emphasised. Stardom as a
> whole holds all four things to be true.[46]

These things are contradictory, but the most powerful stars
manage to hold them in balance: '[Dylan and Baez] were
"absolutely coherent" and yet compounded of heteroge-
neous elements usually foreign and irreconcilable; they were
arrestingly familiar, instantly recognizable, and yet somehow
inscrutable; widely imitated, made themselves of imitation,
mere types, long familiar in the revival and on the wider cultural landscape and yet thoroughly inimitable and original.'[47]
Stardom's emphasis upon the individual means that the politics of a movement become mediated through a particular
star persona and thus through the actions of the star (in this
instance though, I think, not in any of the others discussed
here, Baez is as important as Dylan). The way that stardom
functions means that politics can only be viewed through the
prism of a particular star's actions:

> It would be hard for the press to deal in any other way with
> a star's revolutionary associations. What the star does can
> only be posed in terms of the star doing it, the extraordi-
> nariness or difficulty of her/his doing it, rather than in
> terms of the ostensible political issues involved.[48]

Ultimately it meant that the strength of the folk revival depended upon the image of one individual. For those who saw the folk revival as a way of enabling political change, this was a fragile position.

In the end, of course, the old guard were right from their side: Dylan's split from the folk revival precipitated its demise, and the individualised politics, both in the revival itself and in its transmutation into rock, were not tools to enable working-class emancipation. They were wrong, however, in thinking it could ever be anything else. The folk revival was not a mass movement but a mass-mediated movement. Because of this it could never offer a real alternative, but could only posit change through itself, through the very medium that helps maintain inequality. It could never transcend the conditions of its own production. The revival's origins within the culture industry also explains the emergence of a political sensibility dominated by individualism. While the belief was that only by developing one's individual self-awareness could one change society, such transformation could only occur through consumption in the commercial sphere (this reaches its apex with the evolution of rock). As Robert Cantwell notes:

> Bob Dylan's first album was not a commercial triumph but it was a triumph of the folk revival . . . now it was ratified by the commercial establishment. Play could become an instrument for shaping reality and hence a means of laying claim to the social and historical initiative. This was the contribution of the folk revival to the sixties counterculture.[49]

A mass mediated form of popular music, even one as embedded in political discourse as the folk revival, can only 'capture what it is like to be oppressed; it cannot explain that oppression or remove it'.[50] Similarly, while a star can express or embody the contradictions of a particular time, ideology or group, he can't reconcile those contradictions, can't make them go away. Stardom is a contradictory mixture of subjectivity and collectivity, of the common (wo)man and the unique individual but it is also the marriage of democracy and commercialism[51] – it emerges as a phenomenon only in a commercialised culture and, as such, it can never be the vehicle to transcend that commercial reality.

Dylan emerged as a star at a time when things may not have seemed this way, however. More than anyone else, he came to symbolise the political restlessness of a new generation who, initially, utilised the honesty and simplicity of folk music as a way of expressing their frustration. Whether Dylan ever genuinely believed that political change was possible is doubtful but, for our discussion of Dylan's stardom, irrelevant. What matters are two key points. First, the star image of Dylan as an emblem of politically radical youth; second, the elevation of human subjectivity and individual self-development as a form of political activity. Both of these become intensified during the emergence of rock in the mid-sixties, which fundamentally depended upon the sensibilities of the folk revival. As such, Dylan is the key figure in the emergence of rock culture.

Snapshot: The chameleon poet

Dylan became increasingly uncomfortable with his role in the folk revival. He had regularly disclaimed the Spokesman of a Generation tag and, in 1964, he released the album *Another Side Of Bob Dylan*, which contained a number of love songs and 'My Back Pages', a disclaimer of his 'protest era'. Significantly, it contained no explicit protest songs in the manner of *The Times They Are A-Changin'*. Many of Dylan's fans became increasingly uneasy about his seeming change of direction.

During 1964 and early 1965, Dylan's persona began to transform. He generally became more hip, wearing dandyish clothes in place of the folk singer's uniform of jeans and work boots. The tension between Dylan and his audience increased when, in March 1965, Dylan released *Bringing It All Back Home*. Its first side was recorded with an electric backing band, which outraged many in the folk fraternity. In May, Dylan toured the UK as a solo folk performer, mixing his new work like 'Mr Tambourine Man' and 'It's Alright Ma (I'm Only Bleeding)' with his older protest work.

On his return from the UK, Dylan penned and recorded a new song, 'Like A Rolling Stone'. Recorded with a full band, the song, with its sweeping sound, has become emblematic of Dylan's career. It gave Dylan his highest chart placing (number two) and is regarded as one of the most important songs ever recorded. Dylan played it, along with two other songs from his forthcoming album, *Highway 61 Revisited*, at the Newport Folk Festival in July. By playing with an electric band at this most sacred of folk events, Dylan deliberately broke the unwritten rules of the folk revival. He outraged many of the organisers and was booed by the audience, providing one of the most dramatic performances in rock history.

The conflict between Dylan and his audience continued for
the rest of 1965 and on his 1966 world tour. In these shows,
Dylan would play the first set solo with an acoustic guitar.
These performances were well received. After a break, he
would return supported by The Band and play an electric set
culminating in 'Like A Rolling Stone'. Everywhere Dylan played
these electrified performances were booed by the audience
and Dylan argued with hecklers. These shows soon took on a
mythical quality, available for many years on bootleg before the
'Royal Albert Hall' concert (actually from Manchester) was officially released in 1998.

Albums and major events

November 1963	*Newsweek* publishes an article that reveals Dylan's conventional upbringing in Hibbing
February 1964	Three weeks road trip from New York to San Francisco, during which Dylan first hears the music of The Beatles
May 1964	First public performance of 'Mr Tambourine Man'
July 1964	Newport Folk Festival
August 1964	*Another Side of Bob Dylan*
March 1965	*Bringing It All Back Home*
May 1965	UK tour (documented in the film *Don't Look Back*)
June 1965	Moves out of New York to Woodstock
June 1965	Writes and records 'Like A Rolling Stone'
July 1965	Plugs in at the Newport Folk Festival
August 1965	*Highway 61 Revisited*
November 1965	Marries Sara Lowndes
April–May 1966	World Tour (documented in *The Bootleg Series volume 4*)
May 1966	*Blonde and Blonde*

4

ROCK STARDOM: RECONCILING
CULTURE AND COMMERCE

The apex of the folk revival of the early sixties came at the Newport Folk Festival in July 1963. On the final night of the event, Dylan, Joan Baez, Pete Seeger and Peter, Paul and Mary linked arms and led the audience through renditions of 'We Shall Overcome' and 'Blowin' In The Wind'. Two years later, the same festival provided the site for the symbolic end of the revival, as Dylan outraged the organisers and was booed by the audience for playing with an electric backing band. After that performance, 'what had been understood as folk music would as a cultural force have all but ceased to exist'.[1]

Dylan's Newport 1965 performance is probably the most discussed performance in the history of popular music. Biographically, the performance can be seen as part of a process – beginning at least as early as February 1964 when Dylan began writing 'Mr Tambourine Man', and continuing at least as far as May 1966 when Dylan was booed by British audiences on the last leg of his 1966 world tour. In terms of rock historiography, however, this single act – plugging in at Newport – is used to symbolise the closing of one chapter and the opening of another, both in terms of Dylan's own career and with regard to popular music as a whole. Dylan 'going electric' is a foundational moment in popular music history.

Accounts of Dylan's shift from acoustic to electric music usually concentrate on what Dylan did to popular music – making it literate and giving it a social conscience. While Dylan may have been a folk star, the folk revival was still only a small section of popular music and, so the story goes, it is only when Dylan changes musical forms that his true effect is felt. These narratives are key elements of Dylan's star-image. For example, Peter Wicke argues that 'by [going electric] Dylan had shown a way forward which was not only followed by many former folk musicians but which placed rock music in contexts which led its development to follow increasingly political criteria'[2] while Mike Marqusee states that 'Dylan opened up an established form to a range of words, references, experiences, moods, and modes not previously associated with it'.[3] Now, I'm not about to begin arguing against such a position, but I do want to approach it in a slightly different (though not wholly original) way. The above quotes imply that Dylan moved from 'folk' into a pre-existing 'rock' music which opened the genre up to new possibilities. My suggestion is that rock did not exist before Dylan's shift to electric music. All of the contemporaneous media reports on Dylan's shift to an electric band that I have seen refer to him playing not 'rock' but 'rock and roll'. Rock and roll was a label that described a teenage music assumed to be good for dancing and little else. There are references to a new type of 'folk-rock' but no mentions of 'rock music'. Rock has a long history in popular music as a verb (e.g. 'Rock Around The Clock', or 'Rock Me Baby') but at this time it did not exist as a noun that classified a form of music. Dylan was seen to have become a rock and roll (or, derogatively and synonymously from a number of disgruntled fans, a pop) performer; it is only afterwards (at least 1967, maybe even later) that it is presented as a shift from 'folk' to 'rock'. So when I say that Dylan going electric was a foundational moment, I mean it literally. Dylan was the catalyst for the formation of a new type of popular music, one that dominated the mainstream for at least the next decade. Dylan's mid-sixties albums 'inspired a new sort of writing, rock criticism, and a new sort of pop fan, the pursuer of meaning rather than pin ups'.[4]

Making such a statement means considering 'rock' in a slightly unconventional way because it concentrates on ideology rather than musical structure. Obviously, electrical instrumentation existed in popular music prior to 1965 and so, while Dylan's mid-sixties albums are musically distinctive, they are not necessarily genre-forming. But, while it might seem a perverse claim, 'rock' is not really about music. As Lawrence Grossberg explains, 'although an account of rock cannot ignore its musical affectivity, it is also the case that rock cannot be defined in musical terms. There are, for all practical purposes, no musical limits on what can or cannot be rock'.[5] This is why albums as differently sounding as *Nashville Skyline* and *Street Legal* can both be considered 'rock'. Instead of viewing rock as a particular genre we need, following Keightley, to view it as a musical culture.[6] The distinctive characteristic of rock culture is that it is generated from within the mainstream:

> Unlike jazz and folk . . . rock's history cannot be understood in terms of processes of crossover. At the outset, there is no 'elsewhere' from whence rock is taken and then 'mainstreamed', no 'outside' or place apart from the mainstream that might serve as rock's birthplace. For all of rock's appropriation, modification or outright theft of

African-American, agrarian, or working-class musical cultures, it is not itself a form of crossover, nor a subculture incorporated by the dominant culture, nor a counterculture (the term most associated with rock politics in the 1960s). Rock may wear subcultural clothes, identify with marginalised minorities, promote countercultural political positions, and upset genteel notions of propriety, but from its inception it has been a large-scale, industrially organised, mass-mediated mainstream phenomenon operating at the very centre of society.[7]

Rock emerged in the mid-sixties as a way of *stratifying* mainstream musical consumption, as a means of creating higher and lower levels of popular music. The basis of rock is the claim that certain elements of popular music are worthy of being taken seriously in their own right. Rather than merely assuming a difference in quality between serious/classical music and light/popular music, rock functions to differentiate between serious, worthwhile popular music (rock) and trivial, lightweight popular music (pop). As such, whether someone is defined as 'rock' or not is a question to be addressed not musically but in terms of ideology (how else can *John Wesley Harding* be considered rock?). This means that, in particular, ideas of authenticity are crucial. The notion of authenticity is complex and contradictory and its surface forms change over time. It is, however, underpinned by consistent ideological roots: rock tends to be defended on two grounds. Firstly, a 'folk ideology' supports the idea that rock is music produced by a specific social group and that rock stars thus represent that group. Secondly, an 'art ideology' presents the idea that rock stars are creative individuals expressing their unique personal vision through their work.[8]

The centrality of these ideologies of authenticity for rock's attempts to stratify the mainstream is the reason that

Dylan is the foundational figure in rock culture. Dylan's shift to electric music brought to the mainstream the political authority and communal links of his folk past while his songwriting skills offered the exemplar of what could be achieved artistically within the new form. In a recent book, Bernard Gendron discusses how rock music came to be accepted as a legitimate artistic form. His claim is that The Beatles are the key figures in this process, arguing that the critical acclaim of their later albums is the key force behind rock's critical acceptance.[9] Gendron underplays Dylan's role in this process, suggesting that 'the story of Dylan's canonization does not coincide as neatly with that of rock as does The Beatles'[10] because a) Dylan had cultural legitimacy before moving into rock music; and b) Dylan was absent from rock's cultural high point in 1967. I shall deal with the latter point in the next chapter – Dylan was actually a considerable presence on the rock scene in 1967 – but the point he makes about Dylan's previous cultural authority is both true and, in my view, the key reason for the rise of The Beatles' legitimacy that Gendron takes as his subject. Gendron points out that The Beatles were critically dismissed as juvenile on their first tour to America in 1964, yet by the summer of 1965 were beginning to be taken seriously as artists. My argument is that Dylan's earlier stardom and his electrified output in 1965 helped teen music acquire a legitimacy that became the hallmark of rock culture. I am not suggesting that Dylan single-handedly 'invented' rock – what Dylan achieved could not have occurred without a range of other musical and social factors being in place, including the emergence of The Beatles in 1964 – but his stardom provided a catalyst for a range of social and cultural ideas to coalesce within rock culture. This is why Greil Marcus can claim that, in 1965, 'Bob Dylan seemed less to occupy a turning point in cultural space and time than to be that turning point'.[11]

DYLAN, ROCK AND TRANSITION

In 1965, Bob Dylan was the coolest person on the planet. Not just popular (though popular he certainly was: in September of that year, 48 of his songs were recorded by other artists and 8 of his songs were in the Top 40, 4 of them sung by him), but *cool*. He dressed immaculately, without ever seeming contrived; his hair became increasingly uncontrolled and somehow still managed to look perfect; he held court with icy wit and implacable nerve; he played mind games to destroy journalistic triviality; he wore sunglasses even when indoors and, as one journalist wrote in 1966, even when 'he removed his dark glasses as a bonus to the cameramen, [he] somehow managed to look exactly the same'. In 1965, he was the only person to give the impression that he knew exactly what was going on, always two steps ahead. If one compares the TV interviews of The Beatles, The Stones and Dylan in 1965, the difference is telling: whereas The Beatles and Stones may have engaged in some slightly childish wordplay in response to interviewers, they were essentially well-behaved boys keen to make a good impression. Dylan treated journalists like they were plankton (in his second national TV performance, Dylan constantly called his interviewer, Les Crane, 'Less'). He seemed to manifest a particular aura: aloof and happening, it is no wonder that both The Beatles and The Stones were in awe of Dylan whenever they met.

My argument is that Dylan was the first real Rock Star. His razor-sharp hipness in 1965 and the strung-out excesses of 1966 laid down the prototype for this new social role. Some of the substance of Dylan's new star-image was rooted in his public persona developed as a folk star but his image in 1965–6 is clearly a different type of star-image. We need to ask, therefore, what enabled his image to take on new meanings. Dylan's stardom is not merely led by his artistic output or force of personality. The star-image also acts as a limit on what the star can and cannot do (for example, Schickel discusses how Ingrid Bergman was the subject of a scandal when she had an affair because such behaviour did not correspond to her star-image).[12] It prescribes acceptable and unacceptable behaviour, what music can be released and what cannot. Early in 1963, Dylan recorded a number of tracks with an electric backing band with the intention of releasing one 'electric side' on *The Freewheelin' Bob Dylan*. It was eventually decided to release an album made up almost exclusively of acoustic material performed solo. While we could just see this as an individual decision made by Dylan, it was actually structured, not only by his manager Albert Grossman and his record label, but by wider audience expectations, by what his particular star-image meant. Dylan's fairly fixed image as a folk star placed limits on what Dylan could do.

Dylan did eventually release an album with one electric side in 1965 – *Bringing It All Back Home*. We thus need to investigate what changed to enable him to pursue this direction. To my mind, the most significant event is the publication of an article in *Newsweek* magazine on 4 November 1963. The article had been sought by Dylan's publicist and record company but it turned into something very negative, accusing Dylan of hypocrisy:

> He says he hates the commercial side of folk music, but he has two agents who hover about him, guarding his words and fattening his contracts. He scorns the press's interest in him, but he wants to know how long a story about him will run and if there will be a photograph.[13]

The article even propagated a rumour (still occasionally heard today) that Dylan bought rather than wrote 'Blowin'

In The Wind'. By far the most significant element of the story, however, was that it was the first to publicise Dylan's normal background:

> He has suffered; he has been hung up, man, without bread, without a chick, with twisted wires growing inside him. His audiences share his pain, and seem jealous because they grew up in conventional homes and conventional schools. The ironic thing is that Bob Dylan, too, grew up in a conventional home, and went to conventional schools.[14]

The article publicised his birthname, pointed out that his parents were in New York to see his next show, and even interviewed his younger brother.

Dylan was furious about the article; it marked the starting point of his lifelong antagonistic relationship with the press. The irony is that although Dylan was furious with the exposé, it probably served him well in the long run because it removed the fixity of his star-image.[15] Without the article it is difficult to see a way in which Dylan's renunciations of his protest material would not also have been a renunciation of the whole meaning of the star-image 'Bob Dylan'. If 'Bob Dylan' meant only one thing then taking it away would have reduced Dylan's significance as a star, effectively signifying a withdrawal from the public sphere, a retirement.* By exposing his 'real identity', however, the *Newsweek* article opened up new possibilities for Dylan's stardom. Given the private/public signifying split in stardom, discussed in chapter 2, the revelations added a new depth to Dylan's star-image. It

---

* Dylan did, in fact, take a decision to retire in May 1965, immediately following the British tour documented in the film *Don't Look Back*. This decision was surely the outcome of the tension between Dylan's star-image – still very much a freewheelin' folk singer in the UK – and his own desire to move forwards musically.

made Dylan 'the person' seem considerably more complex than before, and fitted an ideology of upward mobility that implied people could transform their circumstances through strength of will. The article actually made it easier for Dylan to play games with his public identity because the nature of the game was now public and 'being played with the audience's full knowledge. The mask could be worn in public and could be publicly displayed as a mask'.[16] The idea of 'Bob Dylan' suddenly became a lot more complicated and a lot more playful.

This 'opening up' of the Dylan persona is crucial for the rapid transformation of Dylan's stardom in the mid-sixties but it has also been the mainstay of Dylan's star-image ever since: crucially, Dylan's stardom developed so that '"Bob Dylan" stand[s] not for any imposed role but for the very act of resistance to imposed roles'.[17] Thus a key media portrayal of Dylan revolves around his indefinability and his unwillingness to be defined (for example, Malcom Jones opens his 1995 *Newsweek* article with 'the one sure thing about Bob Dylan is that there is no sure thing' while on its release Jon Pareles described *Time Out Of Mind* as 'a typical Dylan album only because it eludes expectations').

The resistance to confinement is a theme that regularly features in Dylan's work. For example, In 'All I Really Wanna Do', Dylan sings to his paramour that he 'ain't lookin' to . . . Simplify you, classify you . . . Analyse you, categorise you . . . Or define you or confine you', with the clear implication that he expects the same in return. It is notable that the two songs Dylan decided to call 'I Shall Be Free' and 'I Shall Be Free #10' are both nonsense songs, stripped of the confinement of rational expectations. Later in the decade, confinement became a political issue, as in 'It's Alright Ma (I'm Only Bleeding)':

A question in your nerves is lit
Yet you know there is no answer fit
To satisfy, ensure you not to quit
To keep it in your mind and not forget
That it is not he or she or them or it
That you belong to.

Related to a resistance to confinement is the idea of transition, of 'moving on'. This can be seen most clearly in songs
such as 'Don't Think Twice, It's Alright' and 'One More Cup
Of Coffee' but is a consistent theme throughout Dylan's
career. Dylan's most famous song of this era – 'Like A
Rolling Stone' – offers a prime example of this commitment
to transition. The theme of the song is that it is only when
stripped of the security of everyday comfort and privilege
that you can find out who you really are but, as Ricks discusses, although the song is superficially vengeful, it contains
a strong undercurrent of yearning.[18] The soaring vocal in the
choruses intimates that being on your own and completely
unknown provides a level of freedom unattainable to the
singer, who can never be completely unknown. Moving on
and starting again are the only ways to start from a clean
slate. Standing still means being defined and confined.
Dylan's response to such a situation is always to move on. It
is a central characteristic of Dylan's star-image, a central
emblem of Dylan's Never Ending Tour, discussed in chapter
7, and best summed up towards the end of 'Tangled Up In
Blue':

When finally the bottom fell out
I became withdrawn
The only thing I knew how to do
Was to keep on keepin' on
Like a bird that flew . . .

This transitoriness – an unwillingness to be tied down to one place or one position – is a central feature of rock culture. Rock emerges within the mainstream, generated through the emotional experiences of a unique generation that relies upon the comfort and privilege of an administered consumer society while at the same time being constrained by the limits of that administration. Grossberg portrays rock culture as an attempt to transcend the possibilities of an administered society through adopting symbols of those excluded from its everyday wealth and privilege:

> Rock appropriated as its own the markers of places outside of everyday life which other musics, other voices had constructed. These voices and the places they marked became the signs of authenticity within the everyday life of rock culture, but they were the voices of peoples who had no everyday life, who existed outside the privileged spaces of the repetitiously mundane world of the rock formation. Rock then attacked, or at least attempted to transcend, its own everyday life, its own conditions of possibility, by appropriating the images and sounds of authenticity constituted outside of, and in part by the very absence of, everyday life.[19]

From this perspective, it seems far from coincidental that 'Like A Rolling Stone' – which emphasises the freedom gained by losing the trappings of going to the finest schools and being forced to 'live out on the streets' – should be considered the quintessential rock song (voted the greatest song of all time in a *Rolling Stone* poll in 2004). What rock culture does is generate an outsider status for its insiders in order to disrupt the everyday life of the mainstream. As with the folk revival, however, such a project is doomed to failure because it fails to take account of the circumstances of its own production: 'it takes for granted the luxury and privilege of everyday life as the condition of possibility of its own struggle against the mundanity of its everyday life; and it fails to articulate a vision of the conditions of possibility for the destruction of everyday life.'[20]

Without constructing a genuine political alternative to its own sites of privilege, rock culture is confined to disrupting the rhythms of its everyday existence through a celebration of instability, transitoriness and insecurity. 'Mobility is given precedence over stability . . . space is given precedence over place.'[21] Rock itself is therefore a culture of transitions, a form of permanent instability that secures the comfort of post-war society but maintains itself as an other, an in-between, a way of gaining control of one's life by abandoning the control provided by the welfare state. This means that, within rock ideology, keeping on keeping on is a crucial motif both for individuals and rock culture as a whole:

> unlike other musical forms, rock's very existence depends upon a certain instability or, more accurately, a certain mobility in the service of stability. Rock must constantly change to survive; it must seek to reproduce its authenticity in new forms, in new places, in new alliances. It must constantly move from one center to another, transforming what had been authentic into the inauthentic, in order to constantly project its claim to authenticity.[22]

And, as for rock, so too for Bob Dylan.

THE ART IDEOLOGY: SELF AND TRANSCENDENCE

The primary ways in which rock culture attempts to transcend its everyday existence are an emotional investment in

the rock culture itself (so that being part of rock's community matters) and an emphasis upon individual self-
consciousness and self-development. The first of these is
linked with rock's roots in the folk movement and will be
discussed later. In this section, I want to discuss the increasing emphasis on self-consciousness in Dylan's work and
detail its relationship to the newly forming rock culture.

Accounts of Dylan's development place great emphasis
upon a three-week road trip that Dylan took in February
1964. Dylan was due to play a concert in San Francisco and
he decided to drive from New York with companions Pete
Karman, Paul Clayton and Victor Maymudes. Although the
trip may not have been the Kerouac-inspired journey
intended (Dylan repeatedly shied away from people who
recognised him), it is notable because on it Dylan began
work on an important new song. 'Mr Tambourine Man' is
widely hailed as a breakthrough song in Dylan's work –
Heylin states that 'it changed everything'[23] – as it lacks any
of the characteristics of conventional protest songs, concentrating instead on finding a way of transcending the singer's
consciousness. 'Let me forget about today until tomorrow',
sings Dylan, and calls on the Tambourine Man to 'cast your
dancing spell my way'.

Dylan performed 'Mr Tambourine Man' at the Newport
Folk Festival in 1964, along with another new song, 'Chimes
Of Freedom'. 'Chimes Of Freedom' is an early stab at what
Dylan would perfect in 'It's Alright Ma (I'm Only Bleeding)' –
an attempt to provide a systemic critique of a complete social
order rather than a specific instance of injustice. This spirit of
critique, however, is tied to a pantheistic experience of the
majesty of nature. In 'Chimes Of Freedom' the experience of
the sublime coincides with a generalised malaise as, caught in
a storm, the singer and his companions see the chimes of freedom flash for a catalogue of outsiders such as the mistreated

mateless mother and the misdemeanour outlaw. In the end, however, the song concludes that alienation and outsiderness are something we all have to endure, as the chimes flash

> For the countless confused, accused, misused, strung-
> out ones, and worse
> And for every hung-up person in the whole wide
> universe.

Dylan's new songs seemed popular with the audience at Newport 1964, but they did not please many significant players in the folk revival. For example, Irwin Silber wrote an open letter in *Sing Out!* stating 'I saw at Newport how you had somehow lost contact with people . . . some of the paraphernalia of fame were getting in the way' while, in *Broadside*, Paul Wolfe wrote that the performance was the 'renunciation of topical music by its major prophet' and that the new songs 'degenerated into confusion and innocuousness'.

Dylan's responses to critics of his new direction mark a significant development in the emergence of rock culture. In an 1964 interview with Nat Hentoff justifying his maligned, and commercially unsuccessful, new album, *Another Side Of Bob Dylan*, Dylan stated:

> There aren't any finger-pointin' songs in here. Those records I've made, I'll stand behind them, but . . . I don't want to write for people anymore. You know, be a Spokesman . . . From now on, I want to write from inside me.

In one sense, such a response merely continues the process of Dylan rejecting his role as a spokesman. It does, however, betray a subtle but significant shift. In his early renunciations of the spokesman tag, the dominant motif of Dylan's argument was that he was merely writing and singing about issues that concerned him (for example, on the liner notes to the *Freewheelin'* album, he wrote 'All I'm doing is saying what's on my mind the best way I know how'). From 1964 onwards, the claim shifted slightly to one that he has to write what is 'inside of him', to express his own self. This subtle change reflects a new awareness of self in Dylan's work. During 1964, Dylan became more self-conscious of his status as an artist, and drew inspiration from the French poet, Arthur Rimbaud, telling friends 'Rimbaud's where it's at. That's the kind of stuff [that] means something'.[24]

The idea that rock music is a form of popular art rather than mere entertainment is a key characteristic of rock culture. Rock stars are expected not only to reflect the excesses of bohemian caricatures[25] but to express individual visions. Critic Jon Landau, for example, writes that 'the criterion of art in rock is the capacity of the musician to create a personal, almost private, universe and express it fully'.[26] We can see this claim repeated many times about Dylan. Paul Nelson, for example, in an article in *Sing Out!* in February 1966, defended Bob Dylan's new style as:

> A highly personal style-vision: Dylan's unyielding and poetic point of view represents a total commitment to the subjective over the objective, the microcosm over the macrocosm, man rather than Man, problems not Problems. To put it as simply as possible, the tradition that Dylan represents is that of all great artists: that of projecting, with the highest possible degree of honesty and craftsmanship, a unique personal vision.[27]

The idea that a rock star is an artist means prioritising the artist's inner self as the source of expressive work. However, in contrast to the old blues singers, for example, who also supposedly expressed the sensibility of their experience in their songs, a further layer of sophistication is added to rock artistry. Singing of one's self was not sufficient to claim artist status: as the latter part of Nelson's statement makes clear, it is also necessary to adopt a high degree of skill and sophistication. Keightley suggests that the measure of an artist in this context is 'one who stays true to the Modernist credos of experimentation, innovation, development and change'.[28] Thus, 'self-consciousness became the measure of a record's artistic status; frankness, musical wit, the use of irony and paradox were musicians' artistic insignia'.[29]

The growing emphasis on artistic self-consciousness can be seen in the increasing focus on originality as a prerequisite of rock authenticity. Whereas in earlier popular music there had conventionally been a division of labour between those who wrote songs and those who performed them, rock musicians were now expected to sing material they had written in order to express their own individuality. The figure of the singer-songwriter thus became the staple of authenticity. The importance placed on originality can be seen in the emerging discourse of rock stars actually being 'poets' and here Dylan is the central figure. Dylan's skilful use of words resulted in his being described as a poet from early in his career. His drift towards self-consciousness exacerbated this tendency. For example, on an early TV appearance, the host introduced Dylan by saying that 'He's primarily a poet. He's a very popular entertainer now, but I think one of the reasons for his popularity is that he has the mind of a poet', while Barry Kittleston, reviewing a major solo concert, wrote in *Billboard* that 'Dylan's poetry is born of a painful awareness of the tragedy that underlies the contemporary human condition'. It is a label that has dogged his whole career. For example, in 1991, Paul Zollo wrote 'he's written some of the most beautiful poetry the world has known, poetry of love and outrage, of abstraction and clarity, of timelessness and relativity'.

The claim that rock stars are poets is at best misguided and itself demonstrates how a particular ideology was used to advance rock's claims to be a superior cultural form. Whatever arguments there may be about early poetry being sung, 'poetry' in contemporary society is not sung. Poetry, as a meaningful category, refers to a particular type of cultural production with particular rules, expectations, forms of production and consumption. It is not a label that marks out a particular standard of excellence – there is bad poetry, just as there are good songs. Bob Dylan is an extraordinarily talented user of words, but he's not a poet, and tired clichés arguing that he is 'as good' as Keats are an attempt to justify popular culture through alien concepts of high culture rather than treat it on its own terms. As Scobie asserts, 'it is a false compliment, based on the intellectual snobbery which assumes that "high culture" is innately superior to any work in a popular medium'.[30] This will be discussed further in chapter 7.

The way that these high cultural discourses about poetry and originality infiltrated our understandings of popular music in the sixties does emphasise how rock emerged as a way of stratifying mainstream consumption, of creating a distinction within commercial music between the serious and the trivial. Another way in which the 'seriousness' of rock culture can be seen is with the rise to prominence of the album as the key rock format. Both the 33⅓ rpm LP and the 45rpm single emerged in the immediate post-war years and these different formats functioned as a means of stratifying the record market by age. Singles were aimed at the teen market, characterised by instability and rapid turnover of product. In contrast, albums were targeted at adult consumers. Due to their longevity, stability and higher price, album sales acted as the bedrock of the industry, accounting for 80 per cent of all expenditure on records by the end of the 1950s.[31] In tandem with their economic importance and age demarcation, albums were seen as more prestigious than singles, and were associated with 'good' and 'serious' music (classical music, jazz, Broadway musicals), whereas singles were associated with throwaway fads and immature consumers.[32] Albums give time for a work to develop, able to go through different 'movements', create various moods. Singles were for quick thrills, specifically dancing, and were over in three minutes before the listener got bored. One of the key features of the emergence of rock is how the album rather than the single becomes its key format: by 1964 sales of 'teen LPs' were rising (though still treated as less prestigious within the music industry at this time, considered a collection of singles rather than a coherent work). By 1967, when 'teen LPs' have become 'rock LPs', youth albums outsold adult albums for the first time.[33] This is a crucial moment in the development of rock's cultural legitimacy (nothing makes a musical form legitimate like stable, long-term sales) as the prestige associated with adult-oriented albums of the 1950s became associated with youth albums of the 1960s. The emergence of the album as the key rock form enables rock to provide a long-term investment (both aesthetic and economic). Rock albums became conceptualised as 'complex and coherent works of art whose value is assessed over the long term' while rock stars became viewed as performers with an extended career in which each album serves as a distinct chapter in their personal aesthetic development (see the quote in the footnote on p. 191 as one example).[34]

The emergence of rock culture, from about 1965 to 1968, thus depends upon a series of ideas concerning how rock music is actually a form of popular art, and rock stars popular artists. Dylan is central to the emergence of this kind of discourse. As part of a 'more mature' folk genre, he had already utilised the album as his main format and thus his electrified albums carried cultural legitimacy into the teen market. During 1965 and 1966, he embodied the idea of an artist following a unique personal vision no matter where (personally and professionally) it took him. Dylan came to represent artistic change itself. The speed of change, from *The Times They Are A-Changin'* (January 1964), through *Another Side of Bob Dylan* (August 1964), to *Bringing It All Back Home* (March 1965), to *Highway 61 Revisited* (August 1965) to *Blonde On Blonde* (May 1966) is breathtaking. The change in concert performance style from his May 1965 UK shows to even the acoustic portions of his 1966 shows must have seemed incomprehensible to audiences. And the conflict between Dylan and his audiences engendered by the electric performances in 1965 and 1966 were evidence of an artist following his own aesthetic vision rather than pandering to the needs of his audience. As Paul Nelson put it, in a *Sing Out!* article discussing the Newport 1965 performance: 'The only one in the entire festival who questioned our position was Bob Dylan. Maybe he didn't put it in the best way. Maybe he was rude. But he shook us. And that is why we have poets and artists.'[35]

THE FOLK IDEOLOGY: THE ROCK COMMUNITY AND THE POLITICS OF THE SELF

The idea that rock was a form of popular art was only one aspect of the new rock culture. Equally important was the idea that rock was a new form of folk music, and here, again: 'Dylan was the key figure. Dylan provided pop artists with a new model of "the star" and a new range of topics for songs. But in creating these opportunities, Dylan also brought with him some of folk's ethos'.[36] 'Dylan' however was not a blank slate when he made his shift from acoustic to electric music – his stardom meant that he embodied many of the character-istics of the folk revival and, while new layers of meaning were added to his stardom when he changed musical forms, the 'old' elements of Dylan's stardom influenced what the new Dylan represented.

Keightley cautiously points out that: 'since rock emerges in the overlapping of a number of musical cultures, however, rock does not simply adopt folk ideology wholesale. Rather, because of crucial differences in the age profiles of their respective audiences and due to diverging attitudes toward success and popularity, rock adapts key aspects of folk ideology.'[37] Keightley is wary of a simple transposition of folk ideology into rock because whereas rock is most obvi-ously associated with youth, the folk revival was inter-generational. Such a contention is substantially correct – the folk revival did include many who had participated in the folk revival of the 1930s – but is also lacking because it does not consider the content of the folk revival in sufficient detail. As already discussed, the folk revival was itself split on generational lines, as younger musicians such as Dylan reflected changing folk sensibility to politics, individuality and commercialism. Thus the new generational conscious-ness described in the previous chapter as underpinning the folk revival is also used by Grossberg to explain the emer-gence of rock culture:

> the rupture which separated youth from adults was not a matter of ideology or interpretation. It was a crisis in the relation between affect and signification, in the [impossibil-ity] of investing in the meanings and values offered to them . . . An affective uncertainty . . . gradually became the common discourse of youth. It is not that youth did not live

the ideological values of their parents; rather, they found it impossible to represent their mood, their own 'affective' relationship to the world, in those terms and to seriously invest themselves in such values.[38]

What does happen in the emergence of rock is that this affective sensibility becomes more widespread and its constituency spreads far beyond the limits of the folk revival. This means that the nascent rock culture became more firmly associated with youth than its folk prototype. This relationship between rock and youth was used to justify rock's status as a form of folk music. The ideology of folk is that the music is generated by a particular community and thus reflects communal experience. In rock culture, the community was understood to be a new generation who shared a common set of experiences, values and beliefs, and rock music was understood as the authentic expression of that generation, created by people who were part of that community. Such an idea is obviously rooted in the folk music revival already discussed.

Rock's rootedness in the folk revival enables it to maintain a specifically political dimension. It was assumed that the content of rock songs dealt with the same issues of injustice and critique as the protest genre, but in a distinctive way. Street argues that, in contrast to folk music: 'Rock's politics . . . emerge in its understandings of private states in public life; and as a result, its politics will have distinct focus and style. They will be concerned with how the individual encounters the world; and they will be interested in comprehending and sympathizing with the individual, not berating or lecturing them.'[39] Such a position is once again a little too black and white as a detailed view of the folk revival shows that it already contained tendencies towards individual experience that became dominant in rock. A focus on how the individual encounters injustice clearly exists in Dylan's early work in the folk revival. In Dylan's post-folk work, however, there is an intensification of such currents as 'consciousness [became] the battleground on which Dylan now plant[ed] his standard . . . Politics had been injected into the theatre of consciousness and consciousness had become the theatre of liberation'.[40] A conception of the authentic individual self and the liberation of that self become the centre of political concern within rock culture as notions of individual experience become entangled with the wider themes of transcendence and transitoriness: 'The impersonal demands of politics create the illusion that one has an investment in society [but] one is nothing and one owns nothing: recognizing that is the only starting point for real freedom and authenticity, the only way to escape social control, to recapture yourself.'[41] A radical rejection of conventional politics is necessary to liberate the authenticity of the individual. Whereas protest songs can present issues in the manner of conventional political discourse, the emphasis on individual consciousness in rock means that rock songs can generally be characterised by an absence of conventional political analysis.[42] Indeed, Wicke is critical of this tendency in rock, arguing that 'the supposed protest character of rock's musical appearance relieved it of the necessity of taking a clear political position in its lyrics'.[43] This highlights the key issue that ties politics and community together within rock's folk ideology – the way that rock culture, by its very existence, was inherently political. Rock's position in the social structure made a rock song political regardless of its musical content. This is why affiliating oneself with rock was a social statement, invested with political significance, and why the folk ideology could be used to promote the notion of a 'rock community', a social group brought together by a shared generational consciousness that was expressed through a specific form of music.* Even if, in the end, rock was more the result of differing affective experiences of the young and old rather than any major ideological shift, it certainly *seemed* as though a major ideological shift was occurring, and that there existed a major clash of values between the old and the youthful. To align oneself to rock culture, therefore, to invest meaning in the values of rock as a way of transcending the present, was itself a political act.

BOB DYLAN, THE ULTIMATE ROCK STAR

Dylan's Newport 1965 performance is often presented as a revolutionary break from folk music. Such claims, and the reifying of a specific performance serve a particular function in justifying broader claims of the revolutionary nature of rock music. They also serve to obscure the continuities between the folk revival and rock culture. Most significant of these continuities is the manner in which rock culture adopted the mass culture critique inherent within folk discourse. The rediscovery of folk music emerged within a wider concern about the spread of mass culture and its supposedly stupefying effects on its audience. Such ideas underpin the folkies' response to Dylan's electrified performance. When Robert Shelton offered support for Dylan's new music, George Wein, the festival's technical director retorted, 'you've been brainwashed by the recording industry!'[44]

---

* The investiture of rock with political significance was initially promoted not from within rock culture but rather from the attacks it elicited from outsiders 'both in public and institutional discourses . . . and in the domestic relationships within which rock's audience was being shaped' (Grossberg, 1992:147). It is only later in the decade, as youth became more self-consciously radical, that rock culture became more clearly politicised from within (Frith, 1983:51). This had a significant impact on Dylan's stardom and is discussed in the next chapter.

Rather than merely 'selling out' to rock and roll, however, Dylan's shift precipitated those same ideas developing within the rock and roll mainstream. Dylan used 'those aspects of the pop process that the folk world had defined itself against in the 1950s – not just the use of amplified instruments, but the trappings of stardom, packaging and promotion'[45] to show the possibilities that popular music offered. The ideology of rock thus emerged as a way of stratifying popular music into a layer of serious music that represented individual sensibility and communal experience (rock) against lower strata subject to all the commercial manipulation and trivial meaning that the folkies so despised (pop). Rather than polemicising *against* popular music, rock polemicises *within* popular music.[46] Both the art and the folk ideologies of rock are ways of measuring rock music against the commercial mainstream, of acknowledging the possibility of serious music within the mass media. As Keir Keightley points out, it is actually this supposed seriousness, and not the alleged recklessness and anti-rationality of rock music, that endows it with its oppositional qualities.[47]

Ideology is not merely a way of describing the world in which we live, it is a way of dealing with the tensions of our lived experience, of ironing out the contradictions and ruptures of the modern world. It works to conceal tensions and this is the case with both strands of rock ideology. The folk basis for rock music, like the communal claims of the folk revival, is delusional. As Frith points out,[48] the problem with the claim is its circularity: rock music is a folk music because it is a genuine expression of a specific community, but that community only exists through its use of rock music. What exists is not a community but an audience: a mass market that tries to reject the very thing that constitutes it. As Wicke states, rock music is 'the expression of a community which rock itself had first established as it became commercially successful'.[49]

There are similar contradictions inherent in the artistic justification of rock as serious music. Two issues are worth noting. Firstly is the contradiction between expressing oneself and being heard. This is not the same as the conventional discussions of selling out but is, rather, recognising the fact that within a commercial medium, a singer's message, however self-expressive, will only be heard if it is commercially popular. Thus, for a record to be an artistic success (to reach people, to communicate), it needs to be a commercial success too. Dylan was aware of this, saying that 'you have to be hip to communicate. Sure, you can make all kinds of protest songs and put them on a Folkways record. But who hears them? The people that do hear them are going to be agreeing with you anyway' (Paul Robbins interview, 1965). The second contradiction inherent in the art ideology is that rock is a mass-mediated form. As such it is collectively produced – technicians, recording artists, producers, record labels all contribute to the making of a song. Wicke argues that 'in this context music as the individual expression of an outstanding personality is *de facto* impossible. Rock is a collective means of expression'.[50] The emphasis upon individual self-expression as a key feature of rock music serves to mask its collective production and thus diminish its commercial origins (this is something rock shares in common with all cultural production).[51]

There are thus at least three ways in which rock ideology is contradictory. Firstly, there is the contradiction between folk community and mass audience – the rock audience defines itself as a folk community even as it is constituted through its role as a mass audience. Secondly, there is the contradiction between the art ideology and the collective, commercial enterprises that actually go into the production of a song. Finally, there is the contradiction between the art ideology and the folk ideology; the 'paradox of representing community with a type of music which is supported by the musician's individuality and the creative realisation of his personality'.[52] What is interesting, however, is not just to show up these core features of rock as 'false' but, rather, to consider the ways in which these contradictions somehow held together, relatively successfully, in rock culture. One way that it is achieved is through stardom. Frith points out that the strength of the rock argument depends on a few individual stars, those who were artists or represented their community *despite* the industry.[53] This is true but does not fully reveal the full significance of stardom. Through individuals coming to represent and embody particular ideas, beliefs, groups and affective sensibilities, stardom functions to relieve contradictory tendencies by reducing 'the cultural meaning of events, incidents and people to their psychological makeup'.[54] The contradictions inherent in the social structure itself can be reduced to the contradictions of an individual personality. Thus an analysis of any star has to question what social roles that individual's stardom plays:

> No matter where one chooses to put the emphasis in terms of the stars' place in the production/consumption dialectic of the cinema [or music], that place can still only be fully understood ideologically. The questions, 'Why stardom?' and 'Why such-and-such a star?' have to be answered in terms of ideology – ideology being, as it were, the terms in which the production/consumption dialectic is articulated.[55]

It is in this way that we can see the importance of Dylan to rock music. Dylan is the uber-rock star in 1965 and 1966 because he manages to hold in balance all of the contradictions of the rock ideology. For a perfect moment, Dylan's 'absolute coherence' as a star personality unites the contradictory elements of self, community and commerce: an individual who rejects politics in favour of inner-consciousness yet still manages to be political; an artist who follows his own unique vision regardless of the consequences yet found new audiences and commercial success; a self-conscious artist speaking for no one except his own self yet upheld as the leader of a youth movement. For about sixteen months, Dylan embodied the values of the emerging rock culture in a way no one else ever has. The coalescing of all these contradictory aspects can be seen in this journalist's description of Dylan in 1965:

> His visionary lyrics to guitar have made him the spokesman for a whole restless, rebellious generation. . . . To his fans Bob Dylan means the ultimate in far-out, the untouchable, the incorruptible, the uncompromising – the man who sees through the Image Makers and the Mass Market and the Big Sell. . . . Dylan's evocative imagery may make him the 1960's answer to the romantic poets of the past.[56]

Such a perfect ideological fit is rare, and unsustainable for long periods – the structural conflicts concealed by stardom are real, and will inevitably surface at some point in a particular star's career. For those stars that really do manage to hold contradictions in balance for a time, the fall from grace can be spectacular, laced with accusations of betrayal or failure to maintain the ideal. This is what happened in Dylan's case. That mid-sixties Dylan has become beatified as the ultimate example of rock authenticity. 'The Sixties' and 'Bob Dylan' with his 'thin, wild mercury sound' stand as markers of an unattainable goal. This has proved difficult for later rock stars expected to live up to these models of authenticity (including several labelled as 'new Bob Dylans'). It has also been the structuring principle of Bob Dylan's subsequent stardom.

Snapshot: The retiring father

The strains of the 1966 tour and the rock and roll lifestyle were clearly taking their toll on Dylan. In July 1966 he had a minor motorcycle accident near his home in Woodstock. The injuries caused by the accident were used as a reason to cancel all of his scheduled appearances, as well as leading to the delay or cancellation of a number of other projects. He then spent time with his family convalescing. Publicly, however, Dylan just disappeared from the popular music scene during this time. For the best part of twelve months, very few people knew what Dylan was doing, whether he was permanently crippled or if he would ever record again.

Right at the end of 1967, Dylan released *John Wesley Harding*. Its pared down acoustic sound was a dramatic change in direction both from his previous albums and from the mainstream psychedelic rock sounds of the era. Dylan followed this with *Nashville Skyline*, an album of country songs, in 1969, and *Self Portrait*, an album mainly of covers, in 1970. This latter release received scathing criticism. Dylan released *New Morning* soon afterwards, which was viewed with relief as a 'proper' Dylan album.

The late sixties is characterised by Dylan's attempt to lessen the burdens created by his stardom. As the new decade began, Dylan remained relatively quiet. In 1974, however, he returned to centre stage, releasing the album *Planet Waves* and embarking on a major tour with The Band, who had backed him on the infamous 1966 tour. Sell-out crowds responded enthusiastically. The mid-seventies are Dylan's most commercially successful spell. *Planet Waves*, *Blood On The Tracks* – often held as his greatest work – and *Desire* reached the top of the charts, but Dylan's private life at this time was troubled. The two *Rolling Thunder*

Revue tours undertaken in 1975 and 1976, and the content of these mid-seventies albums, display a troubled performer and songwriter. After a few years of trauma, Dylan finally divorced in 1977. He spent the majority of this year editing *Renaldo And Clara*. The footage for this four-hour film was recorded during 1975's *Rolling Thunder Revue* and the sensitive subject matter meant that the work was clearly important to Dylan: he engaged in a series of major interviews to explain his aims in making the film. Despite this, the film was critically ravaged.

Albums and major events

July 1966	Motorcycle accident
May–August 1967	Spends much time recording with The Band in Woodstock. The recordings from these sessions become known as *The Basement Tapes*
December 1967	*John Wesley Harding*
January 1968	Performs at Woody Guthrie Memorial Concert
April 1969	*Nashville Skyline*
August 1969	Isle of Wight festival
June 1970	*Self Portrait*
October 1970	*New Morning*
May 1973	*Pat Garret And Billy The Kid* (film)
July 1973	*Pat Garret And Billy The Kid* (soundtrack)
January 1974	*Planet Waves*
Jan–Feb 1974	US Tour (documented on *Before The Flood*)
January 1975	*Blood On The Tracks*
Oct–Dec 1975	*Rolling Thunder Revue* (documented on *The Bootleg Series volume 5*)
January 1976	*Desire*
Apr–May 1976	*Rolling Thunder Revue* (documented on *Hard Rain*)
June 1977	Bob and Sara Dylan get divorced
January 1978	*Renaldo And Clara*

5

BEYOND STARDOM: ROCK HISTORY AND CANONISATION

Stardom and celebrity are inherently social phenomena. You cannot be the only person to know you are a star, a celebrity only in your own home. This means that the public nature of being a star continually affects the individual star's sense of self, even in private. Consider other states of being such as being black or being woman. If you're a woman, your womanhood is a public matter. It affects what people think of you, what is deemed appropriate behaviour in your presence, how you dress, what activities you do. Embodied in your individual personality are a whole series of social norms and expectations that affect how you think, how you act, and what others think of you. Being a woman is inherently social, even when the woman has a 'private life'. The same is true for celebrities. Even if they have a 'private life' – something I questioned in chapter 2 – that private life is always public, always structured by public meaning.

Because stardom is inherently social, it is important to consider it systemically, as a more or less coherent system with specific characteristics. As I said in chapter 1, conventional biographies of stars often ignore the ways in which the life of a particular star is structured in ways similar to other stars. This is no surprise: one of the key characteristics of stardom is that it emphasises individuality and so, as biographies are part of the star system, they also serve to reinforce the primacy of the individual. Specifically, they tend to overemphasise the inherent charisma or talent of the star as the basis of their stardom, and the agency (power) of the star (or, sometimes in cases such as Elvis Presley, the power of a Svengali figure) in creating the star's image. The ideology of stardom here has much in common with discourses of authorship and bohemianism that cohered during the nineteenth century: the innate genius of the artist represented the unique individuality inherent in us all while simultaneously marking off that particular individual as extra special, a hero of the modern age. The same can be said of stardom – the star is represented both as a special individual with particular talent or charisma while at the same time a representation of the ordinary, the proof that anyone can make it in a democratic society.

Subsequent literary theory has undermined many of the conceits of the Romantic myth of genius, however, not only rejecting the possibility of 'pure' originality (all new creations are recombinations of things already in existence) but also rejecting the possibility that the author can control the meaning of his creation. When combined with a systemic understanding of stardom, such postmodern literary theory provides a useful way of considering the meaning of particular star-images. A newly emerging star never has a blank canvas on which to work, there are always the structural constraints of stardom in general as well as specific social and cultural influences that shape a star image. Even someone as 'unique' or 'groundbreaking' as Dylan had these constraints. Despite my claim that Dylan was the first rock star, we can clearly see a range of different star types and influences in his persona. The most obvious of these are Woody Guthrie, James Dean, Buddy Holly and other rock and rollers, Hank Williams and the Beat poets. These are not just musical influences, they are influences that shaped how the public star/artist should act.

At the same time, once a particular star-image has emerged (growing out of narrow social milieu into wider currency, such as a local music scene), it ceases to be controllable by the star. Star-meaning is constructed by the audience and not by the star and/or manager. The star can try to shape their image, can make a 'serious' film, release a folk album, do interviews in particular magazines but, ultimately, it is the public that decide what the star-image means. 'Strictly speaking, the public faces that celebrities construct do not belong to them, since they only possess validity if the public confirms them. The relationship of esteem is also one of dependency.'[1] If you think about it, there are very few stars who have 'retired', stopped being stars at the height of their fame. There are far more cases of stars trying to cling on to their stardom, releasing one more album, making another comeback. It is the public who decide when a star stops being a star, not the individual star.* This is an example of what Turner refers to as 'celebrity from below';[2] the power to maintain celebrity, and the power to construct what a particular celebrity represents, is with the public. This

---

* I am deliberately understating the role that particular media industries play in 'creating' stars here. This would be important for considering stardom systemically (how the music industry produces a range of stars for us to choose from, for example) but can be less important when considering individual stars. All the money and publicity in the world cannot rejuvenate the public's interest in a star if the public doesn't want to be interested. In Dylan's case, as will be outlined, the complementary industries (particularly the newly emerging rock press) have more of an impact on Dylan's stardom than those directly associated with him, such as his record label.

returns us to the thorny relationship between stardom and biography – individual biography is an important component of how stars engender meaning, but the meaning that stars signify does not depend upon biographical accuracy. Take Dylan as an example – forty years after leaving the protest movement, Dylan's stardom still, to a certain extent, represents pacifism and anti-war protest:

> A lot of my songs were definitely misinterpreted by people who didn't know any better, and it goes on today. . . . Take 'Masters Of War'. Every time I sing it, someone writes that it's an anti-war song. But there's no anti-war sentiment in that song. I'm not a pacifist. I don't think I've ever been one. If you look closely at the song, it's about what Eisenhower was saying about the dangers of the military-industrial complex. (Robert Hilburn interview, 2004)

Whether Dylan is or has ever been a pacifist, however, does not matter – if Dylan's stardom represents anti-war sentiment then it represents anti-war sentiment and Dylan can argue otherwise until he's blue in the face, it won't change the fact that it represents anti-war sentiment. Fans can highlight the 'misrepresentation', show how this particular song is not actually anti-war, but that doesn't matter either.*

This 'public ownership' of a specific star-image is not unique to popular music but it does have a particular intensity because of the notion that music stars represent particular groups of people. The folk ideology in rock music

---

* I have a theory, which I'm not developing here in much detail, that the gap between stardom and biography is inhabited by fans. They are the ones who find out the actual biographical detail and who analyse songs/films for 'the real' meaning. This 'superior' knowledge and claims of misrepresentation are key ways in which 'committed' fans distinguish themselves from 'casual' fans. I would also venture that the idea of a star being misrepresented is a key aspect of many stars' stardom. It certainly is in Dylan's case.

dictates that the star is representative of the social group from which she emerges. If the star begins to move away from the group then the audience will be quick to correct or reject her. Popular music stars belong to their fans (Dylan was introduced to his audience at the Newport Folk Festival in 1963 with the statement 'Here he is, take him, you know him, he's yours . . . Bob Dylan.').

This is not to suggest that stars have *no* power, just less than is conventionally presented. A star clearly has more power than an individual fan to construct what the star-image means; the supporting industry (such as managers and record labels), as well as complementary industries like radio and the press, also have considerable power in creating a particular meaning. Much of the interest in individual star biographies lies in the battle over star-meaning, either a star battling with his manager/record company/film studio over control of his image, or the conflict with public meaning of the star. In some cases, this kind of conflict become central to the star's meaning (such as Garbo's 'I want to be alone') and Dylan is one such example. Dylan was so culturally significant that his star-meaning was always more open to contestation than lesser stars. That he emerged within a cultural movement that emphasised collectivity only added to the potential claims of public ownership of Bob Dylan. One of the interesting things about Dylan is how the struggle for the meaning of Dylan's star-image has proved a central strand of that star-image. And whereas for the majority of celebrities, the struggle over image is with managers and publicists, for Dylan, the struggle has been primarily with his audience. The ambivalent relationship between Dylan and his audience has been a central motif of Dylan's career. It can be seen most clearly in 1965–6 when audiences booed Dylan's new electrified music, but it can also be seen in 1979, when audiences booed Dylan playing Christian music, and in 1961 in the folk establishment's ambivalence towards Dylan's eclecticism. It can even be seen in Dylan's ongoing Never Ending Tour project. In general, the tense relationship is used as evidence of Dylan's artistic bravery, a marker of his authenticity as he follows his artistic impulse and ignores the demands of the market, but there are times when the battle over Dylan's meaning has been used as evidence against Dylan, as proof of his artistic decline. Such instances include the crucial 1967–70 period which I will discuss in this chapter, as well as some of the response to the Never Ending Tour. There is in fact, a notable split: those conflicts written about with the benefit of hindsight are used as evidence of Dylan's bravery (how could the audience not hear how great the electric music was?) while those events that were written about as they happened (the release of *Self Portrait*, his turn to Christianity, the Never Ending Tour) tend to be used as evidence of Dylan's weakness (we were right, he was wrong). This is an important split, and I will return to it.

The struggle for the meaning of the 'Bob Dylan' star-image is itself a key component of that image. Returning to the issues discussed in chapter 2, we can see how his star-meaning affects how we interpret Dylan's songs. Many songs are interpreted as at least in part a rejoinder to his audience (I mentioned 'Love Sick' in the introduction; other songs considered this way include 'It Ain't Me Babe', 'All I Really Want To Do', 'In The Garden' and 'What Was It You Wanted?'). Paul Williams writes that 'Dylan has often realized and demonstrated that any man/woman "I"/"you" song can also be about . . . the relationship between a singer/performer and an audience'.[3] Once again, Williams places too much emphasis on Dylan's power to control meaning; surely the point here is that Dylan's stardom structures the meaning of songs which enables them to be heard in a particular way. There is nothing in the words of 'It Ain't Me Babe' that implies it is about anything other than a male/female relationship. It is only knowing what we know about Bob Dylan that facilitates this dual reading. Similarly, Williams himself recounts how he hears 'Seeing The Real You At Last' as being in part about the audience. It's a plausible point but it is driven by Williams' own knowledge of Dylan's relationship with the audience and not from anything 'within' the song. Again, this is not to suggest that Dylan has no power to control meaning. Obviously, song lyrics enable some meanings and close down others – 'Wedding Song' is a man/woman song that is clearly not about the audience. And, as I argued earlier, Dylan is aware of his stardom and does not use it naively (singing 'All I Really Want To Do' at Newport '64 was probably a calculated move; I am less convinced that singing 'It's All Over Now, Baby Blue' after the electric set at Newport '65 was, even though it has subsequently been interpreted that way). When Dylan returned to touring in 1974, after an eight-year hiatus, the first song he played was an unreleased one from 1963 called 'Hero Blues'.

> Yes, the gal I got
> I swear she's the screaming end
> She wants me to be a hero
> So she can tell all her friends

This was ostensibly a man/woman song, and Dylan quite deliberately subverted its meaning in an attempt to assert ownership of his star image.* This tension between Dylan and his audience is a continuing theme throughout Dylan's career. Even as late as 1997, Dylan stated:

---

* In this instance, however, he protested too much: the 1974 tour was a greatest hits package dominated by crowd-pleasers. Dylan later commented bitterly that he 'had to step into Bob Dylan's shoes for that tour' (Toby Cresswell interview, 1986).

Some days I get up and it just makes me sick that I'm doing what I'm doing. Because basically – I mean, you're one cut above a pimp. That's what everybody who's a performer is. (David Gates interview)

I want now to discuss a specific episode in this battle, perhaps the most significant period for constructing the totality of Dylan's star-image. Ironically, it is also the period in which Dylan published less work than any other time in his career, 1967–70.

KEEPING SILENT

In 'Hero Blues', the singer laments that he can never live up to the expectations placed upon him by his lover. He chides that

You need a different kind of man, one that can grab
     and hold your heart
You need a different kind of man, you need Napoleon
     Bonaparte.

The use of Napoleon, the exemplar of Romantic individualism for Lord Byron, is prescient, for in the period 1963–6 Dylan had been granted a similar kind of heroic leadership. When he emerged within the folk movement, he was labelled as the spokesman of a generation, a title he repeatedly rejected. When he shifted into electric music, he was once again feted as the primary leader of the new youth movement, the only man hip enough to know exactly what was happening. The expectations of both kinds of leadership placed extraordinary burdens on Dylan, not least in the way that the media dealt with him, asking him absurd questions about politics, young people, his music, his position as a leader (Do you care about what you sing? Do you think young people understand a word you say? How many folk singers are there?). During the folk singer period, Dylan was generally polite, though sometimes playful, in rejecting any kind of position and any role of leadership. As the decade progressed, however, Dylan's responses became more sardonic and confrontational:

Q: Can you tell me when and where you were born?

Dylan: No, you can go and find out. There's many biographies and you can look to [them]. You don't ask me where I was born, where I lived. Don't ask me those questions. You find out from other papers.

. . .

Q: Of course your songs have a very strong content . . .

Dylan: Have you heard my songs?

Q: I have. 'Masters Of War'. 'Blowin' In The Wind'.

Dylan: What about '[Boots] Of Spanish Leather'? Have you heard that? Why don't you listen to that? Listen, I couldn't care less what your paper writes about me. Your paper can write anything, don't you realise? The people that listen to me don't read your paper, you know, to listen to me. I'm not going to be known from your paper.

Q: You're already known. Why be so hostile?

Dylan: Because you're hostile to me. You're using me. I'm an object to you. I went through this before in the United States, you know. There's nothing personal. I've nothing against you at all. I just don't want to be bothered with your paper, that's all. I just don't want to be a part of it. Why should I have to go along with something just so that somebody else can eat? Why don't you just say that my name is Kissenovitch. You know, and I, er, come from Acapulco, Mexico. That my father was an escaped thief from South Africa. OK. You can say anything you want to say.

(Laurie Henshaw interview, 1965)

He developed the 'anti-interview' method of throwing questions back at journalists so that they had to answer what they thought was true, as well as his famous 'truth attacks', outbursts of Beat-philosophy intended to undermine the interviewer's sense of self:

> I'm saying that you're gonna die, and you're gonna go off the earth, you're gonna be dead. Man, it could be, you know, twenty years, it could be tomorrow: any time. So am I . . . Alright: now you do your job in the face of that – and how seriously you take yourself, you decide for yourself. (To a journalist from *Time Magazine*, 1965)

In rejecting any kind of label, however, in disclaiming any suggestion of leadership, Dylan merely reinforced his position as leader. In the same way that the anti-hero is himself a kind of hero, breaking convention to highlight the problems of the world, Dylan's anti-leadership position (including his instruction 'don't follow leaders' in 'Subterranean Homesick Blues') was itself a form of leadership. Dylan did not have fans, but followers:

> It was like being in an Edgar Allan Poe story. And you're just not that person everybody thinks you are, though they call you that all the time. 'You're the prophet. You're the saviour.' I never wanted to be a prophet or saviour. Elvis maybe. I could easily see myself becoming him. But prophet? No. (Ed Bradley interview, 2004)

The pressure of being Bob Dylan in 1965–6 was extraordinary and it clearly took its toll – a comparison of pictures from 1965 and 1966 illustrate the difference. In 1965 Dylan looks sharp and alert whereas in 1966 he often seems exhausted and spaced out, clearly taking drugs in order to cope. Dylan was later to say that in 1966, you got 'the feeling that I might die after the show' (Craig McGregor interview, 1978). Dylan had to escape New York because of the pressure, and in 1965 he moved to a leafy settlement called Woodstock, a couple of hours north of the city. In July 1966, Dylan had a minor motorcycle accident while riding in Woodstock. Although it did not seem so at the time, the accident marked the start of a period of withdrawal for Dylan. Between the accident and 1970 his public appearances were limited. An interview with the New York *Daily News* in May 1967 was the first public pronouncement from Dylan since the crash. This eleven-month period of silence within the context of the sixties recording industry is in itself remarkable (Dylan had released *Bringing It All Back Home*, *Highway 61 Revisited* and *Blonde On Blonde* within a fifteen-month spell). In the last week of 1967, Dylan released a new album (*John Wesley Harding*) with no publicity; in 1968, his only public performance was at Woody Guthrie's memorial concert and there was no album; in 1969, he released the 26-minute album *Nashville Skyline*, performed three songs on Johnny Cash's TV show and played at the Isle of Wight festival in the UK; in 1970, he released the album *Self Portrait*. And that's it; four years' worth of work (the same length of time that produced all releases from *Freewheelin'* to *Blonde On Blonde*). This is Dylan's least prolific spell in terms of official output; in terms of star-image, however, it is probably the most important spell of Dylan's career.

Dylan had personal reasons for spending time out of the public eye; he clearly needed to recuperate his health and he had recently married and started a family. It also seems clear, however, that Dylan hoped a period out of the spotlight would take the pressure off his star responsibilities. The inherently public nature of stardom, however, meant that Dylan failed in his attempts to withdraw from public life.

Stars are commodities. The only reason that stars exist is because the individual can be turned into a product. Where stars are different than, say, handbags, however, is that they also contribute to the making of the product, 'they are both labour and the thing that labour produces'.[4] Recognising this means recognising that the star is always engaged in the process of creating and maintaining stardom – the star is part of the star's own promotion. The role that the star plays in creating their stardom is one reason why any meaningful distinction between public and private life for the star is impossible. It also means, however, that all attempts to escape from fame are doomed to circularity, with the desire to escape fame becoming a central element of the fame itself. The one thing that everyone knows about Greta Garbo is that she wanted to be alone.

Given the inescapability of stardom, the only option would seem to be silence, and Dylan is not the only star to adopt an 'aesthetic of silence' (Salinger is another example). If the meaning of one's stardom is contested, and one's statements are open to constant misinterpretation, then saying nothing would seem the only eloquent solution. But while silence *could* result in the complete dissolution of stardom – the public could get bored, move on to the next thing – it is the public that decides if this happens, not the star. If the public maintains an interest, then the star remains a star. Even after thirty years of living a reclusive lifestyle, Garbo was still a star and still bothered by the paparazzi. And, if stardom is maintained by the public, then the silence has an audience; it becomes a statement in itself.

This is what happened in Dylan's case. Dylan himself was almost entirely absent from public life in 1967, yet his stardom still dominated rock culture. The reason for this is a historical coincidence – Dylan's crash and withdrawal from public life coincided with the full flourishing of rock culture and, in particular, the emergence of a specific form of rock criticism that defined rock's key features and outlined its history. Any significant cultural form or movement requires cultural 'accreditation', it needs to be acknowledged as worthy of its significant status. This happens both from without, as existing cultural institutions acknowledge the value of the new form, and within, as the new form develops its own body of criticism, its own journals with 'critics who propagate and promote it while they propound and evaluate'.[5] Gendron suggests that for rock this begins to occur in 1966. The first review of a rock record in a major American newspaper occurred in the *New York Times* in February 1966 (Robert Shelton reviewed ten albums, including one by Dylan) and a specific rock column was introduced into the *Village Voice* in June 1966. Sandwiched in-between was the first issue of the first rock magazine, *Crawdaddy*, set up by 18-year-old fan Paul Williams (later to write the *Performing Artist* series of books on Dylan). Over the next eighteen months, rock was accepted not only by bastions of highbrow authority (mainly through the accreditation of The Beatles' highbrow pretensions in releasing *Sergeant Pepper*), but also through the emergence of the specialist 'rock critic', who began appearing in regular newspaper columns and in the emerging specialist rock press, in magazines such as *Fusion* and *Creem*. The most significant new rock journal, *Rolling Stone*, was first published on 9 November 1967.

The important thing to recognise here is not just that rock became accepted as a worthy cultural form at this time, nor that it became the dominant mainstream music. What is important is that through this process of accreditation, *rock itself becomes defined*. If it is an important cultural form, what are its key features? What does it stand for? Who are the key players? The ideology of rock outlined in the previous chapter – the contradictory mixture of self-expressiveness and social reflection – only becomes clearly formulated during this period. The new music magazines clearly differentiated themselves from teen fan magazines that concentrated on pin-ups and industry publicity. Rather than just featuring commercially successful stars, aesthetic achievement would be the most important factor.* They were intended as serious criticism about serious music – *Crawdaddy's* first issue carried an article entitled 'The aesthetics of rock'. Through the new rock press, rock culture itself defined its key characteristics, its key players and works and, in this process, developed a specific historical story of how rock emerged. The period roughly from 1967–1969 is crucial in understanding how 1963–1966 has subsequently become characterised and understood.

All history is written after the event and events are thus 'framed' by the worldview of those writing that history. Do the new 'academics' of rock look at the emergence of rock and roll, or the period 1963–6, neutrally and extrapolate the key features of rock, or do they already have an idea of what 'rock' is and then interpret the historical events through that particular lens? The answer is surely the latter. This is not a question of bias but of how all events are given meaning socially – an absolute objectivity is impossible. Writing history is one of the key ways in which a social group defines its own ideologies, its own social identity. It offers an opportunity to define who is in and who is out and rock historicising was no different (for example, the first full length study of Dylan's work, published in 1972 but very much part of rock's self-definition, contains the declaration that 'country music just isn't that valuable').[6] The period prior to 1967, and alternative forms of music,

---

* Fortunately for them, as a mainstream cultural form, the aesthetically successful were the commercially successful – an issue demonstrated by *Rolling Stone's* coverage of rock superstars.

became framed within 1967's conceptual framework of what rock was and who made up its constituency.

The history of rock music that was developed by rock critics goes something like this. Before 1956, life is very dull and musical consumption is a family affair – artists like Sinatra were enjoyed by adults and children alike. Then, in 1956 – Bang! – Elvis Presley appears and rock and roll is born. This new music is a fusion of black and white music (rhythm and blues mixed with hillbilly). Teenagers have their own music, which liberates them but offends adults and is demonised by authoritarian institutions. Then in 1959, rock and roll dies down, as its main players are sidelined by drafting, scandal, imprisonment and death. Popular music in the period 1960–2 is bland, characterised by Tin Pan Alley songwriting with corny 'moon/June' rhymes and 'How Much Is That Doggie In The Window?' Suddenly – Bang! – the folk revival appears and shows that popular music can have a social conscience and does not have to be limited in its subject matter. Dylan, as part of the revival, illustrates the breadth of language that can be used within popular song. Then, in 1964 – Bang! – the British Invasion produces genuinely exciting and danceable music that reinvigorates popular music. With their homages to rock and roll and rhythm and blues, The Beatles and The Stones show that there had been great music going on in America but people were not hearing it because of racial segregation in the charts. Finally, in 1965 – BANG! BANG! – Dylan's lyrical advances merge with the beat music of the British Invasion and rock music is born. While rock and roll and the music of the beat boom were exhilarating, they were also a bit juvenile; rock music deals with adult themes while maintaining the emotional and visceral power of the earlier musics.

This history is familiar to anyone with a passing interest

in popular music. It is an extremely simplified and misleading history but my purpose in outlining it here is not to correct it.[7] Actually, as I have repeatedly said in relation to stardom, the myth is more important than the facts in this regard – what people believe to be true about rock, or about Dylan, matters. My interest in this history is its emphasis upon radicalism and, in particular, how it presents musical history as a series of revolutionary moments rather than recognising evolutionary continuities. This emphasis on radicalism plays a key role in how Dylan's stardom has been structured. While there are clear continuities both in Dylan's work and his star-image throughout his career, the emphasis is on change – Dylan's chameleon nature – and conflict – the booing at Newport '65 and the 1966 World Tour.

Dylan's period of silence coincides with the time that rock culture is developing its own ideology, writing its own history and creating its own canon. Dylan is placed at the very top of this, above even The Beatles.* Even as he was absent from the scene, Dylan found his cultural cachet increasing as 'the feeling spread among growing numbers of young people that wherever their head was at, Dylan had been there before'.[8] Dylan has commented on this process in subsequent interviews:

> When I got back [into public life] I couldn't relate to that world, because what I was doing before that accident wasn't what was happening when I got back on my feet. We didn't

---

* This may be a surprise given that *Sergeant Pepper*, released in 1967, is now regularly held up as the pinnacle of rock. Gendron's historical account, however, shows that while highbrow critics received the album favourably and lauded the group's avant-garde pretensions, rock critics were generally dismissive, arguing that The Beatles had lost the spirit of rock music. When Dylan released *John Wesley Harding* at the end of 1967, it was highly praised by rock critics because its stripped down sound was more in keeping with rock authenticity (2002:208–15).

have that adulation, that intense worship, I was just another singer really. (Craig McGregor interview, 1978)

It wasn't me who called myself a legend. It was thrown at me by editors in the media who wanted to play around with me or have something to tell their readers. But it stuck. (Robert Hilburn interview, 1992)

By keeping silent, his commercial stock increased too – *John Wesley Harding* and *Nashville Skyline* were his two best-selling records of the decade. The release of *John Wesley Harding* was heralded as a break from the electronic excesses of 1967's psychedelic era and Dylan was once more interpreted as making a major breakthrough, opening the door for a 'return to roots' revival. None of this did Dylan's desire for privacy any good. His privacy was routinely invaded in Woodstock: indeed, he woke up one morning to find someone in his bedroom watching him and his wife sleep. Dylan allegedly resorted to keeping a rifle by his front door to ward off his fans. He even had to move out for a couple of weeks in 1969 when a large music festival held at Bethel, 60 miles down the road, was actually called 'Woodstock' to trade on the countercultural cachet of Dylan's residence. Keeping silent had not succeeded in taking the heat out of Dylan's star-image. He therefore adopted a new strategy: saying nothing.

SAYING NOTHING

In the previous two chapters, I have discussed how the relationship between rock and politics emerged through its origins in the folk revival. Rather than providing an explicit alternative political manifesto, rock's politics were more intangible and therefore, supposedly, more effective than conventional politics. Rock supposedly both reflected and promoted a particular affective sensibility, a way of thinking and feeling that was inherently political in its development of a critical consciousness, but not explicitly political as it wasn't tied to any political organisations. Towards the end of the 1960s, however, rock culture and radical politics did become more explicitly intertwined. With the intensification of feeling against the Vietnam war, flashpoints at Columbia, the Democratic Convention in Chicago, People's Park, and Kent State seemed to be galvanising a broad based youth movement into violent action.* At the same time, there were youth uprisings elsewhere around the world, most notably in Paris in May 1968. With the rise of the Black Panther movement, the civil rights movement in America also became more violent. Rock music was interpreted by many as a central element of youth culture's revolutionary nature, as some rock musicians claimed a more explicitly political role and the underground press claimed ownership of rock stars as the guerrilla warriors of the revolution.

The increasing radicalism of youth culture and its relationship to rock music had effects for Dylan's star-image even as he stayed out of the limelight. Dylan's work, particularly the albums *Bringing It All Back Home* and *Highway 61 Revisited*, featuring songs like 'It's Alright Ma (I'm Only Bleeding)' and 'Desolation Row', were held up as the benchmark of politically aware rock. Marqusee describes the

---

* In April 1968 over 1,000 students forcefully occupied five campus buildings of Columbia College for five days before being forcibly removed by the police; the 1968 Democrat conference in Chicago was subject to anti-war protests that resulted in violent clashes; in May 1969 Governor Ronald Reagan ordered the fencing off and destruction of the People's Park in Berkeley for being a 'a safe haven for commie sympathizers', precipitating violent clashes between riot police and protesters attempting to reclaim the park; in May 1970, four students of Kent State University were killed by the Ohio National Guard as a result of on-campus protests against the Vietnam war.

former as a 'critique of the repressive . . . monstrous totality
of social domination [through which human freedom] . . . is
menaced on all sides'.[9] Dylan's past songs meant that his
star-image became radicalised during the late sixties. As
Marqusee argues, youth radicalism in America

> was clearly seen and felt to be part of a global insurgency.
> Whether Dylan liked it or not, in many parts of the world
> he was heard as the voice of dissident America . . . In the
> USA, no matter how firmly Dylan disclaimed any represen-
> tative function, his voice was heard more than ever as the
> voice of and for the social crisis that everyone now agreed
> was gripping the country by the throat.[10]

The most notable example of this was the formation of a ter-
rorist group in 1969 who called themselves 'The Weather-
men' after a line from a Dylan song.

In what was surely a deliberate attempt to undermine his
star-image, to wrest control of what 'Bob Dylan' meant
away from those who placed him in the vanguard of radical
politics, Dylan's public persona became increasingly apolit-
ical. Earlier attempts to shake off the 'spokesman of a generation' tag had been rejected by the public. In saying that
he just wrote what was on his mind, he had been adopted as
a representative of the generation's individualistic consciousness. In the late 1960s, he therefore produced music
that could not be adopted by the counterculture. In April
1969, he released *Nashville Skyline*, an album of simple
country songs. As youth revolution supposedly raged in the
streets around him, the spokesman for his generation
merely sang:

> Peggy Day stole my poor heart away
> By golly what more can I say?

Love to spend the night with Peggy Day.

While elsewhere on the album he told us:

Blueberry, apple, cherry, pumpkin and plum,
Call me for dinner, honey, I'll be there
. . .
Oh me, oh my, love that country pie!

Dylan's choice of country music is not innocent as the genre is associated with the American South and known as being religiously and morally conservative.* Dylan's voice is also presented differently on this album, a much smoother voice is heard in distinction to the insistent roughness of earlier albums. All in all, *Nashville Skyline* is a nice, if slight, album. One would expect, given the historical situation in which it appeared, that being 'nice' would in itself be cause for criticism. Yet the album received generally favourable reviews, being praised for its overall charm and the craft of the lyrics. The main explanation for this, I think, is that the 'return to roots' revivalism of American rock was still in full swing and the album was viewed as a well-meaning homage. *Nashville Skyline* is one of Dylan's most popular albums among non-Dylan fans. As Dylan's career has unfolded, however, the album is often portrayed as the start of a long decline.

One album of slight country tunes would not be sufficient to alter Dylan's star-image, and his policy of wilful deconstruction continued throughout 1969 and 1970. Any request for a political statement, indeed any kind of state-

---

* Nor is it forced; we now know that Dylan holds country music very dear, though it would have been a surprise in 1969. *Nashville Skyline* and *Self Portrait* have both received something of a reappraisal in recent years, as part of the transformation of Dylan's star-image since 1997.

ment, was politely rebuffed. *Rolling Stone* published a major interview with Dylan in November 1969. For an artist famed for giving nothing away, it is conceivably the least revealing and mundane interview of Dylan's career. When questioned about his social importance, he professed ignorance:

> Q: Many people . . . all felt tremendously affected by your music and what you're saying in the lyrics.
> Dylan: Did they?
> Q: Sure. They felt it had a particular relevance to their lives . . . I mean, you must be aware of the way that people come on you.
> Dylan: Not entirely. Why don't you explain to me.
>
>   . . .
>
> Q: You're an extremely important figure in music and an extremely important figure in the experience of growing up today . . . And I'm curious to know what you think about that.
> Dylan: What would I think about it? What can I do?. . . I play music, man. I write songs . . . I believe, also, that there are people trained for this job that you're talking about – 'youth leader' types of thing, you know? I mean there must be people trained to do this kind of work. And I'm just one person, doing what I do. Trying to get along . . . Staying out of people's hair, that's all.
>
> (Jan Wenner interview, 1969)

In August 1969, Dylan played at the Isle of Wight Festival in the UK. At a hastily arranged press conference, Dylan continued his 'say nothing' policy.

> Q: Can I have your general views on the situation of drug taking among teenagers and young people these days?

> Dylan: I don't have any of those views . . . I wish I did, I'd
> be glad to share them with you . . .

Still Dylan proved a box-office draw, with an estimated 200,000 people descending on the small island. Dylan's performance was criticised for being too short and his new performing style was also underwhelming. He saved the best until last, though, when, in 1970, he released *Self Portrait*.

Self Portrait is a landmark album. It contains 24 tracks, 2 lightweight Dylan originals, 4 songs from Dylan's performance at the Isle of Wight, and 16 covers of contemporary songs, fifties pop tunes and traditional country and folk songs. The album has no coherence (the live tracks are scattered through the album, for example), supposedly Dylan's response to the newly emerging bootlegs of his earlier recordings. More importantly, however, the album was produced with slushy string arrangements reminiscent of the kind of music rock was supposed to displace. It is notorious, perhaps the most criticised album in all of rock. The most well-known review, by Greil Marcus in *Rolling Stone*, famously begins 'What is this shit?' Other reviews were similarly scathing. It is a landmark album because it is the moment that Dylan ceases to be regarded as infallible, as one who opened doors through which others were bound to follow. From this point on, reviewers stopped giving Dylan the benefit of the doubt. Indeed, as I argue below, from this point onward the reverse happens, and no matter how good an album Dylan produced, it was almost always accepted with a 'could do better' review.

Regarding *Self Portrait*, it is possible that Dylan just produced a poor album, but it seems more likely that it was a deliberate attempt by Dylan to reclaim the meaning of his stardom. This is certainly how Dylan has presented its release subsequently:

> That album was put out . . . [because] at that time . . . I
> didn't like the attention I was getting. I [had] never been a
> person that wanted attention. And at that time I was getting
> the wrong kind of attention, for doing things I'd never
> done. So we released that album to get people off my back.
> They would not like me anymore. That's . . . the reason
> that album was put out, so people would just at that time
> stop buying my records, and they did.[11]

This could merely be Dylan rationalising a mistake after
the event – perhaps in this instance the role of audience
conflict in Dylan's star-image makes this reading of *Self
Portrait* more plausible when he actually just released a bad
album! There are a number of factors that support Dylan's
assertion that this was deliberate subversion, however.
Firstly, the album title seems a deliberate statement. A self-
portrait, of course, is meant to reveal the artist's inner sense
of his own self. Following *Nashville Skyline*, there had been
calls for the return of the 'real Dylan', and calling the
album *Self Portrait* seems a deliberate reaction to such calls.
'These trite songs, these casual performances' it says, 'are
the real me.' Then there is the album cover, which contains
no words, either name or title, just a slightly clumsy painting of a face. All of his previous albums had contained
photos of Dylan, so the implication once more seems to be
that this is an accurate presentation of who Dylan is.
Thirdly, there is the fact that Dylan, the most famous songwriter of his age, shows that he considers his self-portrait to
consist of songs by other writers. Fourthly, there is the
opening track, 'All The Tired Horses'. It is one of only two
Dylan originals on the album, yet Dylan's voice is absent
from the song, replaced by female singers. Given the relationship between voice and stardom, particularly in Dylan's
instance, this is again a significant (and, one could assume,

deliberate) gesture. Finally, there is the use of 'Like A Rolling Stone' from the Isle of Wight performance. It is an awful performance, with Dylan forgetting words and singing it entirely without feeling. It is Dylan's most famous song, arguably the best song of all time. No other song could have fulfilled the function of differentiating the new and old Dylan so well, emphasising that the songwriters covered by Dylan on *Self Portrait* included the Dylan who wrote that song.[12]

AFTER THE CRASH: DYLAN'S POST-1960s STARDOM

Dylan once sang 'there's no success like failure' and *Self Portrait* was some kind of success. It did not erase his position as a cultural leader entirely (when Dylan moved back to New York in 1970, A. J. Weberman's 'Dylan Liberation Front' protested outside his house, campaigning for him to return to political songwriting) nor his marketability (his 1974 comeback tour with The Band was the most over-subscribed in rock history). It did, however, succeed in undermining the myth of Dylan's infallibility and the battle for the meaning of Bob Dylan during 1967–70 creates a distinct break, a rupture, in Dylan's star-image that centres on the motorcycle accident of 1966.* The important issue here is that the focus on the motorcycle accident as *the* moment of change has affected the interpretation of *all* of Dylan's career – not just how his later career has been interpreted but also how the pre-crash stardom has been interpreted too. Dylan's pre-'66

---

* There is an excellent cartoon that aptly demonstrates how the accident has come to be defined as the before/after moment in Dylan's stardom. The cartoon depicts Dylan flying over the handlebars of his bike, eyes wide open and a thought bubble that says 'Country Rock!'

output only becomes critically positioned after the fact. This is not to say that it was not popular before the crash, nor that he didn't have a reputation as particularly gifted within the folk revival, but it is to suggest that the work has only taken on such a canonical role within rock culture after 1966. We must remember not only that Dylan's earlier work within the folk revival was part of a minority interest but also that his post-folk work was the site of considerable contestation – a lot of people didn't like it. It is only afterwards that the contestation itself has become part of the justification of the work's worth.

Part of the explanation for this canonisation lies in the rock historiography already discussed, but rock's critics drew upon wider cultural beliefs in codifying the rock ideology. In particular, a significant reason for the way that Dylan's stardom hones in on 1966 is the ideological linkage of youth, genius and mortality. This ideological brew has a notable impact on stardom and there is an oft-repeated idea that death can be a good career move for stars. Death removes the physical body of the person from the image of the star – rather than see the physical decay of the human reality we can instead revel in the idealised star-image (something Warhol recognised in his silk screens). Think of the different ways we consider the two beauties of sixties Hollywood, Marilyn Monroe and Elizabeth Taylor: the former frozen forever as an idealised beauty, the latter tainted by a descent into bloated caricature. Even when we see the perfect Taylor in *Cleopatra*, our image of her is always shadowed by an awareness of what she became. No such shadow is cast over Monroe – she only ever looked that good. Death also creates the tendency to both erase the human failings of a particular star (unless they are part of an image of a difficult, tortured artist) and to create a particular star teleology – a rationalisation of an entire career that creates its own logic and leads to a logical conclusion. Dylan recognised this in an interview/play written by Sam Shepard in 1986. In it, Dylan discusses a significant early influence upon him, James Dean:

> You know where I just was? Paso Robles. You know, on the highway where James Dean got killed? I was there on the spot. On the spot. A windy kinda place. The curve where he had the accident. I mean, the place where he died is as powerful as the place he lived. It's on this kind of broad expanse of land. It's like that place made James Dean who he is. If he hadn't've died there, he wouldn't't've been James Dean.*

Dylan is right on this – that early, dramatic death is a key part of James Dean's stardom; it made Dean who he is, because it creates a finite structure in which his stardom can be interpreted (he's also right to use the present tense – 'who James Dean is' – because the death enables the star-image to maintain itself perpetually in the now). Dean's image was one of restlessness, dissatisfaction and – significantly – youthful good looks. You can't imagine Dean in a satisfied, comfortable, middle-age; it was 'inevitable' that he would die the way he did. The crash affirms Dean's star-image.

Death and stardom thus have an intimate relationship. There are, though, certain limitations. It has to be a particular

---

* *True Dylan* is a play written by Sam Shepard supposedly based on an interview conducted with Dylan. The theme of the play, however, is the authority accorded to stars' statements in authenticating stardom. During the course of the 'interview', the tape recorder (the guarantee of authenticity) breaks and Dylan tells Shepard to just make it up (see Wynands, 2000). Quotes attributed to Dylan in this interview should be treated with caution. Shepard himself had an interest in stardom, and collaborated with Dylan on the song on the same theme, which is discussed in the next chapter.

kind of death – a 'heroic' death – and it has to be at an early age. Both of these emerge from Romantic ideology. The Romantics valorised youth as a time of both political and aesthetic radicalism ('Bliss was it in that dawn to be alive', wrote Wordsworth, 'but to be young was very Heaven'). Youth was a time before the disenchantment of science and rationalism overtook one's self, when the world could be seen through new eyes. It was a time for breaking the rules created by previous generations, and it was a time for excess, to indulge in all the bounteous tastes the world has to offer – drugs, drink, sex, freedom. These excesses were, of course, to achieve a higher purpose, to open up new forms of consciousness, reach 'the palace of wisdom' through the 'doors of perception' (both phrases are Blake's, though they maintained currency in the 1960s), but they also carried a price – the possibility of burning out, and of death. The early death of many of the key figures of Romanticism (notably Keats, Byron and Shelley) all added weight to the cultural ideal that genius blossoms young and then disappears. There is the feeling that it is *better* for these cultural heroes to have died young because then we only have them at their peak. We only know Keats as the bright-eyed youth, and are forever enthralled by the possibilities of what he could have written had he lived beyond twenty-five, whereas we know that Wordsworth became a crusty old Tory.*

As the last mass flourishing of the Romantic ideology, many of these cultural myths are prominent in sixties rock culture. In rock there is a similar valorisation of youth and of heroic excess ('Hope I die before I get old' sang The Who; 'Better to burn out than fade away' reiterated Neil Young, subsequently quoted by Kurt Cobain in his suicide note). The rock myth is to live fast and die young, and we culturally praise those who 'die of rock and roll' (interestingly,

---

* Notably, Keats only achieved fame after his death.

death provides a significant boost to record sales, whereas there is no such effect in the publishing industry).[13] We can forever speculate on what magical music Jimi Hendrix would have made had he lived beyond twenty-seven, but we know Eric Clapton became a crusty old Tory.

If Dylan had died in 1966, he would have received the same kind of beatification as Hendrix later did, probably even more intensely. He would have been held up as the ideal rock star, following in Rimbaud's footsteps in his 'rational disordering of the senses'; the drug-fuelled performances of 1966 held up as the greatest that could be achieved within the genre. Having the feeling that he 'might die after the show' is merely evidence of his ultimate genius, of his willingness to follow his visions.

Now, of course, Dylan didn't die in 1966. My argument, however, is that there is such a dramatic rupture at this moment – a time when rock culture is writing its own history and defining its own canon – that the effect is very similar to if he had died. There is such a dramatic change between the Dylan of 1966 and the Dylan of 1967–70 that there is a kind of pseudo-mortality going on here, almost as if one particular Bob Dylan died in 1966 only for a new one to emerge. We have the process of idealisation, of air-brushing, of the image taking over from reality that normally occurs posthumously. The fact that he had a motorcycle accident is extremely significant because of its glamorous potential (and its resonance with Dean's car crash). Even today, the story of the 'motorcycle accident that nearly cost him his life' is a key part of Dylan's myth (for example, it was repeated in many reviews of the 2005 *No Direction Home* documentary).* To paraphrase Dylan's

---

* The irony is that, by giving him a reason to drop out of the rock scene, the crash quite conceivably saved his life.

quote about James Dean, it's almost like, without the crash, he wouldn't have been Bob Dylan.

Although the crash is the mythical moment of transformation, it is only the period of silence and the battle over meaning after the crash that defines it as such. The period 1967–70 is one in which 'Bob Dylan' is both idealised and rationalised within rock discourse. Across this period, there does seem to be the creation of two Bob Dylan star images. The first is the 'dead' Dylan, who existed up until the motorcycle crash. This Dylan is the model of perfection, but it is an idealisation, a model that never existed in reality. Dylan is presented as an untouchable genius whose instincts are always spot on and who never made a wrong decision:

> After I was knocked off, knocked out [in 1966], I guess people thought that I was gone, y'know, wasn't about to come back, so they started elevating me to a level [from] which no one could come back. (Craig McGregor interview, 1978)

I said earlier that looking back at the 1960s Elizabeth Taylor, the image is shadowed by knowledge of what she became. I don't think the same is true of 1960s Dylan, however. There is such a dramatic rupture caused by this pseudo-mortality that we don't see a future Dylan in that sixties image just as we don't see a future Hendrix. There is, however, an interesting reversal because, from the 1970s onwards, the present Bob Dylan is continually shadowed by that sixties image. This is a visual thing – the way that, every now and then, his image seems to just give us a glimpse of the boyish grin or icy cool that we visualise from old photos, as his face seemingly refracts time rather than light – but, more importantly for Dylan's later career, it is an 'artistic' thing too. Dylan's post-sixties star-image is of someone who never quite lives up to his reputation, never fulfils his potential. Artists' work is often compared to their previous work, so Dylan is not entirely unique in this regard, but with Dylan it does have a slightly different edge. Dylan's idealised star-image represented more than just an individual musician. It represented a whole era. Dylan came to represent rock culture, the sixties, and the promises that both offered but ultimately never quite realised. The subsequent 'failure' of both the sixties and rock culture reflected badly on Dylan's later stardom. There seems to be a transformation of star-meaning, in which we have a new Dylan star-image that is always measured against an old one. Dylan spent the next thirty years of his career being compared to this idealised earlier self:

> Comparing me to myself is really like . . . I mean, you're talking to a person that feels like he's walking around in the ruins of Pompeii all the time. (Mikal Gilmore interview, 2001)

From 1966 onwards, at least until 1997, the abstract notion of Dylan is of someone still capable of producing better work than anyone else in the history of popular music, but never quite managing it. Dylan's reputation among critics is generally more honoured in the breach than the observance. For example, in 1978, when his last three albums had been *Blood On The Tracks*, *Desire* and *Street Legal*, one English critic claimed that 'his talent has been judged by many to be in sharp decline. . . . There has been an alarming dearth of good material in recent years.' For someone as revered as Dylan, he has never received particularly enthusiastic reviews (taking account of the fact that there were hardly any rock reviews before his crash). I would venture that only two

Dylan albums between 1966 and 1996 received a broad range of enthusiastic reviews (*Blood On The Tracks* in 1975 and *Oh Mercy* in 1989). Albums of the quality of *Desire*, *Street Legal*, *Slow Train Coming*, *Infidels* and *World Gone Wrong* have not been critically ravaged but have been treated with indifference. As one journalist noted, 'he seems to be held up to a higher standard because of his own bigger-than-life image'. It's not a wilful dismissal of Dylan, as though arguing he's overrated, more a sense of disappointment that he never lives up to the ideal. It's as though Jesus has returned to Earth to act as a first-aider: the general response is 'Well, this is all okay but, frankly, if you're not going to perform any miracles then why are you bothering?' If the post-'66 Dylan does not match the heights of the pre-'66 one (and no matter what he produces, he can never reach those heights because they are idealised) then even if the work is good, it is never good enough.*

---

* If the analogy with Christ seems a little far-fetched, it is one which Dylan has utilised. In 'Shelter From The Storm', he refers to having his crown of thorns removed, and, in what I consider to be one of the most self-conscious references to his stardom throughout his work, he sings (in 'In The Garden') supposedly of Jesus but also of himself: 'The multitude wanted to make Him king, put a crown upon His head / Why did He slip away to a quiet place instead?'

Snapshot: The rock legend

Dylan embarked on a world tour during 1978, easily the biggest touring commitment of his career thus far. The shows were generally well received outside of the USA (Dylan had not toured outside of North America for twelve years) but were criticised at home; it was dubbed 'The Alimony Tour' and Dylan was criticised for turning into a 'Vegas act'. Towards the end of this year, he experienced a personal epiphany and became a born-again Christian. For the first part of 1979, he spent four days a week attending lessons at the Vineyard Fellowship in Santa Monica. Dylan released two albums – *Slow Train Coming* in 1979 and *Saved* in 1980 – that contained nothing but Christian songs. During live shows in these years, he played only religious material and between songs he preached to his audience. For the second time in his career, Dylan found himself being booed by his audiences.

In 1981, he released the less overtly evangelical *Shot Of Love* and embarked on European and North American tours in which he included some of his old songs. Reviews were less kind than for the 1978 tour, however. Dylan produced no public work in 1982, and his next album, *Infidels*, his first post-evangelical work, received average reviews. A short European tour took place in 1984 and 1985 included the album *Empire Burlesque*. The year was most notable, however, for Dylan's notorious performance closing *Live Aid*. Accompanied by a drunk Ron Wood and Keith Richards, Dylan badly performed three songs and offended many people by suggesting that some of the money raised could be used to pay the mortgages of American farmers.

Dylan's comments acted as a spur to a 'Farm Aid' event, and Dylan regained some credibility with a strong performance backed by Tom Petty and the Heartbreakers. Dylan took the same band on tour with him in 1986, playing Japan, New Zealand, Australia and the US. With a highly competent rock and roll band behind him, the shows were generally well received. Dylan played virtually no songs from his new album, *Knocked Out Loaded*, however, perhaps an indication that he was beginning to struggle to write songs. The remainder of the year was spent filming an awful movie, *Hearts Of Fire*.

Albums and major events

Apr–Dec 1978	World tour (documented on *At Budokan*)
June 1978	*Street Legal*
January–March 1979	Attends School of Discipleship in California
August 1979	*Slow Train Coming*
Nov–May 1979–80	North American tour
June 1980	*Saved*
Nov–Dec 1980	US tour
June–July 1981	European tour
August 1981	*Shot Of Love*
Oct–Nov 1981	North American tour
November 1983	*Infidels*
May–July 1984	European tour (documented on *Real Live*)
June 1985	*Empire Burlesque*
July 1985	Live Aid
October 1985	*Biograph*
Feb–Mar 1986	Pacific tour
June–Aug 1986	North American tour
August 1986	*Knocked Out Loaded*

6

DECLINING STARDOM:
NOSTALGIA AND THE 'DEATH
OF ROCK'

Whether or not Janne Mäkela is correct to suggest that 'rock stardom may celebrate the present moment, but the past is built into the present',[1] it is certainly the case for Dylan. Dylan's mythologised past has been a prominent part of his star-image since at least 1970. During the 1970s, Dylan struggled to not be entirely overshadowed by this past (the release of *Blood On The Tracks* in 1975 is a pivotal event in this regard, giving critics and fans enough evidence to convince them that he was still a creative force). As the eighties developed, however, wider social changes involving a reconceptualisation of both 'rock' and 'the sixties' meant that Dylan gradually began to lose the battle with his history. During this period Dylan became understood almost entirely in nostalgic terms and his live shows and public appearances functioned as living reproductions of past glories. This period of Dylan's career – roughly from 1981 to 1987 – is often portrayed as his mid-life crisis, viewed as precipitated either by his turning forty in 1981 or by his divorce in 1977. While these factors undoubtedly had some impact on Dylan's creativity, to use them as the central explanation for Dylan's errant decade would be as incomplete as solely relying upon a biographical reading of a song. In order to understand what happened, we once more need to consider Dylan's stardom in a broader context, in relation to changes in the music industry as well as broader social developments. This argument becomes more compelling when it is noted that Dylan's creativity did not falter as much as is commonly believed during these years: while he may not have been as prolific as he was in the sixties and seventies, he still managed to produce some of his greatest songs during this decade – though many of them did not make it into the public arena. We need to investigate Dylan's public role, his positioning as a star in the 1980s. The question, it seems to me, is not 'what happened to Dylan's muse?' but rather 'what happened to Dylan's stardom that so alienated him from his music?' How did the burden of being Bob Dylan prevent him from doing the things that Bob Dylan was supposedly so good at?

My argument is that the period in question can be roughly divided into two sections. In the first section, from about 1981 to 1983, Dylan's stardom is marked by ambiguity and uncertainty. In common with many other sixties rock stars, the question of what 'Bob Dylan' stands for cannot be easily answered. This uncertainty can be seen in Dylan's output at this time, in his lack of public presence and his editorial choices. The second part of this period – roughly 1984 to 1987 – marks a period in which the meaning of 'Bob Dylan' is relatively clear. During this period Dylan attains a particular kind of 'living legend' status as his star-meaning becomes dominated by his past. This period is characterised by Dylan's disengagement from his contemporary work – his work is generally competent, but perfunctory, and Dylan displays a seeming unwillingness to challenge media representations of himself.

One of the features of stardom is how it emphasises particular moments in a star's biography, events after which the star (or popular music) were never the same again. Within Dylan's career, his conversion to evangelical Christianity features as just such a moment. The concerts he performed in 1979 and the first half of 1980 featured religious songs exclusively. In between songs, he preached to the crowd and at times was heckled by his audience. This dramatic period of Dylan's life is often used as a convenient punctuation mark in the Bob Dylan story: before he got religion, he was creative, confident and respected; after he stepped back from his role as a preacher he was confused, had lost his muse and everything went wrong. Such a portrayal masks longer-term trends. As discussed in the previous chapter, Dylan was being portrayed as artistically on the wane even before his conversion (*Renaldo And Clara*, *Street Legal* and his 1978 tour had all been fiercely criticised in the US) and, I would suggest, Dylan would still have experienced similar problems in the 1980s even without his conversion. The conversion did have a significant impact on Dylan's stardom, however. Whatever star-meaning Dylan had during the seventies – as a mature artist, as a chameleon – was significantly eroded by his conversion to Christianity, particularly given that one key meaning of Dylan's image is that of resistance to pre-defined roles. The most famous image of Dylan is as an iconoclast imploring that his listeners 'don't follow leaders'. Thus to be on stage preaching at his audience, telling the listener that 'you gotta serve somebody', is fundamentally at odds with his dominant star-image.

When stars take actions that do not match with the public understanding of the star's meaning then the public often turns against them (for example, the public turned against

Charlie Chaplin during a high-profile paternity case in 1943, at least in part out of tiredness of his espousal of left-wing views).[2] In Dylan's case, this rejection can clearly be seen in his sales figures. While *Slow Train Coming* was actually one of his best-selling albums, spending twenty-six weeks on the American charts, *Saved* was the first Bob Dylan album in sixteen years not to make the Top 20.[3] It also had wider implications in affecting what 'Bob Dylan' could mean in the 1980s. That this occurred just as Western societies were structurally reorganising themselves and experiencing dramatic changes in their belief systems means that certain ways of understanding Bob Dylan become more likely while other possibilities were closed down.

1981–3 thus represents a period in which the meaning of 'Bob Dylan' is unclear. I think it is not unreasonable to suggest that this kind of uncertainty affected Dylan's output at this time. It would be wrong to make any great claims about Dylan's state of mind or his artistic consciousness, particularly given that Dylan was likely to be presented as faltering whatever he produced, but there were a series of editorial decisions taken by Dylan during the early eighties that suggest that he himself was uncertain of what exactly he was supposed to do and what role he had to play. This period of Dylan's career can therefore only be understood in terms of Dylan's stardom, not in terms of a diminishing muse. Dylan was still creating work of a high standard during this period. His songwriting between 1980 and 1984 produced major works such as 'Caribbean Wind', 'Angelina', 'The Groom's Still Waiting At The Altar', 'Every Grain Of Sand', 'Jokerman', 'I and I', 'Foot Of Pride', 'Blind Willie McTell' and 'New Danville Girl'. Most of these, however, were not released on his albums. Similarly, while there were sublime moments during concerts, his tours from autumn 1981 to summer 1987 were generally workmanlike and uninspired.

Yet many reports and recordings from studio sessions and tour rehearsals illustrate a performer very much engaged with his music and performing to a high standard. It was the public side of 'Bob Dylan' that was causing Dylan so much trouble at this time. This can be illustrated by the fact that from November 1981 to February 1986 Dylan took only his second – and, to date, last – extended break from touring, punctuated only by a brief European tour in 1984.[4] Indeed, during 1982, Dylan gave only one public performance.

ROCK, POSTMODERNISM AND AUTHORITY

Stars always exist as something more than just themselves; they represent something other than just an individual. This means, however, that stardom and star meaning are constantly structured by factors outside the star's control. They are prey to changing social forces more than anonymous individuals. In the last chapter, I discussed how Dylan came to be understood as the 'leader' of rock music even as he tried to reject that mantle. This linking of Dylan with rock music had an affect on Dylan, because how 'rock' is interpreted and valued will impact on how Dylan is interpreted and valued. In this chapter I want to discuss a range of different processes, both within and without the music industry, that occur in the 1980s and affect the social positioning of rock (as well as a wider reconsideration of 'the sixties') to explain the effect they had on Dylan's stardom. My general argument is that rock's position in the hierarchy of popular music diminished during this era (the 'death of rock' argument) and that, while the death of rock may have been exaggerated, Dylan's indeterminate star-meaning at this time, the way he became represented as increasingly irrelevant, is one outcome of this. On many levels, Dylan's stardom represented 'rock' – his chameleon nature, his continual moving on, his political conscience, his insistence on referring to women as 'baby' – and so as rock's authority becomes diminished, so too does Dylan's stardom. The first factor that I will discuss in this regard concerns what I am labelling 'post-survivorism'. The idea of being a 'survivor' gained currency throughout the 1970s,[5] a notion that probably emerged as a result of the expanding influence of Reich's psychoanalytic theories that emphasise the release of repressed emotions and desires as the key to happiness.[6] Christopher Lasch, in *The Culture of Narcissim* and *The Minimalistic Self*, discusses how the notion of survival became embedded in popular culture and political debate, such as self-help guides on surviving marriage, or divorce, or just about anything you might face in daily life.[7] This notion of survivorism became a key discourse in 1970s rock culture, as one of the central strands of survivorism in America at the time was the idea of having 'survived the sixties', both in terms of surviving the political 'defeat' of the countercultural movement and in terms of the physical toll that much sixties consumption took on its consumers, most obviously in the deaths of several figureheads such as Joplin, Hendrix and Morrison. Survivorism was clearly a significant discourse for those prominent rock stars who had emerged in the 1960s and continued into the 1970s. Janne Mäkela, for example, discusses how Lennon utilised it in many of his 1970s interviews.[8] Mäkela's conclusion is that 'the toll that the so-called rock and roll lifestyle had so visibly taken since the late 1960s in fact gave the "rock survivors" special status, some validation in the 1970s'.

Towards the end of the decade, Dylan also utilised this discourse, portraying himself as a survivor in song. In 'What Can I Do For You?', he asserts 'Well I don't deserve it, but I sure did make it through', while his final pre-evangelical album, *Street Legal*, closes with the lines

There's a new day at dawn and I've finally arrived
If I'm there in the morning, baby, you'll know I've
   survived
I can't believe it, I can't believe I'm alive
But without you it just doesn't seem right
Oh, where are you tonight?

('Where Are You Tonight?
(Journey Through Dark Heat)')

Dylan had certainly had a traumatic seventies, and his private trials had been fought in a very public arena. Several major works of the decade – the albums *Blood On The Tracks*, *Desire* and *Street Legal*, as well as the film *Renaldo and Clara* present a raw and vulnerable Dylan somehow making it through. In a long essay called 'Dylan – What Happened?', Paul Williams argues that Dylan's conversion to Christianity was actually a response to his personal traumas of the late seventies.[9] It seems reasonable to surmise that at the end of the seventies, survivorism played some role in Dylan's stardom.

My reason for mentioning survivorism, however, is not to discuss Dylan's seventies stardom but to question the effect that this had on how he was understood in the 1980s. Mäkela states that the survivor discourse gave sixties rock stars some 'validation' during the 1970s, and provided a justification for their continuation as artists. It therefore seems worth asking: *What happens when the survivor justification expires?* New cultural ideologies that emphasised consumer lifestyles and individual self-sufficiency emerged as part of neo-liberalism and trumped notions of survivorism and collective action. This undoubtedly had an impact on using survivorism as a justification for older rock stars. If their 'validation' as survivors was rejected, what other reason did they have for their continuing stardom?

The weakening of survivorism can be broadly linked to wider arguments regarding the death of rock which developed at the end of the seventies and into the eighties:

> I am now quite sure that the rock era is over. People will go on playing and enjoying rock music, of course (though the label is increasingly vague), but the music business is no longer organized around rock, around the selling of records of a particular sort of musical event to young people. The rock era – born around 1956 with Elvis Presley, peaking around 1967 with *Sgt Pepper*, dying around 1976 with the Sex Pistols – turned out to be a by-way in the development of twentieth-century popular music, rather than, as we thought at the time, any kind of mass-cultural revolution. Rock was a last romantic attempt to preserve ways of music-making – performer as artist, performance as 'community' – that had been made obsolete by technology and capital.[10]

What does the 'death of rock' mean? Just like in discussions of the 'death of the author', the argument is not about a physical annihilation – rock has not disappeared. What has been 'killed', however, is the authority of the rock ideology as well as the assumption that the values and beliefs of rock culture are those to which all forms of popular music should adhere. Rock emerged within the mainstream but it also took over the mainstream, creating a form of 'rock imperialism' in which all forms of music were judged by the standards adopted by rock. The industrial organisation of record labels was dominated by the rock ideology (specific divisions for black musics like soul were frequently marginalised within major labels), while key positions of power within radio and the music press were heavily influenced by those adhering to the rock ideology. Rock was assumed to be synonymous with the mainstream. Following the 'death of rock', however, it is argued that the mainstream has fragmented into a variety of different genres with no one genre being considered dominant. There is no longer an imperialism whereby the ideas and standards of one genre are used as a way of measuring other genres. In this way rock lost its place as the dominant genre of popular music. As Negus explains 'Punk rock had [supposedly] broken the sequential history of pop. The future was to promise a proliferation of the margins, a carnival of styles, rather than a renewed linear narrative based around the concept of a mainstream and musical tributaries.'[11] The reason that punk is used to mark the end point of rock's hegemony is that punk undermined the notion that rock music could offer a genuinely countercultural challenge to capitalism. As previously argued, rock emerged as a way of sorting mass cultural items (and thus consumers) into a hierarchy, with some granted artistic value and revolutionary potential ('rock') and others dismissed as standardised and trivial, wholly implicated by their capitalist production ('pop'). This particular ideology, however, was undermined by punk in the second half of the seventies because punk made clear its status as *constructed* chaos, *manufactured* mayhem. Punk was more concerned with surface than with meaning, with artifice than with naturalism; it showed up the contradiction inherent in the claim that 'the revolutionaries are on CBS'.* The death of rock does not mean that rock music just disappeared. What did occur, however, is that rock ceased to be something that people followed with passion and commitment and became a 'lifestyle choice'. This change can be seen in the emergence of a new UK monthly glossy magazine, *Q*, and the transformation of *Rolling Stone* into a lifestyle magazine. It can also be seen in the most

---

* This was an advertising campaign run by Dylan's record label in 1970.

popular rock stars of the period, such as Phil Collins and Dire Straits. As the key record-buying demographic grew older, rock ceased to be something one believed in but was, rather, something one consumed. We can draw a useful analogy from high culture. At the point where the nineteenth century was becoming the twentieth, there emerged a number of cultural groupings (such as the Dadaists and the Futurists) who believed that art had a special role in modern society. Thinking that high culture was the only part of social life that had not been colonised by the instrumentalism and avarice of capitalism, these avant-gardes engaged in a variety of cultural offensives designed to highlight the contradictions of capitalism in order to awaken the masses and instigate social change. For the first half of the twentieth century, this was the generally understood 'function' of the arts – they were supposed to express a critical voice unavailable in other spheres of life. As modernism became canonised, however, a new generation of artists emerged in the fifties and sixties (such as Jack Kerouac and Andy Warhol) that saw how high culture was itself embedded within the very power relations it sought to overthrow. These new artists believed that culture should be used to describe how we experience the world rather than attempting to provide any overarching critique. This new understanding, which became part of postmodernism, did not seek to challenge capitalism but accepted that culture was thoroughly embedded within capitalism and could not therefore offer any kind of resolution to its problems.

The declining belief that rock could provide a genuine countercultural challenge in some ways mirrors the decline of avant-gardism, while the other changes occurring within popular music at this time – the emphasis on style rather than content; the fragmentation of the mainstream into a variety of different-but-equal genres such as new wave, new romantic and hip hop – all relate to the emergence of post-modernism within Western culture. Postmodernism is complex but can broadly be seen as two distinct but related social processes. The first of these is the merging of 'culture' and 'commerce'.[12] Whereas once culture was seen as the antithesis of commerce, as the only possible space for a critical voice (a view that can be seen in the world view of the English Romantics, the modernist avant-gardes and the voices of the sixties counterculture), today culture is an essential part of commodification in, for example, differentiating between the products that we buy to express our individuality (three stripes on your running shoes or two?). Culture sells and is used to sell; there is no cultural production that is outside of the capitalist game. We can see this in Warhol's reproductions of mass-produced artefacts, in the celebrity status of artists such as Damien Hirst and Jeff Koons, and in how Bob Dylan songs are used to advertise banks and women's underwear.

The second aspect of postmodernism is a cynicism, what Lyotard calls an 'incredulity towards meta-narratives'.[13] Meta- (or 'grand') narrative means a belief system that presents history as following some kind of overarching logic, such as the idea of scientific progress. Marxism is often considered a meta-narrative, as are most religions. According to Lyotard and other postmodernists, people have lost faith in meta-narratives: they don't believe that 'science' or 'technology' will lead us to a better world; they don't trust politicians, or religious leaders, or other kinds of authority figure. People in a postmodern world do not seek to rely on expert knowledge and are instead more interested in experiencing the present rather than worrying about the future.

This growing scepticism towards grand narratives offers a partial explanation for the problems affecting Dylan's star-image in the early eighties. In turning to evangelical religion

– the grandest of grand narratives – at a time when his audience was becoming more self-centred and less socially conscious meant that Dylan was clearly swimming against the tide, as he himself became an authority figure. This is particularly acute given the emphasis on rebelliousness within rock culture and the manner in which Dylan's conversion contradicted his own star-image as an anti-leader. As Dylan pulled back from his explicitly Christian world view, however, wider social processes were undermining rock's claim to be *the* master narrative of popular music. The disintegration of rock's modernist ideals meant that many stars associated with rock lost the justification for their stardom (many sixties stars, such as The Rolling Stones, Paul McCartney, The Who and The Kinks were similarly afflicted during this time). Whatever he may have felt about it, Dylan was seen as responsible for popularising many of the key components of the rock ideology, particularly those aspects such as authenticity and social conscience that were most losing their public appeal.* He was an important symbol of 'rock' at a time when 'it was no longer taken for granted that "rock" represented the most powerful expression of the critique of mass society'.[14] Commenting on Dylan's UK appearances in 1981, *NME* journalist Neil Spencer wrote: 'The expected media fanfare came, but it was muted in comparison to that afforded the '78 trip. . . . [Dylan is now] set at the heart of a rock tradition whose myths are, for a growing number of

---

* One possible way of explaining this is to utilise Stephen Scobie's position that Dylan's persona is a mixture of prophet and trickster (see Scobie, 2003:26–35). Dylan's trickster persona would have been more in keeping with postmodern culture's emphasis on style and surface and if this had been to the fore perhaps he would have been better received at this time (comparable perhaps to how Bowie maintained popularity during the first part of the eighties by adapting different styles). However, around 1980 Dylan was undergoing the most prophetic part of his whole career, which meant he was in conflict with the era's dominant ideas.

young Europeans, now despoiled, overtaken by everyday reality or the new myths of punk and post-punk.'

During the first part of the 1980s, therefore, Dylan's authority as a songwriter and performer – his stardom – was undermined by the social processes that undermined rock's authority. Dylan's work at this time, and its reception, illustrates this. The 1983 album *Infidels* seems to illustrate Dylan struggling to define a new role for himself (such as the decision to include two mediocre protest songs, 'Union Sundown' and 'Neighbourhood Bully'). Significantly, for more interested fans, the story of the album's preparation quickly became part of Dylan's star-image. The production process for *Infidels* was troubled. Dylan's relationship to recording has always been troublesome and his approach has always been to 'cut it live', meaning that the band is recorded together playing the song in the same room. This approach had failed badly with *Saved*, however; even though he took his touring band into the studio with him, the recorded versions were pale imitations of the performances that occurred on stage. For his albums at the beginning of the eighties, Dylan decided to spend more time in the studio working at getting songs to sound right. In one sense this worked – *Infidels* is one of Dylan's best sounding albums. In another sense, however, it went terribly wrong, for it gave Dylan too much time to second-guess himself. The result was that he dropped many of the best songs from the final version of the album and substituted later, poorer, performances of some of the others. Recordings from these sessions soon surfaced among collectors and the whole episode seemed to demonstrate a lack of artistic self-confidence from Dylan at this time.

The forces of stardom are not something that just happen to Dylan, however. He is not a powerless victim battered by the seas of social forces but an active agent able to reflexively engage with his circumstances. One key way he is able to do this is, of course, through songs and there is one song from this period that not only has as its theme the problems of Dylan's contemporary star-meaning but, also, through its own 'biography', illustrates those very problems. It is one of the songs left off *Infidels* – 'Blind Willie McTell'. Dylan begins it by portraying a world reaching its end:

> Seen the arrow on the doorpost
> Saying this land is condemned
> All the way from New Orleans
> To Jerusalem

The song builds a portrait of this modern wasteland, dredging up ghosts of misery and slavery, building to its final statement on the world:

> Well, God is in His Heaven
> And we all want what's his
> But power and greed and corruptible seed
> Seem to be all that there is.

Such an outlook is not particularly unusual within a Dylan song. He has had a vivid sense of living in the End Times throughout his career (in, for example, 'A Hard Rain's A-Gonna Fall') and it is prevalent in Dylan's evangelical and post-evangelical work (again emphasising that the 'prophet' aspect of Dylan's character was to the fore at this time). While the recording of the song offers a masterful evocation of such doom, however, it is not actually the subject matter of the song. As John Bauldie highlights, the question it raises is how can this doom, this desolation, be adequately lamented? For, after each of the song's five verses, the singer, Dylan, states:

And I know no-one can sing the blues like Blind Willie McTell.

As Bauldie writes, 'Dylan conjures the ghost of a long-dead blues singer who might have offered appropriate lamentation were he not dead and gone'.[15] However, the song is not merely about the fact that there is no one who can offer an adequate expression of grief, it is an acknowledgement that this particular singer – Bob Dylan – *knows* there is no one. This is a song in which Dylan reflects upon his status as an artist because the singer knows that whatever he can offer will be inadequate: 'the singer of this song cannot find the words, or the voice, to adequately express what he sees as he gazes'.[16] I don't think that Blind Willie McTell is individually significant here – he chose McTell for its rhyming possibilities rather than to single out that performer specifically (clearly he's not completely irrelevant, but he signifies a particular type of singer rather than an individual; Dylan could just as happily have chosen Leadbelly, or Robert Johnson, or Charley Patton). What is significant is not what the song says about McTell, but what it says about Bob Dylan: it seeks to question the role this singer should play in the modern world.

In delivering this song, both the acoustic version eventually released on *The Bootleg Series Volumes 1–3*, and the electric version currently available only on a proper bootleg, Dylan offers a virtuoso performance. In a last minute decision, however, the song was pulled from the album. The song has taken on legendary status among Dylan fans as an example of what Dylan might have become, how he might have regained his critical and commercial standing in the early 1980s, if only he had released the original *Infidels*.* I'm

* There's another interesting aspect to this: it seems that just about everyone knew about 'Blind Willie McTell', even before its release in 1991. Loads of music journalists suggested it as Dylan's best track of the decade,

not entirely sure that this line of thinking is fruitful, however, given that, to a great extent, *Infidels* turned out the way it did *because* of Dylan's position at the time, because his star-image was so out of step with the times. Short of completely reinventing himself (never really possible for a major star), whatever he had produced in the early eighties would have been treated with suspicion, even if all the great songs left off *Shot Of Love* and *Infidels* had been included. For 'Blind Willie McTell' to have any meaning (both as a song and as a reflection of Dylan's stardom at this time), it *had* to remain unreleased. There is already an irony in the song because, in bewailing the fact that he cannot adequately express the state of the world, Dylan produces a performance that bears comparison to anything produced by the great blues singers. The song is not ironic, however, and Dylan manages to sidestep this irony through his decision to not release the recording. To have released it would have undermined the sincerity of the song and made it necessarily inauthentic. When, in 1997, Dylan (surprisingly) began to play the song in concert, he chose to utilise an arrangement of the song developed by The Band. In this version, the chorus line is changed to:

> I can tell you one thing
> Nobody can sing
> The blues like Blind Willie McTell.

---

and I'm guessing that some of them hadn't even heard it. There's a bit of journalistic pretentiousness in this, but I would also suggest that it was a reflection on Dylan's status as an emblem of rock – those critics with an investment in the rock ideology could use it as proof that the rock dream was still alive but it couldn't be heard. This also goes back to earlier discussions about Dylan's reputation being respected in the abstract as part of his post-1960s stardom. The existence of 'Blind Willie McTell' offered proof that Dylan really is that good but no, actually, you can't hear it, just believe us. The vitality of Dylan, and therefore rock, was a matter of faith.

This changes the entire character of the song. Now, the singer is confident of his abilities ('I can . . . '), the phonetic double negative of the original ('know no', wailed as if crying 'Noooooo! Noooooo!) has been lost, and the extra rhyme (thing/sing) adds a swagger to its delivery. This is a man on top of his game and comfortable with his place within this tradition. The song as originally written and recorded, however, deals with uncertainty in the face of tradition. If the bedrock of Dylan's star meaning was disrupted in the early eighties through postmodernism and the 'death of rock', then 'Blind Willie McTell', to me, represents the first stage of Dylan finding a way to marry his contemporary celebrity with his traditionality, a process which only comes to fruition in the late nineties. Before he achieved this, however, the cultural industries began to shape Dylan's star-image in particular ways that cashed in on the significance of his history.

INDUSTRY RESTRUCTURING AND THE 'LIVING LEGEND'

The period that I have characterised as dominated by an ambiguity in Dylan's star-image coincided with a sustained downturn in the recording industry. The period from 1979–82 witnessed a decline in record sales for the first time since the 1930s. This decline can be partly explained by the changing demographics of the music audience as well as the growth of alternative leisure consumer goods. For our present discussion, the reasons for the decline are less significant than the effects it had on the industry. After a decade of remarkable growth, the labels may have assumed that their business model could continue successfully into the foreseeable future but the downturn resulted in some serious belt-tightening and rosters of recording artists were trimmed. This almost certainly would have impacted upon

CBS's relationship with Dylan. While it seems unlikely that CBS would have considered dropping Dylan, the new climate meant that there was less money available to pander to superstars' crazy ideas like preaching the word of God. In that sense, *Saved* represented a grave blow to Dylan's relationship with his record label.[17] More significant in the long term, however, were the structural reorganisations made by the industry and the changing nature of celebrity and stardom during the 1980s. These changes altered the nature of popular music stardom, transforming it into something we would today more readily recognise as celebrity.*

The recording industry fundamentally changed its overarching strategy during the 1980s. Before this time, a record label's general approach was to nurture a stable of artists, spend moderately on each one and look for a modest return on each investment. It was thus possible to talk of an 'average sales-run' for albums. Dylan's sales would fit into this approach – he has never been a major seller, but his albums sell consistently. The success of Michael Jackson's *Thriller*, however, which sold 47 million copies worldwide, resulted in a shift in record industry strategy. This new approach concentrated on the blockbuster album. Labels realised that they made more money selling 5 million copies of one album than selling half a million copies of ten albums: label staff were thus told to treat every album they worked on as a potential 10 million seller. This significantly increased the importance of celebrity status for pop musicians, because labels began to rely on star names to guarantee major returns, resulting in a number of multi-million dollar contracts (which actually functioned as a form of pre-sales

---

* These changes also contribute to the declining authority of rock and are both a cause and a consequence of broader postmodern trends already discussed. For an interesting account of how all these issues link together, see Frith, 1988.

promotion: talking up the size of the contract in the press created an interest in the star's releases). The celebrity status of the performer also became significant because of its potential to break into new markets – both new territories that were opening up in an increasingly globalised world, and markets for new products and entertainment industries as the record labels became swallowed up by multi-media conglomerates.[18] Popular music stardom, like all celebrity, was a significant feature of media 'synergy' – using one form of media to help sell others (for, example, films using a distinctive signature song became much more common around this time). Again, this trend can be related to the broader cultural currents of postmodernism.

These trends are most clear in the emergence of a television channel dedicated to popular music. MTV materialised as a result of the deregulation of television, which gave rise to multichannel cable TV and multinational channels, as well as the growth of the VCR which made young people more likely to watch TV.[19] Friedlander argues that MTV initially had a democratic effect on the music industry as it introduced less mainstream artists to audiences,[20] but this is difficult to see as by prioritising the expensive video clip as a form of promotion, it gave a further advantage to the major record labels.[21] Certainly by the mid-eighties, MTV was merely replicating existing biases within the industry. MTV has often been criticised for focusing on surface over substance, appearance over artistry (again, another postmodern trait). For example, Jon Pareles wrote: 'in a visual culture like ours, MTV has amplified the importance of image over sound, which has repercussions in everything from stage shows to who gets a chance to record . . . MTV favors pretty people . . . ageing performers, or those whose only talents are musical rather than visual, tend to hide in their own video clips.'[22] There is a danger of romanticising the past in such claims, but it is certainly the case that MTV was another example of the changing nature of popular music stardom in a multi-media world. It was not possible to be just a singer. MTV made an obvious contribution to the changing nature of pop stardom. Although pop videos are often dismissed merely as TV advertisements for a particular record, they are significantly more than that because they help construct a star-image. Pop videos are assumed to be authored in a way that advertisements are not and, though we may acknowledge that many factors are at work in pop videos, we still see the presentation of the star in the video as in some way linked to the 'truth' of the star's personality.[23] As pop videos became more ubiquitous they became an increasingly important vehicle for interpreting what a particular star represented. They provided another example of how Dylan was a man out of time during this period. Almost without exception, his performances in promotional videos show him uncomfortable and shifty. If pop videos are understood to offer a self-portrait of the singer, then Dylan's showed a singer so out of synch that he couldn't even mime his own words.

Two of the strategies deployed by the recording industry in response to its crisis at the start of the eighties, therefore, did not serve Dylan's stardom well. The industry came to depend on blockbuster sales but, even at the height of his stardom, Dylan has never been a major seller. Despite having released over fifty albums, Dylan ranks only forty-third in terms of US sales, with 36 million sales, some way behind The Beatles' 169 million, and also behind artists such as Bob Seeger, Kenny G. and Backstreet Boys.[24] Secondly, the industry came to depend on new types of crossover celebrity, synergistic stardom to conform to the new multi-media landscape. Always uncomfortable in front of cameras, Dylan cut an outmoded figure who did not belong in the new world of surface and style.

One further industry strategy had a significant impact on Dylan's stardom. As a way of compensating for declining sales of current releases, labels came increasingly to rely on their back catalogues as a way of maintaining profitability. Catalogue sales could always be guaranteed from a new generation of record buyers emerging that would want to own 'the classics', but they were given a major boost with the advent of the compact disc which persuaded many people who already owned vinyl versions of the classics to buy them again. The emphasis on catalogue sales created a new structural environment for what 'Bob Dylan' would mean in the mid-eighties. Following this period of ambiguity, record label strategies during the middle of the decade came to structure the meaning of 'Bob Dylan' in a very specific way, one that centred upon his 'Living Legend' status as a means of generating profits. The clearest example of this was the release of *Biograph* in 1985. *Biograph* was a landmark release - the first box-set offering a retrospective of an artist's entire career; fifty-three tracks, including a number that had never before been officially released. The set was a luxury, and therefore expensive, item but sold well and it demonstrated the full potential of the new CD medium to the recording industry. It also conferred a gravitas on Dylan's past (this was before the box-set retrospective was an honour bestowed upon anyone who has walked into a recording studio). As Roy Kelly stated at the time, 'here is an artist of weight, density and history. Here is a man who can fill a box with albums, like Wagner or Mozart or any of those old Europeans.'[25]

The problem is that Dylan had already stated (in the liner notes to *Bringing It All Back Home*) that he didn't want to be Mozart because, like Tolstoy, Joe Hill and James Dean, he was dead. Such a comment illustrates why Dylan would prove ambivalent to the way his stardom developed during the mid-eighties. He has always been wary of the effect that nostalgia plays in idealising the past and paralysing the present, regularly criticising the media's representation of 'the sixties'. During this period he found the same processes happening to him. There was a kind of 'commercial canonisation' of Dylan's work that sought to freeze him as a nostalgia act. During the mid-eighties, Dylan's stardom signified his past, and his present function was to be a living representation of 'the sixties':

> I'm not really a nostalgia freak. Every time you see my name, it's 'the sixties this, the sixties that'. It's just another way of categorizing me. (David Fricke interview, 1985)

Dylan had been victim to canonisation before, of course, as discussed in the previous chapter, but it happened in a particular way during the eighties, as media industries became more adept at opening up new revenue streams that depended upon ransacking the past.*

A clear example of this kind of nostalgia, and Dylan's ambivalence towards it, can be seen in 1984, when Dylan participated in a short European tour. The whole enterprise was dominated by the past. The tour was co-headlined by Santana, a performer hardly at the cutting edge, while promoter Bill Graham even added Joan Baez to the bill in a bid to raise profile and boost sluggish ticket sales. This was a step too far even for Dylan, though, who steadfastly ignored Baez and she quickly left the tour. Dylan was clearly disengaged from the project. Despite spending some of 1983

---

* I'm not suggesting that record labels didn't cash in on Dylan's work before – they clearly did (releasing *Bob Dylan's Greatest Hits* in 1967 while Dylan was out of the public eye, for example). Structural changes in the industry mean that it does begin to happen in a more intensive way during the eighties, however.

jamming with a number of young post-punk musicians (culminating in a successful performance on the *David Letterman Show*) Dylan chose as his band a collection of middle-aged musicians whose best years were behind them. He also left bandleader duties almost entirely to guitarist Mick Taylor, suggesting an 'unprecedented detachment from the whole enterprise'.[26] The nostalgia can be seen in the setlist: only three songs were rehearsed from his three 'religious albums', and only three songs in total from *Planet Waves*, *Desire* and *Street Legal*. By the end of the tour, and in a lengthy setlist, Dylan was playing only four or five songs written since 1974.

The 1984 tour demonstrates what Dylan was in danger of becoming - the rock superstar retreading former glories in front of large audiences. For a period of two or three years, Dylan's response to such developments was disengagement. It seems to me that Dylan refused to invest much of his self into his current work. The end result is a period where Dylan's output is lacklustre. Although Dylan's mid-eighties work is often dismissed as poor by critics, it is actually better described as adequate – not terrible, but not hitting many heights either. The 1984 and 1986 tours, the *Infidels* and *Empire Burlesque* albums all show a level of professional competence that is, frankly, 'alright'.* Most of his public

---

* The significant exception to this rule came when Dylan performed to the largest audience of his career. At 'Live Aid' we see a performer dominated by his past, but not in control of it. Because of his status, Dylan had been asked to close the whole event. Looking overweight and distracted, Dylan set about murdering three of his most famous protest songs – 'Ballad Of Hollis Brown', 'When The Ship Comes In' and 'Blowin' In The Wind'. There are mitigating circumstances to explain Dylan's performance that night (his monitors were turned off, and thus Dylan couldn't hear himself over the thirty-odd celebrities rehearsing their lines for the ensemble finale). Dylan actually achieved something simply by getting through the songs. What appeared on a billion people's TV screens, however, was a performer who could no longer reproduce past glories. This performance had a major impact on Dylan's eighties reputation.

appearances were professional and Dylan had a comfortable media profile from 1984–6 – he was portrayed with dignity, as a member of the old guard. Lip-service was paid to his current 'vitality' but he was predominantly portrayed in relation to his symbolic past. The release of *Biograph* enabled a reaffirmation of the greatness of his past and prompted a series of retrospective appraisals in various media. Dylan suddenly found himself in the centre of the media spotlight: a strong live performance on the nationally broadcast Farm Aid charity show; a 15-minute profile on the national TV show *20/20*; the cover of *Spin* magazine and interviews in *Rolling Stone*, *Time* and the *Los Angeles Times*. Heylin suggests that Dylan 'found himself for the first time adopting an elder statesman of rock persona he felt comfortable with'.[27] To my mind, however, his public performances at this time tell a different story, displaying a disengagement with the present. For example, in his 1985 interview with Robert Hilburn for the *Los Angeles Times*, Dylan offered the following discussion of his new album, *Empire Burlesque*:

> I [don't] want to sit around and talk about the record. I haven't even listened to it since it came out. I'd rather spend my time . . . listen[ing] to other people's records. Have you heard the new Hank Williams album, the collection of old demo tapes? It's great.

And of *Biograph*:

> Columbia wanted to put out a retrospective album on me . . . I didn't care one way or another . . . I guess it's OK for someone who has never heard of me.

This process of disengagement, coasting through interviews on cruise-control illustrates a discomfort as the weight of his own history becomes increasingly oppressive. One of the key themes throughout Dylan's work has been the lifelessness of 'official culture', by which I mean the manner in which canonisation, academic study, evaluation, classification and so on drain the vitality out of cultural items. Any cultural work is a form of communication and, as such, is inherently social. This is a key element of Dylan's work and is why he sees his place of work as the concert hall rather than the recording studio. The process of canonisation, however, generates the notion that a work is so good that it stands above time, for all ages. This removes the work from its social context and means that a work of art is praised not for what it says but merely for what it is – a special object. The specialness of the object – its 'aura' – becomes so overpowering that we cannot see what the work was trying to say.[28] Dylan has always been deeply antithetical to such processes:

> Great paintings shouldn't be in museums. Have you ever been in a museum? Museums are cemeteries. Paintings should be on the walls of restaurants, in dime stores, in gas stations, in men's rooms. Great paintings should be where people hang out . . . You can't see great paintings. You pay half a million and hang one in your house and one guest sees it. That's not art. That's a shame, a crime . . . All this art they've been talking about is nonexistent. It just remains on the shelf. It doesn't make anyone happier. Just think how many people would really feel great if they could see a Picasso in their daily diner. It's not the bomb that has to go, man, it's the museums. (Ephron and Edmiston interview, 1965)

It is an issue he has considered in song. In 'Visions Of Johanna', he sings:

Inside the museums, infinity goes up on trial
Voices echo this is what salvation must be like after a
   while
But Mona Lisa musta had the highway blues
You can tell by the way she smiles

In this verse, Dylan criticises the process of removing 'culture' from everyday experience. By placing cultural artefacts in a shrine – in museums, on university curricula – we rob them of their vitality, of their social nature. Mona Lisa once meant something but now she is condemned to sit behind bullet-proof glass until the end of time. Stuck inside, immobile.

Dylan has thus always been suspicious of the way that culture becomes sanctified through the way we classify and categorise. In the mid-eighties, however, he found this process happening to him: in a commercial way, maybe, but the same process of stasis nonetheless. His past became filed away – an easily digestible piece of social history, another way of making the sixties safe by mythologising them within the current ideological environment. It is unsurprising, therefore, that Dylan's behaviour at the time indicates an ambivalence towards the process even as he contributed to it. Firstly, in the closing song of *Infidels*, 'Don't Fall Apart On Me Tonight', Dylan revisits the theme of 'Visions Of Johanna' but this time makes it directly applicable to the singer:

But it's like I'm stuck inside a painting
That's hanging in the Louvre.
My throat starts to tickle and my nose itches
But I know that I can't move.

The ambivalence to his past living on permeates a variety of Dylan's projects at the time. There was the publication of

Lyrics 1962–1985, a book that collated the lyrics of all his albums, together with liner notes, prose poems and various other songs. The book constituted a major retrospective but was done in a slipshod manner that raises questions regarding Dylan's intent. The book contains a large number of revisions and inaccuracies that undermine its claim to be a definitive summation while there are a number of significant omissions, including all of the songs left off his two most recent studio albums.[29] The collection seems to portray 'Dylan thumbing his nose at or trying to erase . . . his art even as he anthologizes it'.[30] During this period, Dylan completed a number of works that specifically addressed the issue of stardom. He starred in the forgettable film, *Hearts of Fire*, playing an old rock star coaxed out of retirement, and he collaborated with Sam Shepard on the 'one act play' *True Dylan* that ruminates on the media's interest in celebrities.

Shepard also co-wrote 'Brownsville Girl' the most significant statement made by Dylan on the ambivalence of his stardom. The song, an 11-minute epic, was released on the 1986 album *Knocked Out Loaded*. Aidan Day, in his analysis of Dylan's lyrics, argues that the song concerns the ontological status of memorial fragments, 'a collapsing of distinction between actual or real and artificial or fictional' that 'plays with tenses and perspectives as it enacts the lack of chronological structure in the inner life of the mind'.[31] Such a summary illustrates the problems of applying an analysis that prioritises the literary aspect of Dylan's work (the subtitle of Day's book is 'reading the lyrics of Bob Dylan') and returns us to the argument I made in chapter 2 regarding the role that stardom has in creating song meaning. We *hear* Bob Dylan singing these words and, while it may be possible for a singer to adopt a narrator persona, the nature of music stardom means that there is always a layer of meaning in the voice itself that relates what is sung to the life of its singer.

Accounts which concentrate on the biographical detail of the author may be reductive, but to restrict our understanding to a textual 'reading' misinterprets how song itself creates meaning. There is no way that this song cannot not in some way be about Bob Dylan. Indeed, Dylan invites such ideas by failing to distinguish between actor Gregory Peck and the film character he plays – in the last verse of 'Brownsville Girl' it is the actor, and not the character, who is shot in the back.

The song begins with the narrator recalling 'a movie I seen one time'. The title is not mentioned, but it is *The Gunfighter*, a 1950 film starring Gregory Peck. In the movie, Peck plays Jimmy Ringo, a notorious sharpshooter who is haunted by his fame because every town contains a kid wanting to become famous as the man who shot Jimmy Ringo. Ringo was eventually 'shot down by a hungry kid trying to make a name for himself'. The key theme of the song – the tribulations of fame – is thus present in the film that is the subject of the song. Following a summary of the movie in the first two verses, the narrator begins to address an undefined 'you' and recounts a series of memories, though they lack a sense of progression or linear narrative. However, the narrator's flashbacks and his recollections of the movie become increasingly intertwined. In the tenth verse, he says

> Something about that movie though, well I just can't
>   get it out of my head
> But I can't remember why I was in it or what part I
>   was supposed to play.

The singer finds it increasingly difficult to separate the notoriety of Jimmy Ringo and his own experiences. There follows more flashbacks – the singer is caught in the crossfire, doesn't 'know whether to duck or to run' and is 'cornered in the churchyard', before being on trial (Dylan describes himself portrayed in the press as 'a man with no alibi'). In highlighting the trials of fame, Dylan draws attention to his own situation as a star, most notably in two separate lines that drip with irony about his predicament – 'oh, if there's an original thought out there, I could use it right now', and 'I don't have any regrets, they can talk about me plenty when I'm gone' (to which the backing singers add a sarcastic 'oh yeah?'). Hearing *this* star sing such lines – metaphorical or not – and at *this* time, clearly adds a layer of meaning to the song.

Towards the end of the song, we return to the present tense, presumably where the song started:

> Well, I'm standin' in line in the rain to see a movie
>   starring Gregory Peck
> Yeah, but you know it's not the one that I had in mind
> He's got a new one out now, I don't even know what
>   it's about
> But I'll see him in anything so I'll stand in line.

Michael Gray has pointed out the irony that, in offering a song about being a star, Dylan adopts the position of a fan.[32] These lines – 'I'll see him in anything' – surely reflect Dylan's ambivalence towards his own audience at this time, demonstrating a concern that his own audience would turn up no matter what he did. Writing of the 1984 tour, John Lindley suggests that the overwhelming reliance upon sixties material was an understandable response by Dylan given that, in 1981, impassioned performances of 'Slow Train' and 'When You Gonna Wake Up?' received lukewarm responses from the crowd while mundane run-throughs of 'Maggie's Farm' and 'Like A Rolling Stone' were rapturously received.[33]

Lindley is correct to highlight that the most important thing to consider is the relationship between Dylan and his audience. To explain it, we need to consider the wider cultural developments discussed in this chapter, how they enabled and disabled Dylan's stardom in particular ways. During this period Dylan stood for the past, and was part of the emergence of a particular kind of 'living legend' celebrity that linked well with the reliance on back catalogue and cross media promotion in the 1980s music industry. Dylan proved extremely ambivalent, not to say uncomfortable, in this kind of stardom and some of his work can be seen as offering a commentary on the situation. The role of living legend accepts that you're not actually dead yet, but reduces the star merely to repeating the glories of the past. Dylan's 1986 tour, with Tom Petty and the Heartbreakers as his backing band, demonstrates this well: the arena shows were generally well-received by the wider audience but they merely stood for another run-of-the-mill rock show, a rerun of the ideology that elsewhere was being shown up as an empty promise.

Dylan's experience was not unique in this regard: if I am discussing wider understandings of stardom then it would seem odd if I were to claim them as affecting him alone. But they did affect him in a particularly pronounced way because of his existing star-meaning. His association with the earnest, politically committed element of rock did not sit well in the Thatcherite-Reaganite world where 'there was no such thing as society'. The hedonism and excess of previous rock eras fitted well with the new consumerism as new cultural spaces (mainly suburban arenas) emerged for large-scale tours, such as those by Paul McCartney and The Rolling Stones, that offered an opportunity for extravagant consumption in which middle-aged suburbanites could relive the hedonism of the sixties and younger listeners could create their own version of a mythic past. For Dylan, whose image was more associated with the social conscience of the sixties rather than its mythical consumption, the terrain was more awkward. At the same time, other processes of canonisation were in play that had the effect of freezing those past glories; worshipping them but also reducing their potency by stripping them of their lived vitality and elevating them to the status of sacred commodities.

Dylan would later discuss the problems he felt during this particular period:

> I was going on my name for a long time, name and reputation, which was about all I had. I had sort of fallen into an amnesia spell . . . I didn't feel I knew who I was on stage. (Robert Hilburn interview, 1997)

The question remained whether Dylan could find a way of working that incorporated his past without being overwhelmed by it:

> It was important for me to come to the bottom of this legend thing, which has no reality at all. What's important isn't the legend, but the art, the work. . . . If you try to act a legend, it's nothing but hype. (Robert Hilburn interview, 1992)

To get to the bottom of the legend thing, he developed a conscious strategy: the Never Ending Tour.

Snapshot: The wandering minstrel

Dylan played six concerts co-headlining with The Grateful Dead in the summer of 1987. Though these shows were criticised by both Dylan and Dead fans, they had an immeasurable impact on Dylan's career as they were the impetus for the 'Never Ending Tour' (NET), which began in 1988. Before that, however, Dylan released the poor *Down In The Groove* album. It is now possible to interpret the album as an early step to getting back in touch with the music that influenced him, but at the time it was viewed as his weakest ever release. Dylan toured Europe in autumn 1987, again with The Heartbreakers as his backing band, though the manner of the shows was much changed from 1986. The tour was extremely creative, with a wide range of songs played in new arrangements, but it was heavily criticised.

Dylan started the NET in June 1988 and his media presence was high for the next couple of years. *Oh Mercy*, released in 1989, was considered a great return to form. At the same time, *The Travelling Wilburys Volume 1*, a collaboration of unassuming superstars (Dylan, George Harrison, Jeff Lynne, Tom Petty and Roy Orbison), was one of the year's surprise hits. 1990 saw the release of the critically-dismissed *Under The Red Sky* and the Wilburys' less-impressive follow-up, *Volume 3*. Dylan periodically appeared in the spotlight in the early nineties: a Grammy lifetime achievement award in 1991 was followed in 1992 by an all-star extravaganza in which an impressive list of celebrities queued up to pay homage to Dylan.

During the early nineties, Dylan's already tarnished reputation weakened further and, nostalgia-fests aside, his career became less interesting to the media. Following the disappointment of *Under The Red Sky*, his album releases were considered less important and his songwriting talents viewed as defunct. Dylan did not release an album of self-penned material between 1990 and 1997. His next two releases – *Good As I Been To You* in 1992 and *World Gone Wrong* in 1993 – featured acoustic versions of traditional songs, and no Dylan originals. Almost out of sight, the NET continued unabated.

Albums and major events

July 1987	Shows with The Grateful Dead (documented on *Dylan And The Dead*)
Sept–Oct 1987	European tour
October 1987	*Hearts Of Fire* (movie)
January 1988	Inducted into Rock and Roll Hall Of Fame
May 1988	*Down In The Groove*
June 1988	Start of the Never Ending Tour
October 1988	*The Travelling Wilburys Volume One*
September 1989	*Oh Mercy*
September 1990	*Under The Red Sky*
October 1990	*The Travelling Wilburys Volume Three*
February 1991	Receives a Grammy Lifetime Achievement Award
October 1992	All-star gala event – 'Columbia Music Celebrates the Music of Bob Dylan' – held in New York
November 1992	*Good As I Been To You*
October 1993	*World Gone Wrong*
August 1994	Appearance at Woodstock 2
November 1994	Records two shows for MTV's *Unplugged* series

REDEFINING STARDOM:

THE NEVER ENDING TOUR

By the late 1980s, Dylan's stardom had become frozen by sixties nostalgia. This period is generally considered to be Dylan's lowest professional ebb. Dylan himself has subsequently presented it this way, describing his inability to connect with his work at this time:

> I'd kind of reached the end of the line. Whatever I'd started out to do, it wasn't that. I was going to pack it in. You know, like how do I sing this? It just sounds funny. I can't remember what it means, does it mean – is it just a bunch of words? Maybe it's like what all these people say, just a bunch of surrealistic nonsense. (David Gates interview, 1997)

He made a similar statement about his intention to quit in 1965 when he was equally struggling with limitations placed upon him by his star-image (which can be clearly seen in the film *Don't Look Back*). He reversed that decision upon writing

'Like A Rolling Stone'. Dylan attempted to resolve similar problems in the mid–late eighties by initiating the 'Never Ending Tour' (NET). Paul Williams argues that just as 'Like A Rolling Stone' showed Dylan a new way to write, the NET provided Dylan with a new way to perform.[1] This is partially true, but what is actually occurring in both 1965 and 1987 is a wilful attempt to redefine his stardom to open up new possibilities for music making.

Throughout much of this book, I have emphasised how wider social factors constrain a particular star-image and limit the power of the star to shape the public meaning of their stardom. In chapter 5, I discussed how Dylan's attempts to subvert his star-meaning achieved only limited success because of factors beyond his control. It is important, however, not to over-sociologise; the star still has *some* power to shape their public meaning although it is less than conventionally presented. While I would argue that ultimately it is the audience that has the power to accept or reject a star's image, what stars themselves actually do is important for reinforcing or contradicting audience beliefs, for chipping away at the boundaries of their meaning. Certain actions or strategies can have a big impact, positive and negative, in how the audience understands the star.

The directions taken by Dylan in 1965 and 1988 were not obvious, though we may see them that way with hindsight. Neither were they smooth. The change in direction taken by Dylan in 1965 created a tension between the star and his audience, as witnessed at Newport '65 and the 1966 world tour. There is a similar tension between star and public during the first half of the NET, during which Dylan is critically dismissed and often ridiculed by both press and fans. However, whereas the earlier conflict has become a defining part of Dylan's stardom, indicating an artist unwilling to bow to audience pressure, the latter challenge by Dylan to his audience has received inadequate analysis. Indeed, it often seems that people assume he continues the NET – a project which has taken up four-tenths of his working life – because he can't think of anything better to do. My argument is that the NET was a deliberate strategy adopted by Dylan in an attempt to transform his relationship with his audience. He has never explicitly said this (indeed, as I will discuss shortly, he rejects the label 'the NET') but, in interviews during the 1990s, he has mentioned specific elements of what I am discussing. Furthermore, I would argue that he has been pretty successful in achieving what he set out to do, and we need to recognise Dylan's achievement in finding some way out of the problems he faced in the 1980s. Few, if any, of his contemporaries did so, instead either retiring or learning to live with their new star-meaning. That we take his solution to the problem so matter of factly today indicates just how successful Dylan has been in reorienting his star-image. Finally, I would argue that the success of the NET in redefining Dylan's star-image is a key reason for the critical and commercial success that he has achieved since 1997. I will discuss this in the next chapter. In this one, I want to take a more serious look at the NET and discuss some of the issues it raises.

But, first, that tricky issue of definition. Dylan branded his new tour the 'Never Ending Tour' in a throw-away line during a 1989 interview, and it stuck (in part because it was used on the cover of the magazine). He has subsequently, and repeatedly, disavowed the title including an 'official statement' in the liner notes to *World Gone Wrong*: 'don't be bewildered by the Never Ending Tour chatter. there was a Never Ending Tour but it ended in '91 with the departure of guitarist G. E. Smith. That one's long gone but there have been many others since then . . . each with their own character and design.' This has led some to argue that it is inappropriate to use the term analytically (Smith, for example, rather fruitlessly refers to the 'Never Ending Series of Tours' (NEST)).[2] However, it is worth referring back to the discussion of 'Masters Of War' on page 121 explaining how the meaning of Dylan's stardom is not controlled by Dylan. The NET has become the key way in which Dylan's later career is understood. It is a label used by fans and media alike. As with the 'Masters Of War' example, what Dylan thinks about the label doesn't matter. I shall, therefore, be calling it the NET. Dylan is right, however, that we should not let the singular label lead us to believe that all the different legs of the NET sound the same, because they don't. The shows in 2006 sounded much different than those in late 2005, for example. There are, however, particular structural features of the whole enterprise that justify using an overarching name, as it is these structural elements that define what the NET is. These are the subject of this chapter but the different 'eras' of the NET do indeed have 'their own character and design'.

'RECORDING CONSCIOUSNESS' AND LIVE PERFORMANCE

To begin this overview of the NET, it is necessary to discuss the role that records and concerts play in the consumption of popular music. When people attend a concert they are not merely going to hear the music. Rather, they are going to engage in a shared experience in which they unite with others to celebrate the important role that this music, indeed music generally, plays in their lives. The music does not necessarily mean the same thing to every person there, but it means *something* to them all and it is this fact that they celebrate together. The music will have private meaning for people attending the show; this is the music they listened to at university, fell in love to, shared with friends and so on. It will also have a shared generational meaning – this is the music we listened to when we were growing up. And, in some cases, the music (and, indeed, the star) represents some wider social phenomenon, such as 'the sixties'. In all of these circumstances, what matters is not any inherent aesthetic quality the music holds but, rather, the social meaning that the music has – the meaning of the music is socially, rather than musically, prescribed (I will say more on this later).

The social embeddedness of musical meaning in the concert ritual brings with it a set of expectations and preconceptions relating to the particular star and their work. If people attending concerts are engaged in a shared celebration of their experience of music then the performed music needs to provide an adequate reference point. This means two things. Firstly, there is an expectation that the artist will play familiar songs – people want the hits they heard on the radio or at college parties; they generally do not want to hear obscure songs or new material not yet released as these provide no frame of reference for sharing their experience of music with others in the audience. Secondly, they want to hear these songs as they remember them, not in an unrecognisable form. Here the role of the record is paramount.

As explained in chapter 2, 'the work' in popular music is not the written score but its recorded performance. And while the notion of a 'record' may perhaps have been accepted literally in the 1930s and 1940s – records were an imitation of live performances – by the onset of rock and roll, records were not an imitation of anything but were, rather, the musical event itself.[3] The recorded song has come to dominate the idea of 'music' since midway through the twentieth century, so much so that there exists what Bennett calls a 'recording consciousness' that 'defines the social reality of popular music'.[4] It is the record that defines the popular song and, therefore, it is records that are most significant in defining a star's image and career. The dominance of the record affects live performance. Our appreciation of live music is coloured by our experience of recordings. According to Middleton 'live performances have to try to approximate the sounds which inhabit [the recording] consciousness. Even when they fail, or it is impracticable, an audience's collective memory takes over and it "hears" what it cannot hear, in the "sketch" provided by the band.'[5] Live performances are generally heard as crude interpretations of the recorded experience, as variations from the record.[6] This, I think, has always created a problem for Dylan's career; I'm reasonably sure that he has always viewed himself as a 'live performer' rather than a 'recording artist':

> For me, all my albums are just measuring points for wherever I was at a certain period of time. I went into the studio, recorded the songs as good as I could, and left. Basically, realistically, I'm a live performer and want to play onstage for the people and not make records that may sound really good. (Lynne Allen interview, 1978)*

---

* I can only say 'reasonably sure' because, while there are many comments to this effect in the seventies and beyond, there are no such comments from Dylan during the sixties. Explanations for this emerge from Dylan's star-image at that time. Gray (2000:839) argues that Dylan's 'later' view 'replac[es] the previously held Dylan view, which was that each album was a unique step along an unknown road, a deliberate creation under the control of the artist' but this is more a reflection of Gray's view of the work than any comments made by Dylan. My view is that, because of his emergence within a folk music aesthetic, Dylan simply took for granted issues that he would later be forced to make explicit. The clearest 1960s examples of the idea that the songs were blueprints for developing in live performance are his radical revisions of 'Baby Let Me Follow You Down' and 'One Too Many Mornings' on his 1966 world tour.

Dylan's understanding of recording has always been literal –
record what happens in the studio and release the results,
and he has never sought to utilise advanced studio
technology in the way that, for example, The Beatles did
(a revealing comparison: The Beatles spent 129 days of
studio time creating the *Sergeant Pepper* album; Dylan
recorded his first fifteen albums, up to and including 1976's
Desire, in just ninety days).[7] This approach became a hindrance for Dylan, however, as increasingly sophisticated
recording technology seemingly prevented him from realising his ideas quickly. This aspect of Dylan's recording career
is well recognised and provides one explanation for a series
of underachieving albums (notably *Shot Of Love*, *Infidels* and
Empire Burlesque). There is certainly a discrepancy between
Dylan's creative work and his released records during this
period.

There is a more deep-rooted reason for Dylan's discomfort in the recording studio, however. He has repeatedly
voiced disquiet at the effect that records have not only in
freezing a particular moment, but in how they are (and will
be) used to construct a particular image about him:

> Interviewer: But that record will be here, if the world is,
>   for a thousand years . . . long after you're gone, these
>   records will be here and people will listen to them and
>   think . . . well, one thing or another about this guy who
>   made these records four hundred years ago.
> Dylan: Oh, poor me!
>
> (Dave Herman interview, 1981)

Records play an extremely significant part in constructing an
image of the artist and this is contrary to how Dylan seemingly sees himself. Sixteen years later, he claimed that hearing his own albums was 'like looking into a lifeless mirror'

(Robert Hilburn interview, 1997). This resonates with something Dylan wrote in 1964:

do Not create anything, it will be
misinterpreted. it will not change.
it will follow you the
rest of your life.*

As with my earlier discussions regarding his concern over
how culture becomes canonised, Dylan has regularly displayed anxiety that records do exactly the same thing for
music, freezing them and robbing them of their social basis,
their vitality, their capacity to communicate. Dylan's stated
purpose is to communicate directly to people in performance:

> What I do is more of an immediate thing; to stand up on
> stage and sing – you get it back immediately. It's not like
> writing a book or even making a record. . . . What I do is so
> immediate it changes the nature, the concept, of art to me.
> I don't know what it is. It's too immediate. It's like the man
> who made that painting there [points to painting on wall of
> hotel room] has no idea we're sitting here now looking at it
> or not looking at it or anything. (Neil Spencer interview,
> 1981)

For this reason, Dylan has always been interested in *songs*,
rather than records, as songs can be developed and performed live. In 1997, he made repeated reference to the idea
that 'songs [are] just blueprints for what I'd play later on the
stage' (Edna Gunderson interview, 1997). This emphasis on
an ongoing creative process rather than a finished object is

---

* *Advice For Geraldine On Her Miscellaneous Birthday*, included in the concert programme of the 31 October concert at New York Town Hall.

not unique to Dylan and actually has a long history. Emerson, for example, stated that 'books are the death of literature. True art is never fixed, but always flowing.'[8] The etymology of culture, emerging from words like agriculture and cultivation implies that culture is an action, and it is only during the nineteenth century that culture becomes understood as a thing.[9] For artists, the emphasis on culture being a process rather than an object is significant because of an inherent tension from artworks existing in a social formation that attempts to objectify and put a price on everything. Once a cultural idea or expression becomes embodied in a thing, it becomes far more open to commodification. As the purpose of culture has generally been understood as standing against the commodification of all aspects of human life, this creates an unbearable paradox with which both the Romantics and the Modernists struggled: as soon as a work offering a critique of contemporary life is created, it can itself become a commodity. Indeed, Eisenberg suggests that music came to be seen as the most sublime of the arts during the Romantic era precisely because it was the least amenable to commodification[10] and while I am not suggesting that Dylan is engaged in the NET as a kind of anti-capitalist protest (on the contrary, there are many examples of Dylan being rather comfortable with the commercialisation of his music), his interest in music as a communicative process rather than an objectified thing stems from the same ideological root.

It is also a key element of rock ideology. In chapter 4, I discussed the emergence of rock culture as a form of mass culture critique that emerged from within mass culture. One element of this critique was an emphasis upon live performance, which was partly inherited from the beliefs and assumptions of the folk revival.* Whereas music may once have been the art least

---

* It does not entirely emerge from the folk revival as, for example, there

amenable to commodification, the invention of recording fundamentally changed the situation. From the folk perspective, the record creates an unwelcome mediation between performer and listener (worse, a *commercial* mediation) which prohibits direct communication between them. As Eisenberg suggests, 'when I buy a record, the musician is eclipsed by the disk. And I am eclipsed by my money.'[11] The assumption is that only the performance by a singer within physical proximity of his listeners enables an 'honest' performance (there are additional potential layers to this; only performances that do not rely on electrical amplification enable communication; performances where the crowds are too large prohibit direct communication; shows that rely on special effects and video screens prevent a relationship between performer and audience; and so on). I say 'honest' because part of the assumption is that any mediation resulting from the media industries will entail some kind of deception, will enable the performer to pretend to be something she is not.

Within this way of thinking, it is the mechanical nature of the recorded experience that is denigrated and the human relationship of the live performance that is venerated. The very idea of 'live music' only emerges once recorded music becomes the dominant form of music: 'live' as a concept is predicated upon a recorded other.[12] The valorisation of live music can be seen as part of folk culture's mass culture critique. The recorded song never changes, is never affected by its social setting or by the mood of the listener. It sounds *exactly* the same every time it is played, a clear manifestation

---

was an emphasis upon live performance in jazz as well. Also, while the folk ideology of rock prioritised live performance at the expense of records in the way I am outlining here, it is also important to note that the art ideology prioritised the record, as a self-conscious creation, over the live performance.

of the process of standardisation. The listener knows exactly what to expect every time it is played. The live performance, by contrast, is unique. Its uniqueness is guaranteed because it is played by a living being who, by humanity's very nature, will always produce idiosyncrasies in performance. The uniqueness of a performance is aided by the relationship between performer and audience: in a performance unmediated by external factors (amplification, stardom . . .), the audience's response to the performance will generate its own dynamics to which the performer will intuitively respond. And the audience is assumed to be a collective, a group of people who share more than this physical space in common; their shared space, their shared relationship to this music, is taken to reflect a shared social experience, a shared outlook. The record, by contrast, like the novel, offers a mode of individualised reception.

For much of rock culture, therefore, authenticity was located in the live concert. It was in live performance that the relationship between singer and performer was most direct; where the audience could express their collective experience; where, stripped of the supports of the recording industry, the performer had to prove that they could really sing, really play, really move an audience; where the collective effervescence of the event generated a unique excitement that affected that night's performance so that no two shows were ever exactly alike. Like rock culture itself, this ideology held sway at least until the 1980s. As rock culture declined during the eighties, however, so too did 'live culture'. New artists, such as Depeche Mode, New Order and the Pet Shop Boys, made records based on digital technology specifically intended not to be performed live. New music cultures emerged – notably hip hop and rave – that depended upon records rather than live musicians to provide the soundtrack for an evening's entertainment. There was a marked decrease in the number of traditional rock venues. The ideology of the rock gig 'no longer appeal[ed] to the broad base of the population that it once did and [was] no longer economical in many of the circumstances it once was'.[13] Those rock acts still touring in the eighties did so less frequently and increasingly had to rely on spectacular effects (lights, video screens, fireworks) to fill up one end of a large arena and match their audience's expectations generated not just by a recording consciousness, but by an MTV consciousness as well – concerts not only had to sound like they did on record but look like they did on video.[14]

Dylan's position by the end of the mid-eighties was, therefore, severely limited by the structure of his stardom and by the structure of the music industry more generally. Having his star-image dominated by his released albums caused problems as he was generally alienated from the record-making process. He considered himself a live performer at a time when live performance was diminishing in importance and/or descending into spectacle. While he had worked the stadium and arena circuits in 1984 and 1986, Dylan ultimately was not able to follow the same kind of path that other sixties acts like The Stones would follow. Aside from 1974 and 1978, he has never been a big enough draw to consistently fill large halls; and he has never been the kind of performer able to compete with the spectacular effects necessary to entertain in larger spaces. In 1986, *Q* magazine suggested that it was 'undignified' for Dylan to play a venue the size of Madison Square Garden as his style did not suit the larger-than-life MTV consciousness.

RESHAPING DYLAN'S AUDIENCE

The issues discussed so far in this and the last chapter caused a crisis in the relationship between Dylan and his audience.

It seems that Dylan came to resent his audience, believing that they were coming to shows merely because he was a famous name rather than to engage with the nuances of live performance (what he would later refer to as the 'right reasons' for attending). This is something he had complained about even during the 1970s. In 1978, he commented bitterly on his 1974 tour:

> when I went back on the road I was more famous than I was when I'd gotten off the road. I was incredibly more famous. And I had a lot of people who were coming who weren't my true fans, I was just another famous name. These people didn't understand what I had done to get there, they just thought I was a famous name and I'd written songs Jimi Hendrix was singing. (Craig McGregor interview)

In the same year, he told Ray Coleman that his audience 'tend[ed] to come . . . not so much [for] the music, more the side-show', and when interviewer Philippe Adler suggested that Dylan would have been 'intoxicated' by the audience adulation, Dylan retorted:

> No [I wasn't], because I didn't think it was for me. It was an ovation for someone or something else.

Dylan thus became suspicious of his live audience, considering them to be attending his shows purely because he was a famous name or because he symbolised the sixties; for nostalgic reasons rather than to engage with the music. My argument is that the commencement of the NET can be regarded as a calculated attempt to break out of this particular trap. Whether or not Dylan had these things in mind as explicitly as I discuss them, it seems clear that the NET had two complementary, though distinct, purposes. Firstly, it was to create an audience that did not attend shows purely for nostalgic reasons. Secondly, it had to create an audience whose impression of his music was not dominated by his released records. Dylan conflates the two issues when commenting on the success of the NET in 1997:

> I like those people who come to see me now. They're not aware of my early days, but I'm glad of that. It lifts that burden of responsibility, of having to play everything exactly like it was on some certain record. (Jon Pareles interview)

The opening up of this new way to perform was prompted by Dylan's collaboration with The Grateful Dead in 1987. Dylan and The Dead played six stadium shows as co-headliners during the summer. In rehearsing for them, Dylan seemingly reached his lowest point, being completely alienated from his own songs. Dylan credits Jerry Garcia as being the driving force behind reconnecting with them:

> He'd say, 'Come on, man, you know, this is the way it goes, let's play it, it goes like this.' And I'd say, 'Man, he's right, you know? How's he gettin' there and I can't get there?' And I had to go through lot of red tape in my mind to get back there. (David Gates interview, 1997)

A comment such as this, and similar statements made in other interviews, emphasises the relationship between Dylan and his songs. The NET is often considered from a textual perspective – what repeated performances mean for notions of the text of a particular song, for example, or how Dylan radically alters songs in performance. What enabled any such reconnection was not some kind of mystical realignment with the aesthetic content of the songs, however, but a reconfiguration of the relationship between Dylan and his audience. In other words, what made the difference was a re-orientation of Dylan's stardom.

This reorientation is made possible because of the structure of the NET. Its key principle is rather simple – Dylan plays an awful lot of shows. Rather than engaging upon tours periodically, Dylan plays shows continually: touring for a couple of months, followed by a couple of months' break, then back on the road for a couple of months, and so on. Dylan employs his band members and pays them a retainer so that he has first call on their services. This means that Dylan does not have the problems of starting a tour up every couple of years, finding a new band and rehearsing them. The band are available whenever Dylan wants to play shows.

The principle is simple (many artists have musicians on a retainer) but the effect is extraordinary. To gain a sense of the scale of the NET, we need to compare it to Dylan's earlier career. His emergence within the folk revival and his embeddedness within rock authenticity means that Dylan has always been considered as a touring musician. You would therefore expect him to have played a lot of shows. Prior to the NET, his major tours and the number of concerts played in each of these years is listed below.

Tour year										
1966	1974	1975	1976	1978	1979	1980	1981	1984	1986	1987
Concerts										
41	40	31	24	114	26	72	54	27	60	36

This is a total of 525 shows in 22 years, an average of 34.5 shows a year once Dylan returned to the stage in 1974. The NET began in 1988 and, at the time of writing, its last completed year was 2006. The annual concert totals for these years, in chronological order, is: 71, 93, 99, 101, 92, 80, 104, 116, 86, 94, 110, 119, 112, 106, 107, 98, 111, 113 and 97. This totals a staggering 1,909 shows, an average of almost exactly 100 shows per year.* The number of shows played results in frequent and repeated appearances in the same place: rather than turning up in a town every five years or so, the NET rolls up pretty much every year. For example, before the NET, Dylan played in the UK at mostly three-year intervals (1966, 1978, 1981, 1984, 1987) whereas since the start of the NET, Dylan has performed in the UK in every year between 1989 and 2006 except three (1992, 1994 and 1999).

The structure of the NET has given rise to a new type of audience. Firstly, it has diminished the number of fans attending a Dylan show for nostalgic reasons, or because he is a 'legend' that represents an idealised moment:

A lot of the shows over the years was people coming out of curiosity and their curiosity wasn't fulfilled. They weren't transported back to the '60s. Lightning didn't strike. The shows didn't make sense for them, and they didn't make sense for me. That had to stop, and it took a long time to stop it. A lot of people were coming out to see The Legend, and I was trying to just get on stage and play music. (Robert Hilburn interview, 1992)

It is the sheer quantity of shows, and the frequency of Dylan's appearance, that helps to lessen the 'legend-hunter' fans. They make a Dylan concert less of an event and therefore diminish the number of people coming to see Dylan merely as an icon or legend that represents the sixties or their imagined

---

* Most of my statistics in this section come from the incredibly useful, if slightly scary, Olof's Files (http://www.bjorner.com/bob.htm).

youth. To run a rather crude statistical illustration, playing a show in a town annually rather than every three years is likely to diminish the number of legend-hunters. This type of fan may be likely to still attend a show every few years but they will almost certainly not attend the show every time Dylan is in town: the novelty soon fades, the need to relive or recreate a particular moment is not sufficient motivation to annually buy rather expensive concert tickets. This is not to say that there are *no* 'tourists' attending NET shows. There clearly are some at each show, attending because 'Dylan' is a name that is important, but the proportion of them has declined as the NET has continued.* One upshot of this was that the NET's audience was, in its early years at least, much smaller than Dylan's previous audience. In contrast to the 10,000+ capacity arenas he played in 1986, the NET concentrated on smaller venues (2,000–5,000 capacity) as his audience contracted.

This audience is distinctive, however, for, in place of the legend-hunting type of fan, a new kind of audience has developed for the NET:

> I've found a different audience. I'm not good at reading how old people are, but my audience seems to be livelier than they were 10 years ago. They react immediately to what I do, and they don't come with a lot of preconceived ideas about who they would like me to be, or who they think I am. Whereas a few years ago they couldn't react quickly. . . . I was still kind of bogged down with a certain crowd of people. . . . But that's changed. We seem to be attracting a new audience. Not just those who know me as some kind of figurehead from another age or a symbol for a

---

* Heylin suggests early 1995 is the moment at which the NET succeeded in its aim of exhausting those who were coming to see the legend (2000:687).

generational thing. I don't really have to deal with that any more. (Murray Englehart interview, 1999)

Part of this new audience is old fans who have happily followed Dylan's new direction on the NET. However, a significant portion of Dylan's new audience is considerably younger. The number of 15–25-year-olds at current Dylan concerts is certainly notable. Part of this is clearly demographic – Dylan is now outliving some of his original fans – but it is also interesting how Dylan has been able to draw in a new generation of fans in a way that most older performers haven't. In my experience, concerts by The Stones, or even later acts like Elvis Costello or U2 have far fewer young fans attending. Reasons for this are unclear but it seems at least in part the result of a deliberate strategy by Dylan: many of his shows on the NET are in college towns or university campuses, while playing at Woodstock 2 and on MTV 'Unplugged' in 1994 suggest calculated attempts to reach out to a new audience.

I need to make explicit here that I am not suggesting that all of Dylan's old fans have deserted him to be replaced by a wholly youthful crowd. When I talk of Dylan's 'new' audience, I am referring to those who engage with the logic of the NET. There are clearly many fans who followed Dylan in the past and continue to do so today – there are also new 'older' fans, who may not have been that interested in Dylan beforehand but have been drawn into the NET. I have no desire to create a simple binary divide between older and younger fans. At the same time, however, it is important to recognise that the relative youth of Dylan's audience greatly affects how his audience interprets him. Younger members of Dylan's audience (and by this I mean anyone under about thirty-five, though it becomes more acute the younger the fan) conceptualise Dylan differently from older fans who were aware of Dylan in the sixties and seventies. This is partly because of what Dylan has achieved on the NET, but it is also a simple historical fact that the sixties, and Bob Dylan's role in them, mean very different things now than they did in the past. I teach students today for whom 1995 is musical history, let alone the 1960s. The 1960s is as real to them as the Second World War – they may know some people who lived through those times, but conceptualising what it was like to live through them is virtually impossible. This is different even to how people growing up in the 1980s were able to approach Dylan. In the 1980s, the sixties were still recent history, and children of the 1980s imbibed their parents' still fresh experiences. For young people joining the NET in the last few years, the sixties was their grandparents' generation. It is impossible that Dylan should mean the same thing to someone who grew up in the sixties as he would to someone for whom *World Gone Wrong* was before their time. I am not suggesting that all young fans are devoted to the logic of the NET, nor that there is no legend-hunting involved when young people see a Dylan show. Of course there is some. Of course some young people go to see Dylan because he is a sixties icon, and they own *Greatest Hits* and *At Budokan* and want to connect with the past. But even for these people, it is impossible that Dylan could mean the same thing now as he did to his earlier audiences. This younger audience carries less canonical baggage with them when they see a Dylan show, they are 'fans who see him less as a super-star or personal savior than as a gifted artist' (Hilburn, 1992).

Carrying less canonical baggage means that it is easier for Dylan's younger audience to accept Dylan as a performer rather than a songwriter. Anyone under the age of nineteen was not born when the NET began. Anyone under the age of about, say, thirty-five would not have had any significant awareness of music before the start of the NET. To these people, Dylan is a performer. His utterances and his actions tell you that he is a performer. They may know that Dylan wrote a lot of great songs in the past, and they may place great value on the fact that he wrote these songs but, in the world they have grown up in, Bob Dylan is a touring performer, a relentless troubadour. The man on stage is completely different to the mediatised image of the man who wrote the songs (there is more on this in the next chapter).

This historical distance, this awareness and acceptance of Dylan as a performer, makes it easier for younger NET fans to escape recording consciousness. Dylan's contemporary voice is key here. It is so distinctive, and so thoroughly tied to his modern star-image, that there is a radical rupture between the earlier and later versions of the song. The voice and the contemporary arrangement of songs like 'Masters Of War', or 'Positively Fourth Street', make them entirely different songs, with different meanings, from the old recorded versions. The distinction between the old and new versions is so stark that it is almost impossible for the performance to 'stand for' an experience of the sixties recordings for those who were not there. The performance can only represent the experience of now, of the Bob Dylan of the NET.

The main way that Dylan promotes the decline in recording consciousness of his new audience is through encouraging attendance at multiple shows. It is here that The Dead's influence on Dylan is most marked, as they were famous for having a travelling army of fans (Deadheads) who would follow the band from town to town to see shows, sometimes for years on end. Dylan always had some fans who saw multiple shows when he performed in town, but it was certainly fewer than The Dead's, and his audience had less of the 'travelling around' mentality. It seems clear that Dylan recognised the possibilities generated by this kind of relationship between the band and its audience and that the NET was an attempt to establish an audience that saw multiple shows and followed the tour from place to place.*

The NET encourages multiple attendance mainly through its variety, and a clear effect of Dylan's work with The Dead was his willingness to engage with more obscure aspects of his back catalogue. At the first show of the NET, on 7 June 1988, Dylan opened the set with a performance of 'Subterranean Homesick Blues'. He had never played this on stage before. He followed it up with another live debut – 'Absolutely Sweet Marie'. He also played 'Man Of Constant Sorrow', an old folk tune from his first album, and another traditional song 'The Lakes of Pontchartrain', that is not on any Bob Dylan album. Neither of these had appeared at any previous Bob Dylan concert. He also gave a live debut to 'Driftin' Too Far From Shore', a song from his 1986 album *Knocked Out Loaded*, the first ever non-acoustic performance of 'Gates Of Eden' and performed 'Boots Of Spanish Leather' for the first time since 1965. On the second night of the tour, two days later, Dylan repeated only two songs from the previous performance – the opener and the closer ('Maggie's Farm'). He played 'Baby Let Me Follow You Down' from his first album, the traditional song 'Two Soldiers', 'Had a Dream About You Baby' from 1988's *Down In The Groove* and 'The Man In Me' for the first time since 1978. By the fourth show of the tour, Dylan had performed 40 different songs; by the fifteenth, 62.

This pattern of playing a wide range of songs on tour has continued throughout the NET. In 1990, the 93 shows yielded 134 different songs; the 112 shows of 2000 provided 126 unique songs, while the 113 shows in 2005 produced

* According to Sounes, Dylan actually tried to join The Dead in 1989 (2001:440–1).

110 different songs. This variety can be contrasted to Dylan's earlier tours: on his comeback tour with The Band in 1974, Dylan played 40 shows. These produced 45 different songs. The 1978 world tour of 114 shows produced just 64 different songs.* Some songs, of course, do get played more than others. Dylan has not abandoned the songs that made him famous and this has resulted in criticism from some quarters that his shows are still dominated by his sixties material.[15] A close examination of the NET, however, reveals some interesting issues. Firstly, there is less reliance on material from the halcyon days than may be expected (in 1997, for example, only 41 per cent of NET songs were written between 1961 and 1966, while the same period accounted for only 37 per cent of songs in 2002 – it has never risen above 50 per cent). Secondly, Dylan now plays a wider range of songs from that particular period than in the past. To say he plays 'sixties songs' actually provides little information about what those songs may be. If people go to a Dylan show hoping that he'll play his sixties classics, I'm pretty sure they're not expecting 'Country Pie' from 1969's *Nashville Skyline* (104 performances in 2000). The songs Dylan plays are not necessarily his most famous. For example, in 1996 (86 shows), only 4 songs were played more than 40 times that year. One of these was a cover song (The Dead's 'Alabama Getaway'), one was an eighties song ('Silvio') and only two were what could be considered 'classics' ('All Along The Watchtower' and 'Rainy Day Women Nos 12 & 35'). Sometimes songs do stay in the set for the long haul ('All Along The Watchtower' was played at 482 consecutive shows between 14 May 1992 and 3 August 1997; 'Tangled Up In Blue' was played at virtually every show in

---

* I say 'just' but this would still be a high figure compared to many other artists.

1998, 1999 and 2000; currently 'Like A Rolling Stone' and 'All Along The Watchtower' are perennial encores) but a notable feature of the NET is the way in which the expected hits are rationed.*

A quick, highly subjective, case study: in November 2005, I saw Dylan play 5 consecutive shows at the Brixton Academy in London. Over these 5 nights, I heard 50 different songs. Of these 50, 18 were what I would call 'greatest hits' material. Some greatest hits received multiple airings: 'Like A Rolling Stone' and 'All Along The Watchtower' were played for every encore, while 'Maggie's Farm' was the first vocal on 4 nights (the other songs played 4 times were the classic 'Highway 61 Revisited' and 2 songs from 2001 – 'Summer Days' and 'Honest With Me'). Of the remaining 32 songs, 13 were more obscure 1960s–1970s material and 16 songs were from 1980–2003. I heard the live debut of 'Million Dollar Bash' (from 1967's *The Basement Tapes*) and 'Waiting For You' (a 2003 song released on a movie soundtrack). These were accompanied by 3 cover versions: Dylan opened 4 of these shows with a short instrumental cover of Link Wray's 'Rumble', played a version of Fats Domino's 'Blue Monday', and twice played The Clash's 'London Calling'.**

The variety in the setlists is one reason that people attend more than one show (if you only went to the first night at Brixton, you'd have missed 'London Calling'!) but not the only reason. It is actually the entire structure of the NET that encourages multiple attendance. How does the NET

---

* Again, comparison to earlier Dylan tours is instructive. The 1974 tour included 5 songs performed at all 40 shows, and 10 more performed in at least 30 shows. In 1978, 'All Along The Watchtower', 'Blowin' In The Wind' and 'Maggie's Farm' all garnered 111 performances each, while 9 other songs topped 100 performances.

** It's not always quite this varied; there is likely to be more variation when Dylan plays a series of shows in one town, as he did at Brixton. The first 5 shows of the 2006 summer tour yielded 'just' 27 songs.

work? I think it is best summarised as the creation of an ongoing environment which enables the performer to reach inspired moments in performance.[16] The NET is about creating a particular structure in which Dylan can create. This is partly facilitated by a talented band who are comfortable with the way Dylan plays but it is mainly fulfilled by a relationship of trust between performer and audience. If a performer believes that they can trust their audience then they are more likely to take chances and produce something interesting. The audience therefore needs to understand, be versed in, the logic of the NET.

PERFORMANCE AND THE QUESTION OF TEXTS

Fans of the NET do not attend multiple shows because the performances are consistently magnificent. As Scobie says, 'no one plays a hundred masterpieces a year',[17] but the aim of the NET is to create an environment in which special moments can occur, when certain songs, even just certain phrases 'take off' and produce something new which revitalises the song being performed. Individual moments: little phrases; Dylan picking up on a particular lyrical riff and pushing it to see how far it will go; a line in a song sung in a way that inverts the meaning of the song; an extended harmonica solo; these things happen at most Dylan concerts. More substantial moments: a particular run of two or three or four songs together that seem to meld into one spectacular moment and stop time; a show where Dylan just seems switched on from the word go and produces moment after moment in the same show; these things happen at some Bob Dylan concerts and, as you never know which one, you attend several to increase your chances.

I don't think this logic is recognised by those outside of the NET cocoon. Other than obsessiveness, the general explanation for why fans attend multiple shows is that every night Dylan continually rewrites and restructures his songs. A colourful example of this idea comes from Adrian Deevoy who, in a reviewing Dylan's 1993 Hammersmith residency in *Q* magazine, describes

> [p]eople coming to watch Dylan savagely revise some of their favourite songs. It's a unique thing. You won't hear anyone else doing it. . . . no-one sets about their back catalogue quite like Dylan. He gets inside the melodies, inverts them, corrupts them, deconstructs and reassembles them. They may have started life as clean-cut sober tunes but tonight they're going home with someone else's trousers on their heads and lipstick on their thighs.

This is not how the NET works, however. Dylan has explained that what actually makes the NET distinctive is the consistent structure of the songs:

> If you're going to ask me what's the difference between now and when I used to play in the Seventies, Eighties and even back in the Sixties, [back then] the songs weren't arranged. The arrangement is the architecture of the song. And that's why our performances are so effective these days, because measure for measure we don't stray from the actual structure of the song. And once the architecture is in place, a song can be done in an endless amount of ways. (Murray Englehart interview, 1999)

The idea that Dylan routinely transforms songs on stage is 'a myth, probably perpetuated by newcomers who couldn't guess what he was singing until the song was almost over'.[18] The fact of their unrecognisability to outsiders, however, does imply the diminution of the NET audience's recording consciousness. It is certainly true that old songs sound little like their recorded versions. The Never Ending Tour has clearly attempted to reposition Dylan as a performer, escaping the tyranny of recording, living for the moment, existing only in front of a live audience. One notable aspect of Dylan's emphasis upon performing has been the emergence of a new form of Dylan criticism that emphasises the 'performerliness' of Dylan's work, both expounding upon the NET and re-evaluating his earlier work. The most significant writer in this area is Paul Williams, who has produced three volumes discussing the performed nature of Dylan's work, as well as a collection of earlier articles.[19] Since he first wrote about Dylan in the sixties, Williams has always emphasised the performative element of Dylan's work. For example, discussing 'She's Your Lover Now', he writes: 'Dylan is a passionate vocalizer of felt truth, tongue connected directly to the heart, mind following not leading. The rhythm and the performance structure come first, and the language fills in the spaces . . . His songs entertain our intellects but their source is visceral – mind follows feeling.'[20] His approach coincides with the NET, however, because the first volume of his book series about Dylan's work, *Performing Artist*, was published in 1990 and his method has provided a foundation for many fans' own accounts of the experience of the NET. Williams too has written much on the NET. Describing a 1999 performance of 'Visions Of Johanna', he writes: 'What makes this eightminute performance so remarkable is its expressiveness, its artistry, its structure, its musicality, its freshness, its vision. . . . This is not a repeat of a work of art created back in 1966. It is unmistakably a great work of art created at the time of performance. Something new and original and thrilling.'[21]

This approach has been strongly criticised by Michael Gray, who has described Williams' work as 'air-headed apologism'.[22] Gray, by contrast, concentrates on Dylan as a songwriter (actually, a lyricist) rather than a performer and therefore categorises Dylan's later career as one of artistic decline: 'in performance, the Bob Dylan of the 1990s may be continuing to revise or re-write the texts of the mid-1960s and 1970s; but wasn't it the Bob Dylan of back then who did most of the work?'[23] This type of approach indicates the difficulties of repositioning the meaning of a star-image in the way that Dylan has attempted. No matter what he does as an individual, remnants of his old image, how the public itself creates the meaning of 'Bob Dylan', remain. We can see similar processes occur during Dylan's retreat from celebrity in the late sixties. In this instance, Dylan's star-image as the supreme songwriter structures expectations and reception of any new work or change in direction. Thus any emphasis on performing is interpreted as an *absence* of songwriting (for example, Heylin states that Dylan 'has increasingly sought to pursue this aspect of his artistry [performing] – the lesser talent – at the expense of his greater genius [songwriting]').[24] Dylan acknowledged this problem in 1997:

> People identify me with the songs I write. They don't identify me on what I can do with a song that's already been written. I feel that that's just an area that I've never really been able to expound upon because I don't record that much. People expect me to record songs of mine that I've written. So that's my particular dilemma. (London press conference, 1997)

The 'new audience' that Dylan has worked hard to create is one that acknowledges that Dylan wrote a lot of songs in the past and, while he writes sporadically in the present, is now mainly occupied with engaging live audiences. It is an audience that sees the value of performing in its own right rather than in terms of some absent other.

Dylan's work in reconfiguring and re-performing many of his old songs links with developments in postmodern literary theory that question the notion of a finished text and subvert ideas of originality and authorship. Stephen Scobie's work *Alias Bob Dylan Revisited* synthesises an emphasis upon Dylan as a performer with many of the insights of postmodern literary theory (Scobie is perhaps the only literary analyst of Dylan who pays more than lip service to the idea of performance). 'Dylan', Scobie argues, 'never regards a song as unalterably finished' and will instead reconfigure songs, drop or reorder verses, rewrite small phrases.[25] Scobie concludes that 'the text of a Dylan song is not any one of these [performances] exclusively but rather their sum'.[26] Gray criticises the idea that Dylan is continually rewriting the text as 'the main cliché of Dylanology in the 1980s and 1990s'. He suggests that 'it seems rather too convenient for the Bob Dylan who has writer's block, or has lost his way'.[27]

Gray's critique of the idea of an open-ended text returns us to the earlier discussions about recording consciousness. Consider the following critique of a NET performance:

> He always cuts out verses from long songs these days. There is no reason for this, beyond the sheer shrugging-off of the task of the full performance. There you are, say, at the concert in Montreal in May 1990; Dylan launches into 'Desolation Row', which is fresh – having been performed only five times in the previous two decades; and he misses out five verses. How can this not disappoint? Such short-changing of the audience, such short-changing of his own work, is in essence another expression of self-contempt.[28] it

Gray's view that Dylan 'misses out' five verses depends upon a fixed idea of the work to which the performer is expected to adhere. Like the process/product idea discussed earlier, it has a longer history than merely Dylan. Written notation developed to ensure the perfect reproduction of sacred rituals and, in some cultures, incorrect reproduction could prove fatal for the performer; Eisenberg recounts a description of one indigenous culture where 'old men used to stand by with bows and arrows and shoot at every dancer who made a mistake'.[29] A similar sanctification of the text has occurred within modern culture. Lawrence Levine offers a fascinating analysis of how Shakespeare's work became sanctified in America, explaining how Shakespeare's plays were initially performed with little regard to the 'original text' – unpopular sections were dropped, new jokes added, individual scenes performed as part of wider burlesques.[30] Over the course of the nineteenth century, however, the idea emerged that plays should be performed exactly as Shakespeare had written them. Indeed, in 1879, a member of the audience fired two shots at actor William Booth for 'taking liberties with the text'.[31] Luckily, Michael Gray lives in a time which frowns upon such extreme expressions of displeasure.

An emphasis upon the sanctity of a text is founded upon a set of values that prioritises written culture over oral culture. The invention of recording, however, added a new means of preserving an original text. Whereas in the past, fidelity to an idealised script or written score was deemed sacrosanct, in popular music it is the recording that is considered the ideal work. In Gray's approach, any performance is only interpreted within the context of what he refers to as the 'original Dylan recording'. Whether in written or recorded instance, however, the assumption is that the original text is worthy of respect. In referring to a short-changing of the work itself, Gray accuses Dylan of treating his own work disrespectfully. I don't think this is true; it seems to me that Dylan is incredibly respectful of his (and others') songs. As with Dylan's comments about museums and paintings in the previous chapter, however, that respect is manifested by not treating them as too precious to touch (Gray's criticisms echo earlier ones from the folk community who considered Dylan too irreverent with traditional material). The shift away from 'respecting' the text is another element of postmodern theorising, and I will return to it below.

Despite Gray's critique, Scobie's approach and Williams' more impressionistic discussions resonate with the effects of the NET and with the experience of many of the NET's followers. When Gray rhetorically asks 'how can this not disappoint?' he fundamentally misunderstands the ethos of the NET and, I think, misjudges the experiences of Dylan's new audience. The chief effect of attending multiple shows is a reconfiguration of how one hears a text, facilitating what I might as well call a 'NET consciousness' in place of a recording consciousness. Hearing multiple shows, and thus many performances of the same song results in a saturation of listening that intensifies the experience of listening, expanding our experience of the present moment to the point where it takes over the awareness of alternative moments. In the moment of performance, in the act of listening, NET consciousness undermines any awareness of alternative versions of the text. If 'Mr Tambourine Man' has two verses tonight, or three, then that's what 'Mr Tambourine Man' is tonight – you hear the performance in front of you and not absent others. This is especially true with attendance at multiple shows – attending five consecutive nights relieves the pressure that this one has to be 'the night' and therefore opens up one's ears to the intensity of the now. This is something called 'moment time' that I will discuss in the next chapter and one of its effects is that it de-prioritises the 'original' recorded version.* When I hear the officially released version

---

* There is, however, a sleight of hand going on here. There exists another

of 'Highway 61 Revisited', say, or 'Señor', I hear them as a fresh performance, contextualised within the experience of hearing many other performances. I do not hear them as *the* performance, even though in many cases they were the performances I first heard. I know the words and the sound of all of Bob Dylan's released records. They are embedded in my consciousness perhaps more deeply than anything else. When I am at a show, however, I am engaged with the performance in front of me, at that moment, to the point where I couldn't actually tell you what verses he 'misses out'. Other fans have told me the same thing. Again, this fits with a general postmodern aesthetic; what we need to concentrate on is the immediate, visceral, sensual experience of the cultural work rather than any intellectual rationalisation of its meaning or content. How does experiencing the performance affect you? Right from the start of his career, Dylan has made repeated comments that the most important thing is the affective element of music. In 1965, he said that 'the point is not understanding what I write but feeling it' (Frances Taylor interview), while in 1997 he stated:

> You can't interpret a Hank Williams song. He's done the interpretation and the performance, and that's it. Now it's

---

way of experiencing the NET, and that is through bootlegs and live concert recordings. Unlike The Grateful Dead, Dylan does not openly condone the recording of his concerts. Virtually all his concerts get recorded, though, and he knows it. Actually, I think he depends on it as a key element of the NET mentality. The aims of the NET in creating a new audience would not be achievable without the prevalence of live recordings – seeing 5 shows a year is not going to reduce someone's recording consciousness; hearing 100 recordings of live performances might. Live recordings ride the line between process and product, for what we have is a procession of products aiming to document the ongoing process; each recording only given meaning by all the others that surround it (see L. Marshall, 2005).

for the listener to decide if it moves him or not. (Edna Gunderson interview, 1997)

That 'decision' occurs in the moment of listening. If you are moved by a performance on the NET, you are moved by what you see and hear in front of you. That is why I think discussion of 'the text' is a bit of a red herring. Literary scholars are interested in notions of the text, not music fans: for them the issue is not what can be considered definitive but, rather, whether a particular performance moves them.

HIGH AND LOW CULTURAL VALUE

The division between Gray's fixed, closed notion of a text and the more open-ended conceptions of Scobie and Williams reflects at least in part the wider cultural positions of modernism and postmodernism. Significantly, though, they are also a division between the values of high and popular culture – a related but not identical issue. There is some irony here, because when Gray originally published his analysis of Dylan in 1972, the idea of taking popular culture seriously was itself a fairly radical gesture. The problem of Gray's approach, and it's a problem that besets many early attempts to take popular culture seriously, is that it merely accepts the assumptions of traditional high culture over what defines cultural value. Gray seemingly provides a challenge to the mass culture critiques which claim all popular culture to be rubbish, by arguing that, actually, Dylan is very good. However, by using Dylan as the a priori example which disproves the critique ('if Dylan is good, then the whole critique is wrong'), the effect is to maintain the high/low divide but force Dylan into 'high culture' ('see, he's really an artist after all!'). It does nothing to address the problems caused by the binary divide in the first place. The analysis of popular culture that has emerged since the 1980s, intrinsically related to the emergence of postmodernism and now coalesced into the discipline of Cultural Studies, has illustrated that popular culture does different things and has different values to traditional culture. It therefore needs its own forms of analysis rather than those borrowed from an alien culture. At the same time, other academic work has been conducted that shows how the idea of 'culture' endorsed by writers like F. R. Leavis and Michael Gray is itself tied to a historically specific set of ideas that acts to universalise a particular class ideology and, as such, is thoroughly implicated in the inequalities of the modern world.[32]

The first way to highlight the differences between the values of high and low culture relates to an idea of autonomy, how they relate to the day-to-day world. Within traditional high culture there is an idea that culture should maintain a distance, a level of autonomy, from everyday life. Since the onset of modern society, culture has been understood as having a special role, pushing forward our consciousness, differentiating us from barbarians, making us more human. It must do so in a social system that gives everything a price, standardises and objectifies human beings. Therefore culture (particularly 'art') must maintain a distance from the social world, be functionally useless as a rebellion against a system that demands everything have a use. Popular culture (and more recent developments in high culture too, such as pop art) rejects the false claim of autonomy and instead fully integrates into the rhythms of daily life, including its mundane and commercial aspects. Low culture, in its very nature, is not merely 'aesthetic', but social, as the earlier discussion of concert attendance suggests.

This leads to a second point of divergence. In high culture, the value of the work is to be found embodied in the work itself. The work and its meaning exist regardless of other social practices (there are thus repeated examples of artists who were never appreciated in their lifetime but the inherent quality of their work was finally recognised). Great works of art are considered to adhere to some universal standards of greatness – Shakespeare's works are good whether we recognise it or not. In popular culture, however, the meanings of works are generated by the social practices in which they are used. The value of works is accepted as transitory as social practices and tastes change. The question in popular culture is not 'is it good?' but 'what (or who) is it good for?'. This question of usefulness is anathema to high culture.*

The final point of divergence between high and low culture relates to how we interact with cultural works themselves. In traditional high culture, the key mode of reception is one of appreciation and critical distance. One should engage with a cultural work in quiet contemplation in order to fully draw out the subtle meanings in the work itself. We thus go to special churches to worship the works, silently walking round a gallery or sitting quietly at a classical music recital. In high cultural appreciation, as mentioned earlier, one is expected to be respectful towards the text. Engagement with popular culture, in contrast, is marked by its *participatory* aspect. We do not treat the text as sacred; we are sometimes inattentive, dropping out to

---

* I am absolutely not suggesting that there should be no investigation of quality within popular culture. There is a tendency for those promoting popular culture to rely upon a populist defence (if people like it, it must be good). This leads to a simple inversion of the mass culture critique and what Jim McGuigan (1992) calls a 'crisis of qualitative judgement'. We do need to be able to distinguish what is good and bad within popular culture, but the argument here is that we need to develop new forms of criticism that deal with low culture on its own terms. One factor that needs considering is the 'usefulness' of the work.

converse and turning our attention back to the TV; we skip
tracks that we don't like on CDs, or make compilation
tapes. We don't have to go to special places or create the
right spiritual environment for us to interact with the
work; if we go to a pop concert we can stand up and dance,
talk to our friends, can take food in, buy drinks from the
bar at the back of the auditorium – compare the architecture and conventions of a rock concert and a classical
concert to see the difference between the 'distanced appreciation' of high culture and the 'participatory appreciation'
of popular culture.

The split between distanced and participatory appreciation (and the related features just discussed) characterises the
different approaches of Gray and Williams and is why Gray
sees the NET as a story of artistic decline. Consider, for
example, the following criticism:

> In the solo acoustic halves of his 1966 concerts, he got
> polite applause for showering genius around . . . Now, in an
> unhealthy contrast, he gets whoops and wild applause
> between each verse.[33]

Really? At a rock concert? Do you think people dance as
well? This quote shows that Gray really doesn't understand
how popular music works, how the bodily reaction and the
participatory appreciation *are part of the form itself*. This is
the arena in which Dylan works: he is a rock star, not a poet
on a reading tour. It is also the arena in which he *chooses* to
work (unsurprising really, given that music – not poetry –
affected him at a young age and has kept him enthralled for
sixty years). As early as 1965, Dylan was concerned at the
inappropriate level of reverence offered at his shows, stating
that 'it's hard for me to accept the silent audiences' (Ray
Coleman interview). Gray's use of the adjective 'unhealthy'

clearly illustrates the ideological basis of his analysis – the Victorian moralism of Matthew Arnold that sought to civilise the masses and maintain social order. The treatment and purpose of the work is all important for Gray, but the work is some abstract thing that demands our respect. This is despite repeated statements from Dylan that his songs are written for a particular purpose – for him to sing in front of a live audience.

Rather than consider works in splendid isolation, we need to think about the *usefulness* of songs, to both Dylan and his audience. The song that best illustrates the different approaches is 'Silvio'. Released on 1988's *Down In The Groove*, 'Silvio' is an incredibly important song in Dylan's career. The lyrics were written by The Grateful Dead's lyricist, Robert Hunter, and shown to Dylan during the career-changing 1987 rehearsals. Dylan evidently saw something in the lyrics that he liked, added music to them and recorded it for his new album. The recorded version doesn't sound that good: it runs a little too fast and sounds a bit thin and tinny. This provides ample opportunity for Gray to disparage it, describing it as 'numbingly undistinguished', a 'miserable nonentity'.[34] So, why is it important? It's important because it is one of the most played songs on the NET, having been performed 595 times. The question that needs asking is not just 'is it any good?' (I have some sympathy with Gray's portrayal of its recorded version; I entirely disagree with using that as a basis for evaluating it as a live experience) but 'what good does it do?' Paul Williams understands this, and provides a convincing answer:

> Dylan likes the song. He likes the response it often gets from his live audience (not because they're familiar with the song, but because the dynamics of the song's music and Dylan's enthusiasm for it as a singer and bandleader tend to

make it an exciting and satisfying musical experience, even though it's not one of the Dylan songs the audience members were hoping to hear tonight).

Why does Dylan like it? Again, because it's fun to perform. And I think he feels liberated by the fact that it's a Dylan song without baggage; he and the band play it as though it were a big hit or a song that made him famous, and the audience can feel that and respond happily without knowing what the song is . . . which allows the singer to lean into it in a way that's different from the other Dylan songs and covers he's playing. 'Find out something only dead men know!' This is exactly the sort of lyric Dylan enjoys calling attention to (repeating it or slowing it down, doing tricks with it) during a performance – compare 'No one sees my face and lives' from 'I and I' or 'Just like so many times before' from 'Knockin' On Heaven's Door'.[35]

Williams is correct that it is a song that works for the audience – it *is* fun, you can see that Dylan finds it fun, and you can dance to it. I'd much rather hear 'Silvio' in concert than, say, 'Queen Jane Approximately'. I wouldn't want to hear ten 'Silvios' in a show, but that's not the point. We should never ignore the effect that songs like this have on the mood and structure of a concert. It is also a song that provides another rumination on Dylan's stardom; whether Hunter wrote it as a portrayal of Dylan is irrelevant; that we (and presumably Dylan) can see it that way is what matters. 'Stake my future on a hell of a past', the song begins, exclaims 'Seen better days but who has not' before concluding 'Going down to the valley and sing my song / Let the echo decide if I was right or wrong'. Nothing in Dylan's canon captures the attempt to escape the permanence of the record better than the opening and closing lines. For both performer and audience, 'Silvio' provides the rallying call to embark on the NET.

At various times in this book, I have been critical of those who label Dylan a poet. The rationale for my argument should be clear from this explanation of the differences between high and low culture. High and low culture do different things, fulfil different functions. The meaning of works is created in different ways in each sphere; repetition, for example, is more important in low culture than high culture. The institutions of both 'high' and 'low' culture contain different assumptions and are involved in different social practices; to use one as the basis of judgement for the other is inappropriate and will always fail to do justice to the culture in question. Dylan works in a low cultural medium – 'I don't like to think of myself in the highfalutin' area. I'm in the burlesque area' (David Gates interview, 1997). That means that in order to properly appreciate his work we need to understand the social contexts in which it exists, how it is used, the expectations, structures, limitations and opportunities of his chosen area. Dylan is a rock star and, no matter how good he may be, he cannot transcend the social structuring of his medium.

Such an approach greatly undermines the authority of high culture (and, indeed, its critics). The modern notion of culture that came to prominence in the nineteenth century reflects an idealised attempt to unite humanity. Culture – particularly its embodiments in 'the arts' – is seen as the only place in which the conflicts of the everyday can be transcended, the only place where civilisation and perfection can be found. This is a terrible indictment of modern life, as it implies that civilisation and perfection cannot be found in everyday life, but it also places an intolerable burden on the arts, as the symbolic importance of the artist and the critic far outweigh their actual political effectiveness.[36] This

burden is relieved by the emergence of postmodern theorising which has pluralised the idea of culture, made us more
aware that 'Culture' is white, male, European and middle
class. The idea of 'Culture' was initially cultureless, its constituency assumed to be all of humanity. As soon as its
authority is challenged, however, then it becomes impossible
to uphold its assumptions. 'Culture' becomes just one culture out of many, not the standard to which all cultures must
adhere.

On a lesser scale, rock music follows this path too. When
rock emerged it too was cultureless, it assumed that its values
stood for all young people and that its cultural prejudices
reflected a common humanity. It, too, had an intolerable
burden, being required to transcend the everyday, engender
social change, stop wars. Over time, however, it too became
scrutinised (rock is certainly white, middle class and male,
even though it may not be European) and, as other mainstream musical genres emerged, it became seen as one possible culture among many. Rock's ideology mirrors the great
aims of the Romantics and the Modernists who wanted to
use culture to transform society, but just as the dreams of the
modernist avant-gardes were dismissed as just one more
grand narrative, so too did rock's pre-eminent position
within popular music decline in the 1980s. Ultimately, what
propels Gray's critique of the NET is a concern about the
status and purpose of Culture (and, therefore, rock) in contemporary society. Gray laments the 'co-option of real music
by advertising',[37] Dylan's 'decay into celebrity'[38] and criticises Dylan for referring to his performances as 'a show'.
Gray retorts:

> Dylan seemed comfortable with the idea that what he did
> in live performance was a 'show'. . . . It could be that for
> those who grew up in the Reagan-Thatcher years, it *is* all

showbiz, just as, for instance, being a student is routinely just a career move now. But it wasn't always so, and there was a very long period in which a Dylan live performance might have been an event, might even have been a concert but was never merely a 'show'.[39]

He's right, of course; there was a time when Dylan shows meant more than they do today. But to believe, thirty years later, that they *should* be more than a show would almost be quite sweet were it not for the fact such naive idealism is used as the basis of a withering critique of Dylan's later work.

Whether we like it or not, we have to see the emergence of the NET in the context of the death of rock's metanarrative. Dylan's association with the earnest ideals of rock rather than its more pleasurable excesses made his position in the eighties tenuous. The NET began as a conscious attempt by Dylan to reposition his music, to get people to see it not as an attempt to change the world but merely as an attempt to move an audience (something he's actually been arguing since the sixties). To understand that songs are songs, and that they can't change the world even if we once thought they could. Those concerned with authenticity and artistic development should be relieved that Dylan found a rewarding way to achieve these more modest ambitions without, as did so many other performers, substituting spectacle for engagement.

THE NET AND DYLAN'S STAR-IMAGE

Gray is not alone in equating the declining significance of rock's ideals with personal failure: Mike Marqusee, for example, equates the lessening of Dylan's ties with sixties radicalism as an 'artistic decline'.[40] These kinds of criticism illustrate that Dylan has not been able to cast off all aspects of his old star-image and his associations with sixties idealism. Over time, however, I think that the NET has been relatively successful in redefining Dylan's star-image. In particular, the NET has repositioned Dylan as a performer rather than a songwriter, characterising him as a modern-day troubadour. Driven both by Dylan's distinctive aims and wider demographic trends, a new audience has developed for his shows. I would argue that the critical and commercial success he has achieved since 1997 would not have been possible without this realignment.

This repositioning was a slow process, however. Early reviews were critical of Dylan playing 'obscure' songs and of his playing familiar songs in an unfamiliar manner. Generally, however, the strength of the performances began to be noticed and the shows of the early NET gained good reviews. These strong reviews were facilitated in 1989 by the release of *Oh Mercy*, an album hailed as a return to form. Whatever Dylan himself may feel about being a performer, much of rock stardom is directed by the release of albums. These provide the measuring points for a career, the points to which the narrative of biography and performances are tied. *Oh Mercy* painted a favourable impression with critics and this is reflected in an acceptance of Dylan's new performing style.

In terms of Dylan's reputation, therefore, the critical panning received by *Under The Red Sky* in 1990 marked another turning point. Coupled with this, the departure of G. E. Smith, the driving force of the first NET band, left the NET rudderless. Many fans consider the first half of 1991 to be the most painful part of the NET, when a Dylan who was clearly drinking heavily led an under-rehearsed, amateurish band, around Europe. The early nineties is a period in which Dylan's star-status became emaciated. The NET was viewed as the last refuge of a sometimes inspiring, but more often atrocious, performer who could no longer write songs and refused to retire with dignity. To many, he became a laughing stock, a running joke.* The albums he released during this period strengthened the impression of someone with nothing to say. He released two albums of traditional songs featuring just his voice, guitar and harmonica (*Good As I Been To You* in 1992, and *World Gone Wrong* in 1993). The third album released during this period was for *MTV Unplugged* (1995). It is an album unloved by critics and fans alike, deemed to be poor performances of 'safe' songs.

What comes across most from the reviews of the time, however, is a resignation to Dylan's continuing irrelevance. What is noticeable is not whether albums and shows garnered good or bad reviews but simply how much they were ignored: *World Gone Wrong* recorded his worst ever chart position, 70, and the logic of the NET made Dylan shows much less of a media event. In the early 1990s, Dylan simply dropped off the critical map. He later claimed that it was this period that enabled him to transform his stardom, to shape his career as he intended:

In the early '90s, the media lost track of me, and that was the best thing that could happen. It was crucial, because you can't achieve greatness under media scrutiny. You're never allowed to be less than your legend. When the media picked up on me again five or six years later, I'd fully developed into the performer I needed to be and was in a

* Although Dylan's reputation has recovered since 1997, I do think that this idea of inconsistency and extremes – sometimes breathtakingly good, sometimes breathtakingly awful – is still a significant part of Dylan's star-image, particularly for people with only a passing interest in music.

position to go any which way I wanted. The media will never catch up again. Once they let you go, they cannot get you back. It's metaphysical. And it's not good enough to retreat. You have to be considered irrelevant. (Edna Gunderson interview, 2004)

Dylan's 'relevance' returned in 1997, sparked by an event that not even the performer himself could have predicted.

Snapshot: The soul of previous times

The NET suffered a temporary hiatus in May 1997 when Dylan was hospitalised due to an attack of pericarditis (an inflammation of the sac around the heart, brought on by an infection called histoplasmosis). It is unlikely that Dylan's life was ever in serious danger, but this was not known at the time and Dylan's media profile was suddenly raised as stories of his impending demise ran on TV and in the press. He was released from hospital in June and issued a press statement that included the immortal 'I really thought I'd be seeing Elvis soon'. He returned to the stage in August, looking considerably frailer. Within a month, however, he was playing in front of 300,000 people, including the Pope, at the World Eucharist Congress.

In September 1997, Dylan released *Time Out Of Mind*, his first album of original material in seven years. It received greater critical acclaim than anything Dylan had produced in the last twenty years and marks the start of a remarkable upturn in Dylan's reputation. He won three Grammies for *Time Out Of Mind*, and the last ten years have seen Dylan feted by awards bodies, universities and rock critics. In 2000, he won an Oscar for the song 'Things Have Changed', recorded for the movie *The Wonder Boys*. His next album, 2001's *"Love And Theft"* received universally good reviews. In 2003, Dylan wrote and starred in *Masked and Anonymous*, a movie about an old rock star bailed from prison to play a benefit concert. He released the first volume of an autobiography, *Chronicles*, in 2004 and, in 2005, featured in *No Direction Home*, a 4-hour documentary on his early career directed by Martin Scorsese. Critics used these latter two releases as an opportunity to effuse about just how extraordinary Dylan was. In 2006, Dylan began a new career as a DJ, hosting *Theme Time Radio Hour* on XM satellite radio station, playing an eclectic mix of songs. He also released a new album, *Modern Times*, which was once more well received. This album has proved one of Dylan's best-sellers, giving him his first number one album for thirty years. Through all of these years, the NET continued and is now nearing 2,000 shows.

Albums and major events

May 1997	Dylan is hospitalised with chest pains
August 1997	World Eucharist Congress
September 1997	*Time Out Of Mind*
December 1997	Awarded a Kennedy Center Honors Lifetime Achievement Award
January 1998	Still looking frail, Dylan performs at the Grammy Awards ceremony and wins three awards
February 2000	*Wonder Boys* soundtrack (various artists)
May 2000	Wins the Polar Music prize
January 2001	Wins Golden Globe Award for 'Things Have Changed'
March 2001	Wins Oscar for 'Things Have Changed'
September 2001	*"Love And Theft"*
July 2003	*Masked and Anonymous* (film)
September 2004	*Chronicles Volume 1*
September 2005	*No Direction Home* (documentary)
May 2006	*Theme Time Radio Hour* begins
August 2006	*Modern Times*

8

NEVER ENDING STARDOM: DYLAN AFTER *TIME OUT OF MIND*

1997 was one of the most important years of Dylan's career. Two things occured which, together, fundamentally altered the meaning of Dylan's stardom. These were his period in hospital and the release of *Time Out Of Mind*. I said in chapter 2 that although literary critics may argue against the biographical interpretation of songs, stardom is in fact a key way in which songs are given meaning and that, while stardom and biography are intertwined, stardom does not depend upon biographical accuracy. Nowhere is this more apparent than in the release of this album. In 'reality' Dylan's ill health and *Time Out Of Mind* have little to do with each other – the songs were written in late 1996 and recorded in January and February 1997, while Dylan was not laid low until May. In terms of stardom, however, the two things are fundamentally connected. The illness created an understanding of Dylan, a context, in which these songs were received and interpreted. Once released, the songs on the album reinforced that public impression.

Time Out Of Mind was a universally lauded album. Conceivably, it received better reviews than any album Dylan has ever released. My argument is that these excellent reviews are not because of the strength of the songwriting. Nor were they merely an expression of relief that he was alive. The key reason for the success of *Time Out Of Mind* is that the album offers a consistent and coherent sound that was in harmony with Dylan's contemporary star-image. This occurs primarily through the voice, but it is also present in the sound of the album (hot and claustrophobic) and in the lyrics. Michael Gray offers a good synthesis of the album's key themes:

> Endless, almost compulsive walking, desolation, lack of a sense of contact with other people; a suffocating sense of the hollowness of everything, and therefore the purposelessness of life; a looking forward to death, alternating with a wish that time was not running out; the conviction that long ago some crucial wrong turning was taken in life, one that meant the loss of true love; the conviction that there is little to say and ever less point to saying it; the exhaustion of feeling, mingled with a passionate sorrow for all this loss.[1]

I want to synthesise these further and explain how three key themes linked to the specific star-image Dylan had throughout the early nineties. The first is the emphasis on constant movement, walking in particular. Many of the songs begin with reference to walking ('I'm walking through streets that are dead'; 'Gonna walk down that dirt road'; 'I'm walking through the summer nights'. . .). As Gray points out, this walking seems almost inescapable or compulsive. This certainly marries with the conception of Dylan created by the NET. Transitoriness, the concept of continually 'moving on', is a key element of rock culture, and Dylan has always been viewed as a restless character. Since the start of the NET, however, that restlessness has been given a very physical image – that of the itinerant troubadour, the wandering hobo, always heading for another joint, staying in a place long enough to play a show and then moving on. Dylan's contemporary image is thus one of continual movement, always moving on to the next gig. In 1997, journalist Alan Jackson wrote of 'a man who exists solely within a spotlight. Someone brought alive again each night on a stage somewhere around the world, but otherwise forever rootless and a willing slave to that never-ending tour'. This image is reinforced through the references to constant, compulsive, walking on *Time Out Of Mind*.

The second key theme of *Time Out Of Mind* is that of having nothing to say. There are repeated references throughout the album to being unable to say the words that would mean something:

> Feel like talking to someone, but I just don't know who
> ('Million Miles')

> Now you can seal up the book and not write any more
> ('Tryin' To Get To Heaven')

> Well I'm tired of talking, tired of trying to explain
> ('Til I Fell In Love With You')

This clearly ties in with the image of nineties Dylan as someone devoted to performing rather than writing. Dylan made repeated statements during this time that 'the world don't need any more songs' and such statements were affirmed in the release of two albums of old songs, *Good As I Been To You* and *World Gone Wrong* (in 2004, he stated that 'if I made music for myself, I would only cover old Charley Patton songs'). However, as already mentioned, many critics and fans were reluctant to relinquish the idea of Dylan as a songwriter and were critical of his turn to performing. There is, therefore, a certain irony that Dylan's argument about the lack of need for new words was only taken seriously by his audience when Dylan makes it in new songs and this illustrates how Dylan can never be entirely successful in transforming his star-image. But, successful or otherwise, the claim in 'Highlands' that 'there's less and less to say' fits neatly with the image of Bob Dylan in the 1990s.

The final key theme of *Time Out Of Mind* is aging and mortality. Throughout the album, there are references to lost youth, to failing bodies, to a falling of metaphorical darkness. This was the theme most clearly picked up by reviewers and is the one most clearly related to his biographical detail. It is here that star-image and album response directly coalesce. The media were quick to draw links between Dylan's spell in hospital and the doom-laden nature of this album. Some drew incorrect conclusions that the illness must have prompted the melancholic album. Others didn't, but even then, some implied that Dylan must somehow have known that something was going to happen. And even those reviews that explicitly highlighted the biographical discrepancy merely served to bring the two things closer together in public consciousness.

The key to *Time Out Of Mind*'s critical acceptance was that it presented a coherent image of a singer that matched with the public conceptualisation of Dylan the star. This can partly be seen in the words – there is a thematic coherence to this album – but by far the most significant element of it is in the voice. Songs acquire their meaning through the voice more than through the semantic meaning of the words. Nowhere is this more apparent than on this album. On *Time Out Of Mind*, Dylan's voice embodies the key themes of the album. It sounds old; very old; way older than Dylan himself and there is no doubt that this voice was shocking to many listeners:

> The sinister rusted-muffler growl he introduced on *Time Out of Mind* . . . shocked the world because it didn't even echo past glories – it was something totally new.[2]

This new voice had begun to make an appearance on *Good As I Been To You*, *World Gone Wrong* and *Unplugged*, but very few people heard these records. *Time Out Of Mind* was one of Dylan's most successful records, becoming his first platinum album since *Slow Train Coming*. Most of those buying the album had not heard Dylan singing since at least *Oh Mercy*, perhaps *Infidels*, maybe even before that. The voice of *Time Out Of Mind* bears no relation to what Bob Dylan's voice was supposed to sound like.*

This is partly because of his age, but there is also no doubt that the NET has had an impact on Dylan's voice (when he recorded this album, he had played 749 NET shows). With inadequate periods for resting his vocal chords, his range had constricted (since 1997 it has condensed even further), the sound was cracked, gnarly, haggard. Reviews of his recent albums have referred to it as 'superbly cracked', a 'scratchy, cigarette-scarred bark', and a 'cruelly muted rasp that sounds as if it must be drawing blood from Dylan's throat'. It is a voice that sounds as old as Methuselah. But the voice is also astonishingly 'present', it has so much texture that one can almost touch it. Williams suggests that listening to *Time Out Of Mind* is like being in the first few rows of a concert[3] and it is the visceral nature of the voice that gives this effect. This

---

* This is despite the fact that Dylan's voice has often been characterised as old before, most notably with regard to his first album, on which it is hard to believe that the singing voice belongs to a 20-year-old.

voice certainly has a grain, a thick, coarse grain with a natural dignity and beauty: the grain of a 400-year-old oak tree, burning with the bark still on.

To my mind, the 'age' of the voice is fundamental to how Dylan's star-image has developed since the release of *Time Out Of Mind* (which I will discuss later). The voice is understood as being able to reveal someone's true personality. As Frith points out, 'we assume that we can hear someone's life in their voice – a life that's there despite and not because of the singer's craft'.[4] Dylan is now conceived of as old, not middle-aged (perhaps more of a problematic label for rock music) – he was 49 when *Under The Red Sky* was released, he was 56 going on 70 when *Time Out Of Mind* came out. Now, age is not an inherent virtue. It can be interpreted in different ways, for example, as representing senility and decrepitude. In this instance, however, Dylan's age came to stand for wisdom and fortitude. Again, it is the voice that provides this impression – the singer on *Time Out Of Mind* expresses alienation, desolation, a sense of disconnectedness with the world but in a way that asserts the indomitability of the singer's inner character. There is strength in the face of resignation. The singer is able to assert his inner strength not so much in the words he speaks but in the authoritative way they are stated. Dylan 'speaks authentically of having lost any sense of authenticity'.[5] This characteristic, this dignity and defiance in the face of age, is a key feature of the NET, and of Dylan's post-'97 stardom generally.

Since the release of *Time Out Of Mind*, Dylan has been lauded in a way he hasn't been since the 1960s. Between 1997 and 2001 he has been feted with awards: the Dorothy and Lillian Gish Prize; a Kennedy Center Honors Lifetime Achievement Award; three Grammies for *Time Out Of Mind*, including his first major Grammy (album of the year); the Polar Music Prize; a Golden Globe award; and, to his personal delight, an Oscar. He was also nominated for the Nobel prize for literature in each of these years. His work since 1997 – the albums *Time Out Of Mind*, "*Love And Theft*" and *Modern Times*, his autobiography *Chronicles*, and the documentary *No Direction Home* – have received rave reviews. "*Love And Theft*" was the first album in nine years to be given five stars by *Rolling Stone*. His commercial standing has risen too – all three albums made the Top 10 around the globe, while *Modern Times* has given Dylan his first US number one album since 1976.

There is clearly an irony in how, despite Dylan's attempts to reposition himself as a performer rather than a songwriter, it is only with the release of an album of new Dylan songs that he regains critical acclaim. Despite attempting to realign his star-image through the NET, the idea of Dylan as the greatest songwriter of his age is still important. It also illustrates the wider cultural idealisation of originality. This irony doubles back on itself, however, because what Dylan released in 1997 was not 'original' in the conventional sense. Instead, it was a deliberate juxtaposition of earlier sources, a patchwork quilt of lines and images from the blues, folk and pop canon. The opening song title, 'Love Sick', recalls Hank Williams' big hit, 'Lovesick Blues', while the second song, 'Dirt Road Blues', mimics Charley Patton's 'Down The Dirt Road Blues'. 'Smoking a cheap cigar' from 'Standing In The Doorway' is taken from Jimmie Rodgers' 'Waiting For A Train'. The clouds in 'Highlands' are compared to 'sweet chariots that swing down low', and so on and on and on. There are musical quotations too: the melody of 'Make You Feel My Love' is lifted from 'You Belong To Me' while the opening notes of 'Standing In The Doorway' bring to mind Elvis Presley's hit, 'Can't Help Falling In Love'.* This way

---

* Songs already covered and officially released by Dylan!

of composing continued onto later work, on 'Things Have Changed' ('I'm a worried man with a worried mind' echoes many blues songs, while 'Forty Miles Of Bad Road' was a hit for Duane Eddy) and *"Love And Theft"* (the line 'I'll believe I'll dust my broom' (from 'High Water') is the title of a common blues song, while Charley Patton recorded a song called 'High Water Everywhere'; 'I got love for you, and it's all in vain' from 'Tweedle Dee and Tweedle Dum' replicates Robert Johnson's 'Love In Vain'. The final line of 'Sugar Baby', 'Look up, look up – seek your Maker – 'fore Gabriel blows his horn' is actually from Frank Sinatra's 'The Lonesome Road'). There was a bit of a media furore when it was discovered that Dylan had borrowed several lines from a Japanese novel, *Confessions of a Yakuza*, by Junichi Saga, without attribution.* This use of quotation has been discussed by many commentators. It is often discussed as undermining conventional ideas of authorship.[6] The use of quotations from other songs also serves to reinforce the central theme of *Time Out Of Mind* that there is less and less to say, as well as reiterating an earlier Dylan sentiment that 'It's all been done before / It's all been written in the book' ('Too Much Of Nothing').** In this chapter, however, I want to approach the issue from a slightly different angle;

---

* And a similar rumpus when several lines from *Modern Times* (2006) were sourced back to the American Civil War poet, Henry Timrod. *Modern Times*, released after this chapter was first written, continues the trend of making use of explicit quotations: 'Rollin' and Tumblin'' is a rewrite of Muddy Waters' song of the same name while 'The Levee's Gonna Break' harks back to Memphis Minnie's 'When The Levee Breaks'. Familiar lyrical lines float through all of the songs, such as 'I sleep in the kitchen with my feet in the hall', 'Put on your cat clothes' and 'Blues this morning fallin' down like hail'.

** 'All the words have been used; it's just how we put them together. And even that – though we might think we've come up with something super, fantastic, I think if you look in the right place you'll find someone else has done it' (Bill Flanagan interview, 1985).

to consider how the use of quotations affects the musical experience of time, how they link Dylan to 'tradition', and how these dual processes affect Dylan's star-image. My view is that it is in the relationship between time and tradition that we can find the explanation for Dylan's remarkable resurgence in status.

'SITTIN' ON MY WATCH':
THE MUSICAL EXPERIENCE OF TIME

The most interesting comment I have read about *Time Out Of Mind* was in an email to Paul Williams that he published in his 2005 book. It states that 'the album is also like a website full of hypertext links to the history of blues and folk, with lots of references all the way'.[7] The reason I find it interesting is that it raises issues about the role that 'technology', in its broadest sense, affects how we experience a particular work. To put it another way, how the nature of the work (what kind of 'vessel' it is) rather than just its content (what it says) affects how we experience the work.* The emergence of hypertext (HTML), with those hyperlinks so familiar to us on the world wide web will, it has been argued, change the nature of reading. When reading a novel, the reader's progress is structured by the nature of the work – you read progressively, from the beginning to the end. This imposes a sense of linearity on the act of reading –

---

* For example, the emergence of the printed music score changed perceptions of what 'music' was and, therefore, what individual works of music could mean. As composition could now be separated from performance, it generated a new music-maker, a 'composer'. This created a specialisation of knowledge that not only produced a hierarchy of production (composers are assumed to be more talented than instrumentalists) but also a hierarchy of consumption (listening to classical music 'properly' requires knowledge of compositional techniques) (Frith, 2001:29–30).

the author lays down the tracks and you follow them. In this sense, the author is in control of the pace of your experience – slowing you down for a couple of chapters to build suspense, quickening the pace at times of drama. This linearity is structured by the nature of the novel itself – there's no other way to read it; you can't read pages randomly. The emergence of HTML, however, has created alternative ways of reading. Rather than being forced to read from beginning to end, the reader can link to something else, to a digression or even to a different webpage. They may never reach the end of the article at all, instead following a series of links to end up at something completely different. This diminishes the power of the author to guide us, and increases the reader's control over the reading experience. The key issue for my purpose, however, is a decline in the linearity of reading and its replacement by a more, say, expansive kind of reading, one that has more spatial dimensions. What I am interested in is how these changed practices affect our experience of time. With a novel, the author can attempt to impose a set time on how we experience the created universe in the fiction, giving us information when we need it, fast-forwarding a few months or spending many chapters on one day. Simplifying this quite a lot, how time unfolds within a novel is determined by the author. What the author cannot do, however, is structure how this experience of 'reading time' matches our experience of real time. Some people read faster than others; you may choose to read an entire novel in a day, or one chapter each night before sleep, and so on. The reader has the power to determine the time in which they experience the novel. This is not the same as our experience of music. Although the pause and shuffle buttons offer some control to the listener, 'music lives in time, unfolds in time', it 'imposes[s] a common time' on the listener.[8] You cannot 'listen quicker' – forcing the music to play a bit faster makes it sound funny. When listening to a piece of music, you are in the hands of the composer and/or performer.

Our *experience* of time in music, however, is not necessarily the same as the 'actual' time it takes a piece of music to unfold. Our experience of musical time affects our experience of real time. Philip Tagg, for example, has shown that we tend to think that fast songs last for a shorter time than they actually do, while slow songs seem to last longer.[9] The relationship between musical experience and time has been a central preoccupation of modernist and postmodernist classical composers. It has also been a central concern of Bob Dylan. Throughout his career, a key theme of his work has been the indeterminacy of experienced time. More specifically, Dylan has made repeated comments of his desire for songs to 'stop time'. In 1985, he said that 'for a moment they stop time. Songs are supposed to be heroic enough to give the illusion of stopping time' (Bill Flanagan interview). So, how can this apparent paradox – using something that intrinsically unfolds within time to provide the illusion that time has stopped – be achieved? The solution is offered by Frith, who asks 'how *long* is the present? More specifically, can music extend this? The answer, not so peculiar after all, is that if "the present" is actually defined by a quality of *attention*, then music does indeed expand the moment, by framing it. And it is precisely this "time attention" which defines musical pleasure.'[10]

The composer, songwriter or performer must develop strategies for framing the moment that enable the listener to place time out of mind. Dylan has adopted a couple of strategies in this regard. In the mid-seventies, particularly on *Blood On The Tracks* and in *Renaldo And Clara*, Dylan sought to unify past and future into an intensified present. Dylan said of 'Tangled Up In Blue':

I was trying to be somebody in present time while conjuring up a lot of past images . . . What I was trying to do had nothing to do with the characters or what was going on. I was trying to do something that I don't know if I was prepared to do. I wanted to defy time, so that the story took place in the present and the past at the same time. (Bill Flanagan interview, 1985)

In the same interview, he also said that 'Idiot Wind' 'was just the concept of putting in images that defy time – yesterday, today and tomorrow. I wanted to make them all connect in some kind of strange way.' This is a strategy that structures 'You're Gonna Make Me Lonesome When You Go', a song that simultaneously looks backwards to before the relationship and projects forwards to the effect of parting as a way of intensifying the pleasure of the present. The extensive use of quotations from other sources on his later albums is another way that Dylan attempts the same kind of process: the use of traditional sources incorporates the past into the present, while the continuity of the tradition ensured by Dylan's use of these works points to the certain future of this tradition. As Dylan sings on 'Bye And Bye', 'The future for me is already a thing of the past'. This repeats a theme from his sleeve notes to *World Gone Wrong*, in which he said the songs showed you a way of 'learning to go forward by turning back the clock', which itself recalls the exclamation on the sleeve of *Planet Waves* that 'the ole days are gone / forever and the new ones aint far behind'.

Dylan's singing style also plays around with the idea of time. His singing can reflect the experience of time described in the lyrics, but also can itself affect the listener's experience of time and thus intensify the meaning of the words being uttered. Dylan is a master of using his voice to stretch time, almost to the point of uncoupling the vocal from the musical structure to which it is tied. This is what Allen Ginsberg referred to (on the sleevenotes to *Desire*) as Dylan's 'long-vowelled voice'. I shall offer three brief examples. Firstly, on 'Idiot Wind', when he sings 'I waited for you on the running boards while the springtime turned slowly into autumn', that 'sl-o-o-o-w-w-ly' is stretched out so long as to contain the memory of the entire season as he waits for future to become past. Secondly, on 'Solid Rock' the pause in the opening line 'I'm hanging on . . . to a solid rock' manages to contain all of the tension of 'hanging on', time passing slowly as you fear falling, as well as the future of refuge and relief because of the nature of what the singer is hanging on to. Past danger and future salvation are united in the vocal pause. Finally, on 'Not Dark Yet', he sings 'I can't even remember what it was I came here to get away from'. Dylan's vocal delivery is so drawn out on this long line that you can almost forget what the start of it was by the time you reach the end, the earlier words lost in time.

So, in lyrics and vocals, there are times when Dylan is able to grasp past and future in the present moment. Alfred Schutz argues that this is a necessary feature of musical composition: 'The composer, by the specific means of his art, has arranged it in such a way that the consciousness of the beholder is led to refer what he actually hears to what he anticipates will follow and also to what he has just been hearing and what he has heard ever since this piece of music began.'[11] Schutz refers to this as 'inner time'. While Dylan has attempted to achieve this lyrically, I·do not think it is the most appropriate way to understand how we experience time in Dylan's music. An alternative way of understanding the experience of musical time is what Kramer calls 'moment time'. In moment time, the trick is to obliterate past and future so that the listener is only able to focus on the immediate moment. The present moment is expanded to fill our entire perception. Kramer: 'emphasizes the importance in music of the "now," an experience of the *continuous* present. Moment time, that is to say, makes memory impossible (or, the same thing, irrelevant): it does not offer rehearsals of what is to come or rehearings of what has been . . .'[12]

The key to achieving moment time is repetition as it reduces the listener's conception of an unfolding linear 'narrative'. This, of course, is an inherent paradox, for it means that, as Kramer says, 'moment time uses the linearity of listening to destroy the linearity of time'.[13] Kramer describes his experience of a 'vastly extended present' when listening to Erik Satie's *Vexations* (1893). The piece consists of four eight-bar phrases repeated 840 times in succession, during which time got

> slower and slower, threatening to stop. But then I found myself moving into a different listening mode. I was entering the vertical time of the piece. My present expanded, as I forgot about the music's past and future. I was no longer bored. And I was no longer frustrated because I had given up expecting. I had left behind my habits of teleological listening. I found myself fascinated with what I was hearing . . . True, my attention did wander and return, but during the periods of attending I found the composition to hold great interest. I became incredibly sensitive to even the smallest performance nuance, to an extent impossible when confronting the high information content of traditional music.[14]

Dylan works in a popular music rather than high culture and such a test of stamina would prove too much for most of Dylan's audience. There are, however, certainly some similarities between Satie's proto-minimalism and Dylan's music. This is most notable in Dylan's live performances but, on occasion, he has successfully attained 'moment time' on record. Probably the most successful instance is 'Highlands', of which Dylan said that it has 'got that hypnotism that sounds like it would go on forever. And that's the point. It can go on forever' (Edna Gunderson interview, 1997). The key to 'Highlands' is that nothing changes. The little country-blues riff continues unabated throughout the whole song, there is no bridge, no middle eight, nothing except verse after verse. The music offers no possibility of resolution, no sense of an ending. In this way it is similar to 'Sad Eyed Lady Of The Lowlands' and it is notable that both songs utilise a fade-out. This is not uncommon, of course, but it gives the impression of the band playing the song forever, with the listener merely closing the door to the recording studio (songs in live performance, by contrast, have to reach a definite conclusion). In 'Sad Eyed Lady Of The Lowlands', however, the introduction of the harmonica signifies that the end of the song is near, implying that the singer has said all he needs to say. 'Highlands' offers no signal that things might change. The song itself is about nothing happening ('Woke up this morning and I looked at the same old page'; 'Every day is the same thing out the door') and even when something does happen (he meets a waitress) the singer sings it in a way that shows the event as utterly meaningless (reminiscent of 'Clothes Line Saga' from *The Basement Tapes*). The 'message' of this song, in lyrics, vocals and music, is that everyday is the same, and everyday nothing happens. The length of the song – 17 minutes, 20 verses, 100 lines – reiterates the point with interest. But the song is far from boring. All I can do here, like Kramer, is record personal experience. I was listening to the song recently, and it seemed like it had been going on *forever*. I looked at the CD display which informed me that the song had been playing for 3 minutes and 42 seconds, approximately two-thirds the length of 'Cold Irons Bound' which had passed in the blink of an eye less than ten minutes earlier.* Time had certainly slowed, but this moment of 'clocking' liberated the song, or me. Suddenly, the repetition, the mundanity, was alleviated. The sound of the voice, rather than the meaning of the words, became more important. Dylan's voice itself offered a kind of solace. It seemed to intone that the relentless sameness didn't matter, that things won't change, but don't worry, things would be alright if you just roll with the absurdities. From this moment on the song intensified as the sound became almost mantra-like. The remaining thirteen and a bit minutes passed far quicker than the first four.

Despite this particular instance being achieved on record, it is Dylan's performances on stage that offer the clearest example of Dylan working to achieve moment time. One example is the acoustic portions of the 1966 tour, the key to which is the harmonica solos. The solos in 1966 go on forever, or at least seem like they do. They are disproportionate to the length of time taken to enunciate the lyrics (even though there are many times in 1966 when the singing is incredibly drawn out, slowing down time). There are also times when Dylan finds two or three notes on the harp, bending them, stretching them, repeating them over and over. All this has the effect of stopping time, of bringing the listener to a point where there is no conception of the start of this solo and no expectation of its end. It's as if you're waiting for a train that doesn't arrive: you wait and wait and it doesn't arrive, and then you've missed the meeting you

---

* It is important to recognise the influence that technology has on our experience of musical time. The advent of CD technology has enabled us to become more aware of how we experience time and has, therefore, changed our experience of music.

were going to anyway and you enter a new time zone in which it doesn't matter any more.*

The other era in which Dylan has been most successful in 'stopping time' is on the NET. The small, repeated phrase, like a minimalist tape loop, is a feature of all aspects of Dylan's NET performances – vocals, harmonica and guitar. Dylan's guitar playing has been criticised in recent years – Heylin describes it as 'like an autistic child with a blade of grass, playing the same riff until the neck snapped'.[15] Such comments illustrate the audience demands placed on Dylan by working in a different cultural sphere than Satie (Heylin probably wouldn't appreciate *Pages mystiques*) but they also show a lack of appreciation of what Dylan is trying to achieve:

> [My guitar playing is] not incidental stuff and it's not inconsequential. I don't play lead guitar, like you have probably heard a lot of people say. I don't see that. What I do is restructure a song and my guitar is more or less like my vocal style. (Edna Gunderson interview, 1997)**

Dylan does not 'stop time' in everything he does on the NET, but the times when he becomes most engaged in his performances owe something to repetition and relate to this idea of stopping time: picking up on a particular rhythmic phrase which he repeats, or transfers into the next line of the song. This is something he works at with his voice, guitar and harmonica. Again, I will try to record my personal experience of how this works. At a recent show I attended, Dylan got into a particular groove with his vocal delivery on

---

* I am in debt to Dai Griffiths for offering this analogy to me.
** Since 2002, Dylan has stopped playing guitar on stage – it has been suggested that arthritis makes it impossible for him to play regularly. He now plays piano or keyboards, which I think have proved far less successful in his attempts to stop time.

'All Along The Watchtower'. Rather than singing each line as a line, Dylan broke each line down into duo-syllabic chunks, with the rhyming word at the end left to hang. The pause between the mini-lines was relatively short (the gap between 'All a' and 'long the' was roughly the amount of time to say 'long') but each gap distinctly punctuated each line. Dylan added small words to the initial text in order to keep the rhythmic couplets scanning (detailed below). The third verse of the song was, therefore, sung roughly like this:

All a
Long the
Watchtower   (sung as two syllables, as 'watchtowr')
Princes
Kept the
View

All the   ('while' is dropped)
Women
Came and
Went the   ('the' is added)
Barefoot
Servants
Too

Outside
In the
Distance
Know a   (either a 'you' is dropped or a 'know' is
                   added – depending on whether he is
                   covering his or Hendrix's version!)
Wildcat   (he can't quite cram this into two
                   syllables – it's more 'wy-uld-cat' –
                   instead it is sung at a higher pitch than
                   previous lines)

| Did a | ('a' added) |
| Growl | |

Two riders	(sung as three distinct syllables, at the
	same pitch as 'wildcat')
Were a	
pproaching	
And the	('and' is added)
Wind be	
gan to	
Howl.	

What does this achieve? It breaks the linear narrative of the story and, therefore, of our experience of the music. It becomes impossible to focus on these four lines as lines, as telling any particular story. Rather than hearing the complete line, the presentation forces you to concentrate on the two syllables you are hearing at that moment. It becomes virtually impossible to maintain an awareness of even the previous line. This means that particular elements of the words may come to the forefront (I had never noticed the little 'outside-in' phrase at the start of the verse's third line, for example) and new internal rhymes are created (All a / long the). The single syllable rhymes gain intensity from their positioning, and are given particular emphasis by Dylan – growl and howl were elongated to cover the space given to two syllables and a pause in the other lines. All in all, experiencing the *sound* of the words becomes important. This is something I have already discussed in relation to the 'meaning' of the words, but it also has an effect on the experience of time. Because the linear narrative of the words has been broken (you cannot concentrate on what the words are saying), the moment of hearing the little phrase becomes the focus of your concentration, creating an instance of 'moment time'.

DYLAN AND MUSICAL TRADITION

Discussing the NET in the last chapter, I emphasised what we might want to call the experience of moment time for the NET's audience. Within NET consciousness, what matters is the intensity of experiencing the performance in front of you and not any other possible performances, 'original recorded versions' or otherwise. There is, however, another element to NET consciousness that relates to the 'inner time' described by Schutz. If NET consciousness is successful in reducing recording consciousness, then the listener is aware that the performance they see in front of them is part of a wider chain of performances from the past and into the future. A particular performance of a song is always heard within the context of all the other performances of that song, already heard and still-to-hear; phrasing is semi-consciously 'compared' to previous phrasing; motifs are subconsciously united to earlier versions. Each individual performance straddles the line of sameness and difference so that: 'You're always hearing tonight's performance as, in some sense, a variation on a theme you already know. The April '93 "Mr Tambourine Man" is a great performance in itself, but a part, a very large part of its pleasure lies in its variation from every other performance of "Mr Tambourine Man" you've ever heard.'[16] Scobie suggests that the effect of this is to 'de-emphasize the linear progression of the song and to see its structure more in spatial terms, as if all the images were laid out alongside each other in a continuous present tense'.[17] This shift from linearity to spatial awareness is similar to the effect that hyperlinks have on written texts and is characteristic of postmodern culture generally.[18]

One dimension of this spatiality concerns how Dylan's stardom has become wedded to an idea of 'tradition'. My argument is that in the latter part of his career (since the

start of the NET but much more noticeably since 1997)
Dylan has become much more firmly associated with a conception of traditionality, a traditionality which is considered
inherently virtuous. I am not saying that Dylan's work has
dramatically changed in its relationship to 'tradition' in the
last few years – it has a bit, but there are also many continuities with his earlier work. What matters, however, is not
textual or biographical accuracy but how these issues are
understood and presented. This also explains why I am using
the label 'tradition' uncritically in this chapter. The notion
means a lot of different things and, invariably, traditions are
more complex than they first seem. I do not need to interro-
gate the concept here. People have an assumption of what
'tradition' means, and it is this intuitive or impressionistic
understanding of the concept that is significant when considering how it overlaps with Dylan's stardom. I am, therefore, keeping the notion of 'tradition' deliberately vague. It
is not necessary to be more specific for the current project.
This is not about 'Dylan and the folk tradition' or 'Dylan
and the blues tradition' but, rather, how Dylan has come to
stand for and represent the maintenance of a link with the
past, of the importance of a tie with an idealised tradition for
reclaiming the authenticity of the present. For a variety of
reasons, this has resulted in a dramatic intensification of
Dylan's status in recent years and, I would argue, this contemporary star-image is characterised by an association with
an ineffable tradition rather than, as previously, with an ideal
of 'the sixties'.

A variety of wider factors are significant in creating a context in which this realignment of Dylan's star-image can
occur. The strength of the work alone is not sufficient – I
would argue that if Dylan had released *Time Out Of Mind* in
1992 it would not have resulted in such a radical reconceptualisation of Dylan (quite apart from the fact that he couldn't

have released *Time Out Of Mind* in 1992 because his voice wouldn't have been the same). One notable event in this reframing was the reissuing of Harry Smith's *Anthology of American Folk Music* in 1997. In an interesting article, Katherine Skinner discusses the change in status of the *Anthology* since its original release.[19] Skinner argues that when initially released in 1952, the *Anthology* was actually fairly inconsequential. In 1953, it sold only 50 copies, 45 of which were to university and college libraries. Because of a copyright dispute, the *Anthology* was withdrawn from sale from late 1953 until at least 1956 and its average annual US sales between 1959 and 1978 was a mere 74 copies. There were very few reviews or references to the *Anthology* in the popular press – *Sing Out!* did not publish a full article on it until 1969 – and infrequent references to it in scholarly journals.[20] On its reissue in 1997, however, the *Anthology* was considered a canonical work and a formative influence on the folk revival of the fifties and sixties. 'According to critical reviews that accompanied its reissue, [the *Anthology*] is the cornerstone upon which much contemporary American music rests.'[21] David Fricke, in *Rolling Stone*, stated that 'today, it is impossible to overstate the historic worth, socio-cultural impact and undiminished vitality of the music in this set'.[22] Skinner's intention, like mine, is not to argue that the latter reviews were simply wrong but, rather, to try to explain the reasons for the change in the *Anthology*'s status. These reasons are not to be found in the text themselves but instead are in the wider social practices of 'cultural valorisa-tion'. Even if you think that the *Anthology* has always been *that* good and *that* influential, why is it that its quality and value only become recognised at this particular time? Simi-larly for Bob Dylan. Dylan's work has always – always! – been deeply embedded within an awareness of the traditions of American (and, indeed, British) song, even during the radical mid-sixties. So why is it at this moment – 1997 – that it suddenly becomes the dominant element of his star-image?

Skinner's explanation for the reception of the *Anthology*'s reissue centres on the repositioning of 'folk music' within American popular music more generally. In particular, she suggests that by the 1990s the academic study of popular music had been institutionalised within the discipline of Cultural Studies and that 'scholars and critics increasingly sought to create a taxonomy of the roots of popular music forms'.[23] These roots included an 'expanded definition of "folk" or "roots" music' that incorporated the commercial recordings of the 1920s and 1930s that were contained on the *Anthology*. At roughly the same time, there emerged a new popular interest in traditional-type music, labelled as a new genre, 'Americana'. These provided a new context for the *Anthology*. Finally, Skinner argues that the fact that the Anthology was among the first reissued box sets of these kind of recordings enabled it to represent, to stand for, a much larger body of music.[24] Skinner's points are reasonably convincing. There are, however, aspects of the music industry that are not sufficiently considered, notably how a combination of cheap, digital storage opportunities in the CD era and the expiration of copyright in sound recordings and songs resulted in an explosion of traditional music being made available, very cheaply in many instances. This would have increased general awareness of the foundational role that these early recordings made to popular music both at a scholarly and popular level (for example, weekly magazines with free CDs on the history of the blues, or cheap roots CDs available in petrol stations). We also need to consider the wider social context of the interest in traditionality. David Boyle argues that there has been an upsurge in the cherishing of notions of the 'authentic' as people become increasingly concerned about artificiality and the endangering of what they consider real.[25] This can be seen in, for example, a rising interest in eco issues such as organic food or the desire for authentic rather than touristy holiday experiences.

The event that links the *Anthology*'s re-release with Dylan's 1997 re-canonisation is the publication of Greil Marcus' book *Invisible Republic*. The book is ostensibly about *The Basement Tapes*, the songs recorded in Woodstock by Dylan and The Band in 1967 (not just the officially released recordings but the 106 songs available on bootleg). It isn't wholly about Dylan, however, but instead offers a broad, impressionistic sweep across the realm of 'American music'. In particular, it unites the *Anthology* with *The Basement Tapes* as collections of recordings that document 'the old weird America'. The book was criticised by many Dylan fans as being unreadable. This criticism normally translates as 'it's not all about Dylan', but it was repeated in a range of media. The criticism of the book tends to come from the fact that it is not 'biographical' – there is little detail of how these songs were recorded, who dropped in, how Dylan treated his wife, what drugs were taken, who said what to whom, and so on. Instead, Marcus' interest lies in consideration of shared cultural ideals and cultural memory. The book explains how 'Dylan and The Band explored new songs and old, digging deep into their own private mythologies and the collective unconscious of North America to mine a fresh-minted folklore, simultaneously ancient and modern'.[26]

The eclecticism of *Invisible Republic* can be a hindrance (it is difficult to follow if you are unfamiliar with the basement recordings and the *Anthology*), but it offers a thoughtful consideration of popular music that does not rely on high cultural ideals without merely descending into uncritical populism. And, like *The Basement Tapes* themselves, its influence was felt beyond merely those who read it. The publication of the book was a significant event in the non-music press (it received a large number of commentary articles and reviews in the British serious press, for example). Given its coverage in the broader media, it played a significant role not only in the canonisation of the *Anthology* but also in the subtle reconceptualisation of Dylan as a contemporary exponent of an ancient tradition. The logic of the NET had managed to chip away some of Dylan's star meaning, but it was not total (the release of two albums of traditional songs in 1992 and 1993 had not effected this reconceptualisation, for example). It seems that the confluence of a range of factors – CD reissues, the reconceptualisation of roots music, the continuation of the NET, Marcus' book, Dylan's health scare – came together at a particular historical moment that was finding authenticity in organic, pre-modern entities. None of this would have mattered, however, were it not for the release of *Time Out Of Mind*. I have already discussed some of the ways that the album reflected and reinforced Dylan's star-image, but I want now to specifically discuss the way that the use of quotations, on this album and subsequent work, has helped to embed Dylan within this idea of tradition.

Dylan's album titles often relate to the overall theme of the music, but there are few that have the manifesto-like quality of *Time Out Of Mind* and "*Love And Theft*". *Time Out Of Mind* makes a clear reference to the idea of a tradition; the phrase is applied to something that has been done for so long that its origin can no longer be recalled, beyond not just a living memory but beyond a shared, cultural memory. "*Love And Theft*" is also an extremely evocative title, explicitly drawing attention to itself as an opening statement of intent. The quotation marks surrounding the words highlight that the title itself is taken from elsewhere.*

---

* In this instance from an academic book on blackface minstrelsy written by Eric Lott in 1993. There are certainly links with minstrelsy on the

The use of quotations on *Time Out Of Mind* and *"Love And Theft"* is the clearest way that Dylan draws attention to his relation to tradition. What matters is not that there are lines from other sources within these 'original' songs. This is something that Dylan has always done (for example, the line 'railroad men drink up your blood like wine' (from 'Stuck Inside Of Mobile With The Memphis Blues Again') is lifted from Bacsom Lumsford's 'I Wish I Was A Mole In The Ground', a 1928 song on Harry Smith's *Anthology*, while 'I don't mind a reasonable amount of trouble' from 'Seeing The Real You At Last' is taken from the film *The Maltese Falcon*, one of a number of lines from Bogart films used on *Empire Burlesque*). The important issue is not Dylan's use of these 'stolen' lines; what matters on *Time Out Of Mind* and *"Love And Theft"* is his explicit drawing attention to their use. These are not just borrowed lines, they are deliberate quotations. Many of the lines used on *Time Out Of Mind* are so obvious, from such common stock, that they are clearly there to be recognised by the listener. Most people interested enough in popular music to be interested in Dylan will pick up on references to 'That's Alright Mama' (Arthur Cudrup and Elvis Presley) and 'Rock Me Baby' (Muddy Waters and B. B. King) in 'Million Miles'. Lines like 'I'll eat when I'm hungry, drink when I'm dry'

---

album in its burlesquing of Shakespeare and use of jokes, but whether Dylan has read this book or not doesn't matter. The further intertextual linking of Dylan to another form of traditional music does matter, however, especially given Shank's argument (2002) that the legacy of blackface minstrelsy is the 'structuring principle' of American popular music, providing 'a history of more or less successful attempts at self-recreation', of whites pretending to be blacks, of naifs pretending to be sophisticates (and vice versa). (See also Meisel's argument (1999) that rock music is characterised by a 'crossing over' of cowboy and dandy.) Shank argues that, rather than real political unity, the folk revival's relationship with the civil rights movement is actually one of blackface appropriation. This bears similarities with Grossberg's analysis of the emergence of rock discussed in chapter 4.

('Standing In The Doorway'), and 'The cuckoo is a pretty bird, she warbles as she flies' ('High Water') come from songs that Dylan performed early in his career ('Moonshiner' and 'The Coo-Coo Bird'). Such blatant borrowing emphasises Dylan's absolute comfort and confidence in his knowledge of traditional music. It is as though he holds the entirety of these traditions in the palm of his hand.

Scobie argues that Dylan's use of quotations on these albums creates an ambivalent relationship to tradition: 'the use of quotations signals Dylan's sense of continuity. . . But at the same time, his use of them as quotations signals his sense of distance from the tradition'.[27] Because of the necessary temporal distance from the tradition from which Dylan borrows (times have changed), there is an ironic distance inherent within the songs and in Dylan's place in the tradition. I understand why Scobie would argue this. Theoretically it may even be correct. I don't think it is appropriate, however, when considering how Dylan is perceived. In this aspect of Dylan's contemporary image there is no space for irony. That voice just doesn't *sound* ironic.* This is clearer with the vocal style on *Time Out Of Mind* and *Modern Times*, but even the much more playful tone of *"Love And Theft"*, does not suggest an ironic relationship to the songs themselves, or to the traditions from which he borrows. It is, rather, the confidence of the singing on *"Love And Theft"* that suggests someone at one with the entire panoply of American popular music, a musical version of Whitman's claim that 'I contain multitudes'.

The second reason that Dylan's relationship to the tradition of American popular song is not ironic is because, in many ways, his position in that tradition is genuine, is

---

* Michael Gray draws a useful comparison between Dylan's voice and Leonard Cohen's later singing style (2000:791).

authentic. 'Dylan, remember, has been out there a very long time. He spent time with the Rev. Gary Davis, and Robert Johnson's rival Son House, and Dock Boggs . . .'[28] Robert Cantwell wrote that in the pre-war folk revival, 'Leadbelly was a living representative of an inaccessible past'.[29] Dylan plays a similar function today. He is the only significant link to the musical culture of the 1930s. Pete Seeger may still be alive, and Joan Baez and Ramblin' Jack Elliott still playing songs but they are on the margins of popular music (and have been since 1964). No one with Dylan's pull, or his central role in popular music, offers that genuine connection to the culture of a bygone era.

In interviews since 1997 (indeed, since before then, but people didn't pay so much attention at the time), Dylan has repeatedly highlighted not just his debt to traditional music but how that traditional music constitutes almost his very being:

> Those old songs are my lexicon and my prayer book. All my beliefs come out of those old songs, literally, anything from 'Let Me Rest On That Peaceful Mountain' to 'Keep On The Sunny Side'. You can find all my philosophy in those old songs. I believe in a God of time and space, but if people ask me about that, my impulse is to point them back toward those songs. I believe in Hank Williams singing 'I Saw The Light'. (Jon Pareles interview, 1997)

Similarly, he claimed that his new songs on *Modern Times* were 'my *genealogy* . . . when I was singing them, they seemed to have an ancient presence' (Jonathon Lethem interview, 2006). I don't think this is ironic (of course, I am structured by Dylan's stardom in how I interpret the statement). What I think I can say to be true is that such statements have not been interpreted as ironic by critics and fans. The use of quotations in his recent albums, and the recent interviews in which he has emphasised traditionality, have affected Dylan's star-image so that he is now thoroughly wedded to a concept of tradition. Dylan is not interpreted as a contemporary songwriter playing around with the signs and signifiers of musical genres (like, say, Beck). Instead he is conceptualised as a living embodiment of the entire tradition of popular song, as evidenced in the following extracts from reviews of "*Love And Theft*":

> "*Love And Theft*" comes on as a musical autobiography that also sounds like a casual, almost accidental, history of the country.

> We are whirled into a maelstrom of voices and perspectives, as though Dylan is a human switchboard, directing the babble of history and culture.

> The only artist alive who can fully embody the living stream of American folk music in all its diverse currents and muddy depths.

Five years after "*Love And Theft*", the reviews of *Modern Times* offered a similar conception of its creator. One reviewer described him as 'America's living, breathing musical unconscious', while another claimed that his use of 'American folk forms . . . doesn't make Dylan less; it makes him more, because he contains all of these songs within himself'. One went even further, asserting that 'Bob Dylan doesn't use the blues any more – he *is* the blues'.

STARDOM, TIMELESSNESS AND IMMORTALITY

In claiming an inherent distance in Dylan's relationship with tradition, Scobie suggests that the phrase 'time out of mind' is double edged because while it suggests continuity (a process existing longer than anyone can remember), it also suggests rupture (the point past which no one can remember). Regarding songs, Scobie suggests that 'the paradoxical effect of a song's existing "time out of mind" is to introduce a point of discontinuity into continuity; the loss of origin, the occluding of source, the becoming-anonymous of the author.'[30] This can clearly be witnessed in traditional music, in which the authenticity of a song is often asserted by a lack of authorial reference point. I also wonder, however, whether it may not be a useful way into considering some of Dylan's own songs too. Clearly, the processes are not *exactly* the same – the fact that these songs can be attributed to a particular author is of great significance to how they, and Dylan, are understood. But we can perhaps draw something of an analogy here; there is some kind of rupture between the performer on stage and the person who wrote the songs. In a sense, the person who wrote the songs is long gone, a myth, part of our cultural memory. The same kind of cultural memory as the blues. To some of us – the new NET audience discussed in the last chapter – that songwriter never existed in our lifetime but exists only in traces of the collective memory that surround us. That songwriter is only as real as Robin Hood, or Beethoven (or, perhaps because of the film footage we have of him in his pomp, as real as John F. Kennedy or Jimi Hendrix). The performer we pay to hear now bears little relation to the guy who supposedly wrote the songs – he doesn't look the same and he certainly doesn't sound the same. The singer may be in front of us, but the songwriter is from another lifetime.

The songs, too, seem to have existed for time out of mind (even the new ones sound old!). They have an apparent time-lessness, not in the old-fashioned sense of 'having stood the test of time', but in the sense that they have been removed from their historical origins, existing in a perpetual present. This is a central strand of the NET and is insufficiently recognised by those who criticise Dylan's 'over-reliance on sixties material'. When, in 1997, Dylan was asked if he thought Johnny Cash would get bored singing the same songs night after night, he instantly dismissed the possibility, replying 'they're just so automatically perpetual. They always existed and they always will exist. Who would get bored singing those?'[31] He has said similar things of his own songs too:

> For me the songs are alive. I don't get bored singing the songs because they have a truth to them. (London press conference, 1997)

> When Joan [Baez] and I sing ['Blowin' In The Wind'], it's like an old folk song to me. It never occurs to me that I'm the person who wrote that. (Neil Hickey interview, 1976)

The reason he feels that his songs have this 'perpetual' quality is because they are rooted in a particular tradition rather than in a particular historical moment:

> There's a lot of clever people around who write songs. My songs, what makes them different is that there's a foundation to them. That's why they're still around, that's why my songs are still being performed. It's not because they're such great songs. . . . they're standing on a strong foundation, and subliminally that's what people are hearing. (Jon Pareles interview, 1997)

> [Songs are] not worth much if they don't have permanence. A lot of [my songs] will last. A lot of them won't. I came to terms with that a long time back. What made my songs different, and still does, is [that] they all came out of the folk

music pantheon, and those songs have lasted. So if my songs were written correctly and eloquently, there's no reason they wouldn't last. (Edna Gunderson interview, 2004)

It is clear to me that one of the purposes of the NET was, if not to stress the timelessness of the songs to his audience, then to at least be in service to that timelessness, to a tradition of which these songs are a part. 'The songs are the star of the show, not me' (Robert Hilburn interview, 2004). In several interviews during the NET, he has reiterated the longevity of the songs. In doing so, however, his aim is not self-aggrandisement but to emphasise the strength of the tradition from which they arise. The NET puts into practice something which Dylan has repeatedly argued throughout his career – that he sings his old songs for their presence and not because of nostalgia. By situating his own songs within a tradition, and thus removing them from the particular historical moment in which they were born, he eliminates the possibility of nostalgia:

> For me, none of the songs I've written has really dated. . . . People say they're 'nostalgia', but I don't know what that means really. *A Tale of Two Cities* was written 100 years ago; is that nostalgia? (Mick Brown interview, 1984)

> I'm always trying to stay right square in the moment. I don't want to get nostalgic or narcissistic as a writer or a person. I think successful people don't dwell in the past. (Robert Hilburn interview, 2004)

This emphasises the relationship between tradition and the experience of time. It seems odd that a 200-year-old song should not be considered a thing of the past but this is because traditions themselves stop time. They have no beginning and will continue forever. The present moment contains all of its past and all of its future. As T. S. Eliot argues:

> Tradition is a matter of much wider significance. It cannot be inherited, and if you want it you must obtain it by great labour. It involves, in the first place, the historical sense . . . not only of the pastness of the past, but of its presence; the historical sense compels a man to write not merely with his own generation in his bones, but with a feeling that the whole of the literature of Europe . . . has a simultaneous existence and composes a simultaneous order. This historical sense, which is a sense of the timeless as well as of the temporal and of the timeless and of the temporal together, is what makes a writer traditional. And it is at the same time what makes a writer most acutely conscious of his place in time, of his contemporaneity.[32]

By containing the past and the future in the present moment, traditions stop time (*Rolling Stone* picked up on this in their review of *Modern Times*, stating that 'Dylan has captured the sound of tradition as an ever-present'). This means that by being 'traditional', an artist is not merely looking back nostalgically but actually existing 'square in the moment'. As I've already discussed, there is also something in the structure of the NET that achieves a similar timelessness. The NET creates a perpetual present, never looking back to the last show, always looking forward to the next. Its past stretches back, if not to a time out of mind, then at least a long way (before some of its audience were born), and it gives the illusion that it will go on forever.

It is worth thinking about the effect of this upon Dylan's stardom. Like musical time, 'star time' also has a chronological dimension – our understanding of a star is never fixed but unfolds in time.[33] Dylan's star-image has conventionally been understood chronologically: the earnest folk singer, the hip ruler of the pop scene, the refined country gentleman, the troubled performer of the *Rolling Thunder Revues*, the Born Again Christian, and so on. My argument is that the structure of the NET, and the way that the NET and the concept of tradition have shaped Dylan's stardom have enabled *Dylan himself*, through his star-image, to become timeless. One of the effects of the NET has been to alter this experience of star time; in effect, to 'stop' star time. In becoming so firmly intertwined with tradition, Dylan's *stardom*, not just Dylan's music, has taken on this element of timelessness. He has become, in a curious way, 'immortal'.

The issue of (im)mortality and reputation is one that has pre-occupied artists since the Romantic era. Dwindling belief in religion meant that death became interpreted as the ultimate end, with no reward in Heaven for earthly achievements. Given they could not rely on the literary market for recognition, Romantic poets thus spent much time considering how they were to be properly appreciated, and a consensus developed that truly great writers would only be appreciated after their deaths (you can imagine how soothing this would be for truly terrible writers too, whose lack of success merely affirmed their own greatness). Indeed, the desire for posthumous glory became one of the primary impulses behind the desire to write as it became understood that 'the function of writing is to achieve – in the sublime and impossible moment of inscription – immortality, posthumous life, life after death'.[34] For the Romantics, it was the criterion of originality that would ensure an artist's survival, with the author 'creating the taste' for his work that only subsequent generations would appreciate. The value placed on the aesthetic radicalism of Dylan's sixties work is one version of this ideology. Another way of achieving 'immortality' through one's work, however, is to become part of a greater tradition. In this case, the author embeds himself in a greater tradition, both subsuming his self to that tradition while at the same time ensuring his continuation through the reproduction of his work within the tradition, which continues eternally. Again, Eliot offers a subtle appreciation of this, suggesting that, contra Romanticism, 'the most individual parts of [an artist's] work may be those in which the dead poets, his ancestors, assert their immortality most vigorously'. This is worth comparing to something Dylan said in 1993, around the time that *World Gone Wrong* was released:

> There was a bunch of us, me included, who got to see all these people close up – people like Son House, Rev Gary Davis and Sleepy John Estes. Just to sit there and be up close and watch them play, you could study what they were doing. Plus a bit of their lives rubbed off on you. Those vibes will carry into you forever, really, so it's like those people, they're still here to me. They're not ghosts of the past or anything. They're continually here. (Gary Hill interview)

A similar process has happened with Dylan, only while he is still alive. He has, in a sense, stepped outside of his own career and become something else, a living monument to the strength of the tradition. The 'brush with death' in 1997 (the second such event of Dylan's career) plays a significant role in this transformation. I have already discussed the effects that death can have upon an individual star-image. Among other things, the death of a star has a tendency to tidy things up a bit, to place a linear emphasis on the narrative of the star's history (which is often quite teleological – all elements of a star's biography are understood to lead to a certain point). Let us for a moment imagine that Bob Dylan had died in 1997. What would have happened? Assuming *Time*

Out Of Mind had been given a posthumous release, then the album would have provided the 'perfect' conclusion to the Bob Dylan story. The NET would have been interpreted as a late-in-life meandering caused by a lack of inspiration and writer's block before, intuitively aware of his impending mortality, he had written one final work of real quality. It would all have been so *neat*.

But, as he sings in 'Cold Irons Bound', 'some things last longer than you think they will'. Once again, he didn't die and whereas in 1966 Dylan suffered from the effects that pseudo-mortality had on his stardom, he benefited in 1997. The events of 1997 provided a finishing point to the linear narrative of Dylan's career. That neatness, that linear packaging that normally occurs after an artist is dead and gone, happens to Dylan in 1997. Even though he doesn't die, Dylan's history stops. He has a history, an important one that gives his current status its gravitas, but now he is not making history but encompassing history. The NET's perpetual present, the timelessness of the songs, the embeddedness within tradition, all work to make Bob Dylan exist outside of history. If you stop time, you cannot exist within time. If you contain all history, you cannot exist within history. That chronological narrative of Dylan's career offered above – where does it go after 'Born Again Bob'? Maybe a 'confused, father-of-rock Bob' for some of the eighties, and then . . . what? Nothing except the perpetual present of the NET. It is this standing outside of history that I am getting at when suggesting that Dylan's star-image is now characterised by a kind of immortality.

This 'immortality' is something that particularly takes hold after 1997; an effect of the change in star-image generated by *Time Out Of Mind* rather than being part of the album itself. It can be seen in the response to the two major releases that followed *Time Out Of Mind*: Greil Marcus suggests 'Things Have

Changed' incorporates Dylan 'inhabit[ing] a fictional construct in which he imagines what it would mean to outlive oneself' while an extremely insightful Robert Christgau reviewed *"Love And Theft"* by saying 'if *Time Out Of Mind* was his death album – it wasn't, but you know how people talk – this is his immortality album'. That 'immortality' comes from his relationship with tradition as another (less insightful) reviewer suggested: 'Realising his own mortality on *Time Out Of Mind*, [Dylan] set out to lose himself in the immortality of music itself.' We can see the same kind of thing in the reviews of *Modern Times*. One reviewer stated that 'even in his youth, [Dylan] could tap the spirits of early American music. The difference now is he seems to have joined them on the other side' while another presented him as 'an emissary from a reinvented yesteryear'.

In an earlier chapter, I discussed how a process of pseudo-mortality in the late sixties had impacted upon Dylan's stardom in the seventies and eighties. Since the early seventies, Dylan's stardom was constrained by the idealised myth of the iconic Dylan of the sixties; his later work always shadowed by the earlier achievements. The ironic thing is that, in 1997, it was the same kind of process that, in some ways, alleviated Dylan's historical burden. The pseudo-*immortality* has enabled Dylan to transcend many of the limitations of his earlier stardom. The classifying and rationalising that happens to stars after death provides a structure that gives all the individual images within that career a finite coherence, a way of understanding all of the particular moments as part of a greater whole. Something similar has happened to Dylan. By stepping outside of his stardom's history, his contemporary stardom is able to hold all of his earlier images in balance. His current persona stands not only as an equal to them all, but as embodying a greater whole.

The 'tradition' that Dylan represents is thus not just that of blues or folk music; it is a wider concept that includes the tradition of Dylan's own history, of 'the sixties', as well. I have already discussed how *Time Out Of Mind* contains many references to traditional songs, but it is notable how many lines on the album echo past *Dylan* songs. The opening words of the album, 'I'm walking . . . ' immediately bring to mind the famous question 'how many roads must a man walk down?', but there are more. 'Tryin' to get to Heaven before they close the door' clearly echoes 'Knockin' On Heaven's Door' while a line from the same song – 'When you think that you've lost everything, you find out you can always lose a little more' – holds within it the spectre of 'Like A Rolling Stone's 'When you ain't got nothing, you got nothing to lose'. The length and position of 'Highlands' draws parallels to 'Sad Eyed Lady Of The Lowlands'. At least one reviewer used a line in 'Highlands' to question whether the album was 'a real Blonde [On Blonde] or a fake'. Stephen Scobie has commented that the vocal pause that follows 'I'm hangin on' in 'Can't Wait' is just waiting for the listener to conclude '. . . to a solid rock'[35] while Paul Williams suggests that the line in the final verse of 'Highlands' ('There's a way to get there') is an 'obviously intentional sequel' to the opening of 'All Along The Watchtower' ('There must be some way out of here').[36] And so on.*

Whether these lines are intentional or not (it seems to me that some of them have to be, though some could be coincidental) is irrelevant. What matters is such references have been grasped that way by their listeners. It has the effect of making Dylan's old songs seem 'traditional', part of the same stock of songs as 'Swing Low, Sweet Chariot' and 'See That My Grave Is Kept Clean'. The contemporary Dylan borrows from the stock of old songs, and those old songs include his own and

---

* It also seems to me that the title and chorus of the follow-up recording, 'Things Have Changed' – 'I used to care, but things have changed' – are a quite calculated reference to 'The Times They Are A-Changin''.

everyone's. At the same time, wider than merely the response to *Time Out Of Mind*, there has been a general re-evaluation of Dylan's older material. In the past there was an emphasis upon the radicalism of Dylan's early work, of aesthetic ruptures, of audience confrontation, of relentless progress. Today, even when discussing that older work, my impression is of a change in emphasis, a shift to considering the traditional elements of Dylan's work, of continuity, of rootedness. In 2006, David Hepworth wrote: 'In an interview in Britain in 1965, he joked about [his age], claiming that he'd made his first record in 1935. None of his peers would have said anything of the kind. Most of his '60s contemporaries were *aggressively* contemporary.'[37] This is a fair point, but what is most interesting is not what it says about Dylan but what it says about how the media perceive him. No journalist would have picked up on this comment in any significant way before 1997. Within the Dylan fan community, there also seems to be an increasing recognition of Dylan's rootedness in a range of musical traditions. There has been a reconsideration of the significance of Dylan's late sixties work (*The Basement Tapes*, *John Wesley Harding* and *Nashville Skyline*) – in part driven by Dylan's own playing of many songs from these albums on the NET – that sees these albums as extremely important, as the link between early and late Dylan and the proof of the rootedness of the mid-sixties flux. Marcus' book on *The Basement Tapes* was influential in this regard. Even *Self Portrait* is acquiring a moderate re-evaluation. There has also been a reappraisal of *Good As I Been To You* and *World Gone Wrong*, seeing them recontextualised as purposeful reconnections with traditional music rather than aimless contract filler by someone who couldn't write. Dylan's entire career is becoming understood in terms of its relationship to tradition.

This is not to suggest that there has been a complete inversion of Dylan's star-meaning. 'Dylan' still represents the radicalism and aesthetic revolution of the sixties, particularly to those whose only contact with him comes from short tabloid and magazine references. The standard caption for a picture of Dylan is still 'sixties icon' or 'former folk singer'. But within more serious analysis, and within Dylan's fan community, there has been some realignment that places emphasis on continuity. Whereas Dylan conventionally has been understood as chameleon-like, frequently changing persona, emphasis is now being placed upon the coherence of Dylan's relationship to music and stardom. All of Dylan's career is being reconceptualised, given a particular coherence and teleology, through the prism of his contemporary stardom. This rationalising, this ironing out of inconsistency, is conventionally something that happens to a star after their death. This is the star-time equivalent of what is achieved musically on the NET and on *Time Out Of Mind*. The effect is that we see Dylan's entire career in spatial rather than linear terms, subliminally conceptualising the whole of Dylan's career in any one of the parts. Instead of hearing all the different tambourine men in a particular performance of 'Mr Tambourine Man', we are able to see or hear all of the old Dylans in this particular moment's Bob Dylan. Here are two journalists' accounts of interviewing Dylan:

> As you sit across from him, his face keeps changing. Sometimes it's that I-see-right-through-you look from the cover of *Highway 61 Revisited* – you barely notice the white hairs among the curls, the two days' worth of stubble and the 30 years' worth of lines. Now he turns his head: there's the profile from *Blood On The Tracks*. Now he thrusts his chin up, and he's the funny, defiant kid who used to wear that Bob Dylan cap. (David Gates, 1997)

> The expressions on Dylan's face, in person, seem to compress and encompass versions of his persona across time . . .

Above all, though, it is the tones of his speaking voice that seem to kaleidoscope through time: here the yelp of the folk pup or the sarcastic rimshot timing of the hounded hipster-idol, there the beguilement of the seventies sex symbol . . . (Jonathon Lethem, 2006)

I know many Dylan fans who say similar things: how a specific phrase in an interview reminds them of some earlier interview they've seen; a wiggle of the leg and he looks just like he did in 1978; the way he stands and bears down at the piano, a cross between a gunslinger and a kitten, reminiscent of him playing 'Ballad Of A Thin Man' in 1966. Sometimes, for a moment, he can seem incredibly young.*

My argument, therefore, is that Dylan's contemporary stardom has, in some weird way, stepped out of its own history. His stardom emphasises its spatial dimensions rather than a sense of linear progression. This means that, in perceiving the Bob Dylan of the now, we simultaneously perceive the faces and voices of his entire career, not as a series of discrete moments but as some kind of unity, in the same way that we hear individual folk and blues songs not as discrete units but as embedded within a greater tradition. Dylan's contemporary stardom is no longer shadowed by the ghosts of past images; instead, his current stardom contains the images of his past. He has the past in his pocket, not on his back, as the following review makes clear:

The remarkable achievement of *"Love And Theft"* is that Dylan makes the past sound as strange, haunted and allur-

---

* This actually is another form of continuity. Speaking of some recording sessions in 1976, T-Bone Burnett claimed 'I don't know whether he time-travels or shape-shifts or what you would call it, but you would look at him one moment and he would like a fifteen-year-old kid and you would look at him the next moment and he would look like an eighty-year-old man, and at the time he was in his mid-thirties' (in Sounes, 2001:342).

ing as the future – and this song-and-dance man sings as though he's drunk too deeply of the past to be either scared or impressed by anybody's future, least of all his own.

This reorientation of Dylan's stardom has had a great impact on Dylan's status as a contemporary artist. Reviews of Dylan's 2001 album *"Love And Theft"* were almost universally flattering, and the response to the 2006 follow-up, *Modern Times* was almost as good.* *Modern Times* proved a remarkable commercial success too, reaching the Top 10 in many countries. In between these albums, responses to two non-musical releases offer evidence of how the contemporary Dylan image stands shoulder-to-shoulder with his sixties myth. These were his autobiography *Chronicles* (2004) and the movie documentary *No Direction Home* (2005). Both releases garnered an extraordinary amount of press coverage; as one film reviewer pointed out, Dylan is a rare breed of star who can make headlines simply by speaking. The majority reaction to both releases was positive. *Chronicles* was described as 'a landmark in musical memoirs', with praise for 'Dylan's extraordinary command of language, married in the book to an uncanny recall of events and a masterly narrative sensibility'. An equally enthusiastic response greeted Martin Scorsese's documentary *No Direction Home* ('the finest rock documentary you'll ever see'). What is notable about both releases is that they did not give cause for nostalgia; there was no sense of longing for the old Dylan, and no grumbling about the new Dylan's inadequacies. The documentary in particular gave an impression of the enormity of Dylan's achievements in the

---

* The very useful website Metacritic (http://www.metacritic.com/) collates and averages published reviews of films and music released since 2000. *"Love And Theft"* was the most highly rated album of 2001, averaging 93 per cent across all reviews. Currently, *Modern Times* was the third rated 2006 release, averaging 89 per cent.

sixties, but this did not detract from the older figure being interviewed. It was possible to see how the man in front of us was, in another lifetime, able to achieve such heights. All reviews portrayed Dylan as existing 'square in the moment', providing a distinct sense of who he is now. The interview Dylan gave for the documentary showed a wise man offering an omniscient view of history, giving 'his appearance . . . something of the quality of a statue come to life'. *Chronicles* was described as a 'book bursting with life' with the sense of Dylan as 'absolutely present'. Ultimately, the book 'serves a vital purpose in reminding us of Dylan's genius'.

Dylan's remarkable media presence in the last few years (conceivably greater than any time since the sixties) and the upturn in his reputation have given Dylan's star-image a particular swagger at this time. One reviewer suggested that he 'has never been more comfortable in his own skin'. When I said earlier that there was no place for irony in Dylan's contemporary image, it was a half-truth. There is scope for irony, not in relation to the songs, or to wider tradition, but with regard to Dylan's own myth. A notable feature of *"Love And Theft"* is the confidence of the whole presentation – the audacious borrowing, the musical swing, the vocal gymnastics. *"Love And Theft"* has the aura of a man so at ease in his idiom that he knows he is untouchable:

> You say my eyes are pretty and my smile is nice
> Well I'll sell 'em to you at a reduced price
> ('Honest With Me')

Whereas *Time Out Of Mind* had a consistent overall mood and sound, *"Love And Theft"* is defined by its eclecticism. Dylan takes on a variety of forms of American song – from rockabilly to crooning to bluegrass to urban blues – and the effect is to demonstrate his mastery of all of the currents of

American popular music.* 'Relaxed, magisterial, utterly confident in every musical idiom he touches' declared one reviewer. 'A greatest hits album', Dylan told Edna Gunderson in 2001, 'without the hits.'

No line better encompasses everything I'm suggesting here than one from 'Summer Days':

> She says 'You can't repeat the past.' I say, 'You can't?
> What do you mean you can't? Of course you can.'

This one line does so much! Firstly, it can be interpreted as a comment on Dylan's later career, of how he has managed to find endlessly creative ways of renewing the past. Secondly, the entire line, as so much of *"Love And Theft"* is stolen. In this instance taken not from a song but a novel, *The Great Gatsby*. Thirdly, its source actually brings to mind an earlier Dylan song, 'Ballad Of A Thin Man', in which he exclaims 'You've been through all of F. Scott Fitzgerald's books / You're very well read, it's well known' (which, in turn, produces the irony of Dylan claiming himself to be very well read, a particularly sharp one given the 'plagiarism controversy'). Finally, and most importantly, the sheer vocal audacity in being able to sing this ridiculously long line *as* a line emphasises Dylan's supreme confidence and 'ownership' of these stolen words. 'I contain multitudes', the singer tells us.

This confidence goes beyond singing style; it inhabits all of Dylan's contemporary stardom. Dylan knows the game being played and he knows he's good at it. Perhaps for the first time in thirty-five years, Dylan today speaks as someone

---

* His radio series, *Theme Time Radio Hour* has a similar effect. The eclectic and obscure songs selected by Dylan, and the information he gives about the artists between songs, give the impression of someone who just knows *everything* about all of this music.

in control of his myth. Who else, with a glint in his eye, could make you this offer?

> You're talking to a person who *owns* the sixties. . . . I own the sixties – who's going to argue with me? I'll give 'em to you if you want 'em. You can have 'em. (Jonathon Lethem interview, 2006)

And who could refuse?

NOTES

Chapter 1 Introduction

1 Bourdieu, 1993:162.
2 Schickel, 2000:108.
3 Evans and Hesmondhalgh, 2005:4.
4 Turner, 2004:14–15.
5 Scobie, 2003:85.
6 Schickel, 2000.
7 Rojek, 2001:9.
8 Frith, 2001:35.
9 Evans, 2005:2.
10 Rojek, 2004:173–4.
11 P. D. Marshall, 1997:37.
12 Turner, 2004:103.

Chapter 2 Stardom, Authorship and the Meaning of Songs

1 In Heylin, 2000:4.
2 Heylin, 2000:xv.
3 Smith, 2005:x.

4 Frith, 1998:185.
5 Dyer, 1998:61.
6 Dyer, 1998:153.
7 Sounes, 2001:100.
8 P. Williams, 1990:xvii.
9 Abrams, 1953.
10 Day, 1989; Ricks, 2003; Scobie, 2003.
11 Scobie, 2003:88.
12 Scobie, 2003:48.
13 Scobie, 2003:162.
14 Abrams, 1953:272.
15 Laing, 1990:327.
16 Ricks, 2003:19.
17 Gray, 2000.
18 Moore, 2001:181.
19 Frith, 1998:158–9.
20 In Moore, 2001:185–6.
21 Frith, 1998:164.
22 P. Williams, 2005:207.
23 Frith, 1998:166.
24 Frith, 1998:169.
25 P. Williams, 1996:16-19.
26 Moore, 2001:186.
27 Frith, 1988:120.
28 Hitchcock, 2006:89.
29 Bauldie, 1985:39.
30 Frith, 1998:172.
31 Hitchcock, 2006:89.
32 Barthes, 1990:297.
33 Barthes, 1990:295.
34 In Corcoran, 2002:11.
35 Frith, 1998:196–7.
36 Frith, 1998:186.
37 P. Marshall, 1997:90.

38 Brown, 2002:193.
39 Schickel, 2000.
40 Heylin, 2000:ix.
41 Roe, 2002:86.
42 Dyer, 1991:133–6.
43 Scobie, 2003:40.
44 Moran, 2000:23.
45 Gilman, 1989:5–6.
46 Stone 1990:169–72.
47 Barbas, 2001:35–57.
48 Dyer, 1998:21.
49 P. Williams, 1990:xvii.
50 Frith, 1998:210.
51 P. Williams, 1996:15.
52 Berger, 1972:27–8.
53 Ricks, 2003:360.
54 Dyer, 1998:62.

Chapter 3 Folk Stardom: Star as Ordinary, Star as Special

1 Street, 1986:5.
2 P. D. Marshall, 1997:195.
3 Rojek, 2004:2.
4 Cohn, 1996:16.
5 P. D. Marshall, 1997:196.
6 Hampton, 1986:164.
7 Hampton, 1986:150.
8 Hampton, 1986:158.
9 Cantwell, 1996:324.
10 Cantwell, 1996:337.
11 Goldmann, 1973:131.
12 In R. Williams, 1971:12,
13 Goldmann, 1966:250.
14 Hampton, 1986:214–15.
15 Cantwell, 1996:26–7

16 Harker, 1980:147–9
17 Lhamon, 1990:112.
18 Boyes, 1993:98.
19 Marcus, 1997:28.
20 Marcus, 1997:21.
21 Marcus, 1997:21.
22 Cantwell, 1996:319.
23 Street, 1986:154.
24 Street, 1986:155.
25 Cantwell, 1996:21.
26 In Cantwell, 1996:280.
27 In Cantwell, 1996:22.
28 In Heylin, 1991:74.
29 Cantwell, 1996:281.
30 Ricks, 2003:233.
31 P. Williams, 1990:93–4.
32 Hampton, 1986:55.
33 Ricks, 2003:324.
34 Ricks, 2003:263–4.
35 Hampton, 1986:55.
36 Hampton, 1986:198.
37 Carl Oglesby, one-time president of SDS (Students for a Democratic Society), in Scaduto, 1996:137–8.
38 Marqusee, 2003:3.
39 MacDonald, 1957:60.
40 Denisoff, 1971:185.
41 Cantwell, 1996:282.
42 Denselow, 1989:39.
43 Hampton, 1986:5.
44 Gibbens, 2001:4.
45 Rojek, 2001:28.
46 Dyer, 1998:42.
47 Cantwell, 1996:337.
48 Dyer, 1998:78.

49 Cantwell, 1996:346.
50 Street, 1986:162.
51 Rojek, 2001:9.

Chapter 4 Rock Stardom: Reconciling Culture and Commerce
1   Marcus, 1997:13.
2   Wicke, 1990:102.
3   Marqusee, 2003:132.
4   Frith et al., 2001:79–80.
5   Grossberg, 1992:131.
6   Keightley, 2001.
7   Keightley, 2001:126–7.
8   Frith, 1983:49-57.
9   Gendron, 2002:162–3.
10 Gendron, 2002:162.
11 Marcus, 1997:ix.
12 Schickel, 2000:83–4.
13 Svedburg, 1963.
14 Svedburg, 1963.
15 Scobie, 2003:55.
16 Scobie, 2003:56.
17 Scobie, 2003:55.
18 Ricks, 2003:183–4.
19 Grossberg, 1992:150-1.
20 Grossberg, 1992:155–6.
21 Grossberg, 1992:156.
22 Grossberg, 1992:208–9.
23 Heylin, 2000:154.
24 In Heylin, 2000:151.
25 Pattison, 1987:111–25.
26 In Frith, 1983:52–3.
27 In McGregor, 1972:74.
28 Keightley, 2001:136.
29 Frith, 1983:53.

30 Scobie, 2003:93.
31 Keightley, 2004:378.
32 Keightley, 2004:380.
33 Keightley, 2004:384.
34 Keightley, 2004:388.
35 In McGregor, 1972:55.
36 Street, 1986:143.
37 Keightley, 2001:122.
38 Grossberg, 1992:204.
39 Street, 1986:159.
40 Marqusee, 2003:124.
41 Marqusee, 2003:106.
42 Street, 1986:157.
43 Wicke, 1990:103.
44 Shelton, 1986: 303.
45 Frith et al., 2001:81.
46 Keightley, 2001:127.
47 Keightley, 2001:129.
48 Frith, 1983:50.
49 Wicke, 1990:106.
50 Wicke, 1990:15.
51 L. Marshall, 2005.
52 Wicke, 1990:107.
53 Frith, 1983:55.
54 P. D. Marshall, 1997:247.
55 Dyer, 1998:34.
56 Steen, 1966.

Chapter 5 Beyond Stardom: Rock History and Canonisation

1 Rojek, 2001:19–20
2 Turner, 2004:91.
3 P. Williams, 2005:241–2.
4 Dyer, 1998:5.
5 Gendron, 2002:190.

6 Gray, 2000:111.
7 See Negus, 1996:136–63, and Keightley (2004) for examples of critical accounts.
8 Marqusee, 2003:201–2.
9 Marqusee, 2003:122–3.
10 Marqusee, 2003:241–2.
11 Unknown, 1981 interview, in Heylin, 2000:313.
12 Scobie, 2003:124.
13 Eisenberg, 1987:61.

Chapter 6 Declining Stardom: Nostalgia and the 'Death of Rock'
1 Mäkela, 2004:242.
2 Schickel, 2000:85.
3 Heylin, 2000:506; 526.
4 Heylin, 2000:563.
5 Marcus, 1994:57–8.
6 Curtis,2002.
7 Mäkela, 2004:185–6.
8 Mäkela, 2004:184–96.
9 P. Williams, 1996:63–133.
10 Frith, 1988:1.
11 Negus, 1996:151.
12 Jameson, 1991:xv.
13 Lyotard, 1984: xxiv.
14 Keightley, 2001:140.
15 Bauldie, 1987:199.
16 Bauldie, 1987:202.
17 Heylin, 2000:524.
18 Burnett, 1996:23–4.
19 Frith, 1988:208.
20 Friedlander, 1996:264.
21 Frith, 1988:210.
22 In Burnett, 1996:96–7.
23 Frith, 1988:215–16.

24 http://www.riaa.com/gp/bestsellers/topartists.asp (last visited 10 Dec 2006).
25 Kelly, 1987:244.
26 Heylin, 2000:564.
27 Heylin, 2000:577.
28 Benjamin, 1992.
29 Heylin, 1987.
30 Paul Williams, in Scobie, 2003:114.
31 Day, 1989:73–4.
32 Gray, 2000:582.
33 Lindley, 1987:205.

Chapter 7 Redefining Stardom: The Never Ending Tour
1 P. Williams, 2005:54.
2 Smith, 2005:374.
3 Thornton, 1995:47.
4 Bennett, 1980, in Middleton, 1990:88.
5 Middleton, 1990:88.
6 Eisenberg, 1987:110.
7 Heylin, 1996:xi.
8 In Eisenberg, 1987:15.
9 Eagleton, 2000:1.
10 Eisenberg, 1987:14–15.
11 Eisenberg, 1987:24.
12 Thornton, 1995:41.
13 Thornton, 1995:49.
14 Frith, 1988:124–5.
15 See for example, Gray, 2000:851–2.
16 P. Williams, 2005:124.
17 Scobie, 2003:25.
18 P. Williams, 2006:92.
19 P. Williams (*Performing Artist*) (1990, 1992, 2005) and *Watching the River Flow* (1996).
20 P. Williams, 1990:180–1.

21 P. Williams, 2005:xi.
22 Gray, 2000:257.
23 Gray, 2000:835.
24 Heylin, 2000:xvii.
25 Scobie, 2003:118.
26 Scobie, 2003:118.
27 Gray, 2000:389.
28 Gray, 2000:855.
29 Eisenberg, 1987:51.
30 Levine, 1990:11–82.
31 Levine, 1990:72.
32 Storey, 1993:21-33.
33 Gray, 2000:850.
34 Gray, 2000:854.
35 P. Williams, 2005:35.
36 Eagleton, 2000:39.
37 Gray, 2000:846.
38 Gray, 2000:848.
39 Gray, 2000:845.
40 Marqusee, 2003:239, 270–1.

Chapter 8 Never ending Stardom: Dylan after Time Out Of Mind
1 Gray, 2000:822.
2 Sheffield, 2001.
3 P. Williams, 2005:311.
4 Frith, 1998:185–6.
5 Day, 2002:290.
6 Scobie, 2003: 296.
7 Johnny Borgan in P. Williams, 2005:309.
8 Eisenberg, 1987:27.
9 Tagg, 1984.
10 Frith, 1998:150–1.
11 Cited in Frith, 1998:145–6.
12 Frith, 1998:148.

13 Kramer, cited in Frith, 1998:149.
14 Cited in Frith, 1998: 154–5.
15 Heylin, 2000:686.
16 Scobie, 2003:108.
17 Scobie, 2003:97.
18 Jameson, 1991:25.
19 Skinner, 2006.
20 Skinner, 2006:61.
21 Skinner, 2006:59.
22 In Skinner, 2006:57.
23 Skinner, 2006:71.
24 Skinner, 2006:71.
25 Boyle, 2003.
26 Murray, 1997:6
27 Scobie, 2003:100.
28 Wilentz, 2002:305.
29 Cantwell, 1996:75.
30 Scobie, 2003:296.
31 In P. Williams, 2005:164.
32 Eliot, 1922.
33 Dyer, 1998:63.
34 Bennett, 1999:16.
35 Scobie, 2003:298.
36 P. Williams, 2005:310.
37 Hepworth, 2006:93.

BIBLIOGRAPHY

Abrams, M. H. (1953) *The Mirror and the Lamp: Romantic Theory and the Critical Tradition*. New York: Oxford University Press.

Barbas, S. (2001) *Movie Crazy: Fans, Stars and the Cult of Celebrity*. New York: Palgrave.

Barthes, R. (1990), 'The Grain of the Voice', in S. Frith and A. Goodwin, *On Record*. London: Routledge, pp. 293–300.

Bauldie, J. (1985) 'Tonal breath control', *The Telegraph* 19: 38–40.

Bauldie, J. (1987) 'The Oppression of Knowledge: No-One Can Sing the Blues Like Blind Willie McTell', in M. Gray and J. Bauldie, *All Across The Telegraph*. London: Futura, pp. 198–202.

Benjamin, W. (1992) 'The Work of Art in the Age of Mechanical Reproduction', in *Illuminations*. London: Fontana, pp. 211–44.

Bennett, A. (1999) *Romantic Poets and the Culture of Posterity*. Cambridge: Cambridge University Press.

Berger, J. (1972) *Ways of Seeing*. Harmondsworth: Penguin.

Bourdieu, P. (1993) *The Field of Cultural Production*. Cambridge: Polity.

Boyes, G. (1993) *The Imagined Village: Culture, Ideology and the English Folk Revival*. Manchester: Manchester University Press.

Boyle, D. (2003) *Authenticity, Brands, Fakes, Spin and the Lust for Real Life*. London: Flamingo.

Brown, R. (2002) 'Highway 61 and Other American States of Mind', in N. Corcoran, *Do You, Mr Jones? Bob Dylan with the Poets and the Professors*. London: Chatto & Windus, pp. 193–220.

Burnett, R. (1996) *The Global Jukebox: The International Music Industry*. London: Routledge.

Cantwell, R. (1996) *When We Were Good: The Folk Revival*. Cambridge, Mass.: Harvard University Press.

Cohn, N. (1996) *Awopbopaloobopalopbamboom*. London: Minerva.

Corcoran, N. (2002) 'Introduction: Writing Aloud', in N. Corcoran, *Do You, Mr Jones? Bob Dylan with the Poets and the Professors*. London: Chatto & Windus, pp. 7–24.

Curtis, A. (2002) *The Century of the Self*, BBC TV. Rebroadcast on BBC4 in 2004 (29 April, 30 April, 1 May, 2 May).

Day, A. (1989) *Jokerman: Reading the Lyrics of Bob Dylan*. Oxford: Blackwell.

Day, A. (2002) 'Looking for Nothing: Dylan Now', in N. Corcoran, *Do You, Mr Jones? Bob Dylan with the Poets and the Professors*. London: Chatto & Windus, pp. 275–93.

Denisoff, S. (1971) *Great Day Coming: Folk Music and the American Left*. Urbana: University of Illinois Press.

Denselow, R. (1989) *When the Music's Over: The Story of Political Pop*. London: Faber and Faber.

Dyer, R. (1991) 'A Star is Born and the Construction of Authenticity', in C. Gledhill, *Stardom: Industry of Desire.* London: Routledge, pp. 32–40.

Dyer, R. (1998) *Stars.* London: British Film Institute.

Eagleton, T. (2000) *The Idea of Culture.* Oxford: Blackwell.

Eisenberg, E. (1987) *The Recording Angel: The Experience of Music from Aristotle to Zappa.* New York: Penguin.

Eliot, T. S. (1922) *The Sacred Wood.* London: Methune. Available at http://www.bartleby.com/200/ (last visited 22 September 2006).

Evans, J. and D. Hesmondhalgh (2005) *Understanding Media: Inside Celebrity.* Milton Keynes: Open University Press.

Friedlander, P. (1996) *Rock and Roll: A Social History.* Boulder, CO: Westview Press.

Frith, S. (1983) *Sound Effects.* Bury St Edmunds: St Edmundsbury Press.

Frith, S. (1988) *Music for Pleasure: Essays in the Sociology of Pop.* Cambridge: Polity.

Frith, S. (1998) *Performing Rites.* Oxford: Oxford University Press.

Frith, S. (2001) 'The Popular Music Industry', in S. Frith, W. Straw and J. Street, *The Cambridge Companion to Pop and Rock.* Cambridge: Cambridge University Press, pp. 26–52.

Frith, S., W. Straw and J. Street (2001) *The Cambridge Companion to Pop and Rock.* Cambridge: Cambridge University Press.

Gendron, B. (2002) *Between Montmartre and the Mudd Club: Popular Music and the Avant-Garde.* Chicago: University of Chicago Press.

Gibbens, J. (2001) *The Nightingale's Code: A Poetic Study of Bob Dylan.* London: Touched Press.

Gillman, S. (1989) *Dark Twins: Imposture and Identity in Mark Twain's America.* Chicago: University of Chicago Press.

Goldmann, L. (1966) 'The Subject of Cultural Creation', *Boston Studies in the Philosophy of Science* 4: 241–60.

Goldmann, L. (1973) 'Introduction to the Problems of a Sociology of the Novel', *Telos* 18: 122–35.

Goldmann, L. (1975) 'Dialectical Materialism and Literary History', *New Left Review* 92: 39–51.

Gray, M. (2000) *Song and Dance Man III: The Art of Bob Dylan*. London: Cassell.

Grossberg, L. (1992) *We Gotta Get Outta This Place: Popular Conservatism and Postmodern Culture*. New York: Routledge.

Hampton, W. (1986) *Guerrilla Minstrels*. Knoxville: University of Tennessee Press.

Harker, D. (1980) *One for the Money: Politics and Popular Song*. London: Hutchinson.

Hepworth, D. (2006) '"He's a '60s guy"', *Word*, January, pp. 92–3.

Heylin, C. (1987) 'Lyrics 1962–1985: A Collection Short of the Definitive', in M. Gray and J. Bauldie, *All Across The Telegraph*. London: Futura, pp. 229–42.

Heylin, C. (1991) *Behind the Shades*. London: Penguin.

Heylin, C. (1996) *Dylan Behind Closed Doors: The Recording Sessions 1960–1994*. London: Penguin.

Heylin, C. (2000) *Behind the Shades: Take Two*. London: Penguin.

Hilburn, R. (1992) 'What becomes a legend most? A never-ending tour, a new audience and keeping the mystery alive', *Los Angeles Times Magazine*, 9 February.

Hitchcock, R. (2006) '"He can't sing"', *Word*, January, p. 89.

Jackson, A. (1997)' 'Bob Dylan revisited', *The Times Magazine*, 15 November.

Jameson, F. (1991) *Postmodernism or, the Cultural Logic of Late Capitalism*. Durham, NC: Duke University Press.

Keightley, K. (2001) 'Reconsidering Rock', in S. Frith, W. Straw and J. Street, *The Cambridge Companion to Pop and Rock*. Cambridge: Cambridge University Press, 109–42

Keightley, K. (2004) 'Long Play: Adult-Oriented Popular Music and the Temporal Logics of the Post-War Sound Recording Industry in the USA', *Media Culture and Society* 26(3): 375–91.

Kelly, R. (1987) 'Fans, Collectors and Biograph', in M. Gray and J. Bauldie, *All Across The Telegraph*. London: Futura, pp. 243–9.

Laing, D. (1990) 'Listen to Me', in S. Frith and A. Goodwin, *On Record*. London: Routledge, pp. 326–40.

Levine, L. (1990) *Highbrow/Lowbrow: The Emergence of Cultural Hierarchy in America*. London: Harvard University Press.

Lhamon, W. (1990) 'Dylan's living lore', *The Telegraph* 37: 102–31.

Lindley, J. (1987) 'Highway 84 Revisited', in M. Gray and J. Bauldie, *All Across The Telegraph*. London: Futura, pp. 204–8.

Lyotard, J.-F. (1984) *The Postmodern Condition: A Report On Knowledge*. Manchester: Manchester University Press.

MacDonald, D. (1957) 'A Theory of Mass Culture', in B. Rosenberg and D. Manning White, *Mass Culture: The Popular Arts in America*. New York: MacMillan, pp. 59–73.

McGregor, C. (1972) *Bob Dylan: A Retrospective*. London: Picador.

McGuigan, J. (1992) *Cultural Populism*. London: Routledge.

Mäkela, J. (2004) *John Lennon Imagined: Cultural History of a Rock Star*. New York: Peter Lang.

Marcus, G. (1994) *Ranters and Crowd Pleasers: Punk in Pop Music, 1977–1992*. New York: Anchor.

Marcus, G. (1997) *Invisible Republic: Bob Dylan's Basement Tapes*. London: Picador.

Marqusee, M. (2003) *Chimes of Freedom: The Politics of Bob Dylan's Art*. New York: The New Press.

Marshall, L. (2005) *Bootlegging: Romanticism and Copyright in the Music Industry*. London: Sage.

Marshall, P. D. (1997) *Celebrity and Power: Fame in Contemporary Culture*. Minneapolis: University of Minnesota.

Meisel, P. (1999) *The Cowboy and the Dandy: Crossing over from Romanticism to Rock and Roll*. New York: Oxford University Press.

Middleton, R. (1990) *Studying Popular Music*. Milton Keynes: Open University Press.

Moore, A. (2001) *Rock: The Primary Text*. Aldershot: Ashgate.

Moran, J. (2000) *Star Authors: Literary Celebrity in America*. London: Pluto.

Murray, C. (1997) 'Monty Dylan and the Holy Greil', *The Independent*, 24 May, books section, p. 6.

Negus, K. (1996) *Popular Music in Theory: An Introduction*. Middletown: Wesleyan University Press.

Pattison, R. (1987) *The Triumph of Vulgarity: Rock Music in the Mirror of Romanticism*. Oxford: Oxford University Press.

Ricks, C. (2003) *Dylan's Visions of Sin*. London: Penguin.

Roe, N. (2002) 'Playing Time', in N. Corcoran, *Do You, Mr Jones? Bob Dylan with the Poets and the Professors*. London: Chatto & Windus, 81–104.

Rojek, C. (2001) *Celebrity*. London: Reaktion Books.

Rojek, C. (2004) *Frank Sinatra*. Cambridge: Polity.

Scaduto, A. (1996) *Bob Dylan*. London: Helter Skelter.

Schickel, R. (2000) *Intimate Strangers: The Culture of Celebrity in America*. Chicago: Ivan R. Dee.

Scobie, S. (2003) *Alias Bob Dylan Revisited*. Calgary: Red Deer Press.

Shank, B. (2002) '"That Wild Mercury Sound": Bob Dylan and the Illusion of American Culture', *Boundary 2* 29(1): 97–123.

Sheffield, R. (2001) '"Love and Theft" review', *Rolling Stone*, 27 September, p. 878. Available at http://www. rollingstone.com/reviews/album/235544/love_and_theft (last visited 22 September 2006).

Shelton, R. (1986) *No Direction Home: The Life and Music of Bob Dylan*. London: Penguin.

Skinner, K. (2006) '"Must be born again": Resurrecting the Anthology of American Folk Music', *Popular Music* 25(1): 57–75.

Smith, L. D. (2005) *Writing Dylan: Confessions of a Lonesome Traveller*. Westport: Praeger.

Sounes, H. (2001) *Down the Highway: The Life of Bob Dylan*. London: Black Swan.

Steen, M. (1966) interview by Margaret Steen, *The Toronto Star Weekly*, 29 January. Available at http://www.punkhart. com/dylan/interviews/nov_1965.html (last visited 22 September 2006).

Stone, L. (1990) *The Family, Sex and Marriage in England 1500–1800*. London: Penguin.

Storey, J. (1993) *An Introductory Guide to Cultural Theory and Popular Culture*. London: Harvester Wheatsheaf.

Street, J. (1986) *Rebel Rock: The Politics of Popular Music*. Oxford: Blackwell.

Svedburg, A. (1963) 'I am my words', *Newsweek*, 4 November.

Tagg, P. (1984) 'Understanding Musical Time Sense', at http://www.tagg.org/articles/xpdfs/timesens.pdf.

Thornton, S. (1995) *Club Cultures: Music, Media and Subcultural Capital*. Cambridge: Polity.

Turner, G. (2004) *Understanding Celebrity*. London: Sage.

Wicke, P. (1990) *Rock Music: Culture, Aesthetics and Sociology*. Cambridge: Cambridge University Press.

Wilentz, S. (2002) 'American Recordings: On "Love and Theft" and Minstrel Boy', in N. Corcoran, *Do You, Mr*

Jones? Bob Dylan with the Poets and the Professors. London. Chatto & Windus, pp. 295–305.

Williams, P. (1990) *Bob Dylan Performing Artist 1960–1973.* London: Xanadu.

Williams, P. (1992) *Bob Dylan Performing Artist: The Middle Years 1974–1986.* London: Omnibus.

Williams, P. (1996) *Watching the River Flow: Observations on His Art in Progress 1965–1995.* London: Omnibus.

Williams, P. (2005) *Bob Dylan: Performing Artist 1986–1990 and Beyond.* London: Omnibus.

Williams, P. (2006) '"Today Dylan radically reinterprets his own material when he plays it live"', *Word,* January, p. 92.

Williams, R. (1971) 'Literature and Sociology: In Memory of Lucien Goldmann', *New Left Review* 67: 3–18.

Wynands, S. (2000) 'Celebrity Stardom and the End of Mimetic Identity: Sam Shepard's "True Dylan"', *Essays in Theatre/Études Théâtrales* 19(1): 59–70.

Zollo, P. (ed.) (1997) *Songwriters on Songwriting.* New York: Da Cupo Press, pp. 69–86.

LIST OF INTERVIEWS

The interviews I have used for this book come from a variety of sources: original magazines, edited collections, transcripts in fanzines, websites and tape recordings of the actual interviews. Where possible, I have used full transcripts and/or tapes rather than the published interview in order to reduce journalistic selectivity. Listed below are the interviewer and the date of the interview referenced in the text, as accurately as possible, followed by the original publication details for each interview. A good place to start looking for transcripts are the following websites: http://www.interferenza.com/bcs/interv.htm; http://www.taxhelp. com/interviews.html.

Edwin Miller, June or July 1962
'Bob Dylan sings in Washington Square', *Seventeen*, September 1962.
Nat Hentoff, 9 June 1964
'The crackin', shakin', breakin' sounds', *The New Yorker*, 24 October 1964.

Jack Goddard, 3 March 1965 (scripted)
'Dylan meets the press', *Village Voice*, 25 March 1965.
Paul Robbins, 27 March 1965
Unknown title, *Los Angeles Free Press*, 10, 17 and 24 September 1965.
Laurie Henshaw, 12 May 1965
Unknown title, *Disc and Music Echo*, 22 May 1965.
Ray Coleman, 12 May 1965
'Dylan in depth', *Melody Maker*, 22 May 1965.
Frances Taylor, August 1965
Unknown title, *Long Island Press*, 17 October 1965.
Nora Ephron and Susan Edmiston, August 1965
Published in C. McGregor, 1975, *Bob Dylan: A Retrospective*, London: Picador.
Sydney press conference, 13 April 1966
Reported by Craig McGregor in the *Sydney Morning Herald*, 13 April 1966.
Jules Siegel, 1966
'What have we here?', *Saturday Evening Post*, 30 July 1966.
Jann Wenner, June 1969
'The *Rolling Stone* interview', *Rolling Stone*, 29 November 1969.
Neil Hickey, mid-1976
Unknown title, *TV Guide*, 11 September 1976.
Craig McGregor, April 1978
'Tangled up in blue', *New Musical Express*, 22 April 1978.
Philippe Adler, 16 June 1978
Unknown title, *L'express*, 3 July 1978.
Ray Coleman, 20 June 1978
'Why Dylan stays forever young', *Melody Maker*, 1 July 1978.
Lynne Allen, 12 December 1978
'Interview with an icon', *Trouser Press*, June 1979.
Dave Herman, 2 July 1981
Broadcast on WNEW-FM (New York), 27 July 1981 and released by CBS as a promotional album.

Neil Spencer, 20 July 1981
'That diamond voice within', *New Musical Express*, 15 August 1981.

Mick Brown, June 1984
'Jesus, who's got time to keep up with the times?', *Sunday Times*, 1 July 1984.

Bruce Kleinman, 24 November 1984
'Dylan on Dylan', audio interview for *Westwood One* US radio series.

Bill Flanagan, March 1985
Published in B. Flanagan, 1990, *Written in my Soul*, London: Music Sales Ltd.

Cameron Crowe, August 1985
Accompanying booklet for *Biograph* box set.

Robert Hilburn, October 1985
'At 44 Bob Dylan looks back', *Chicago Sun Times*, 17 November 1985.

David Fricke, late 1985
Unknown title, *Rolling Stone*, 5 December 1985.

Toby Cresswell, early 1986
'Gates of Eden revisited', *Rolling Stone* (Australian edition), 16 January 1986.

Christopher Sykes, 18 October 1986
Recorded for the BBC documentary 'Getting to Dylan', part of the *Omnibus* series, broadcast September 1987.

Robert Hilburn, February 1992
'What becomes a legend most? A never-ending tour, a new audience and keeping the mystery alive', *Los Angeles Times Magazine*, 9 February 1992.

Gary Hill, 3 October 1993
Unknown title, *The Boston Herald American*, 18 October 1993.

Ellen Futterman, early 1994
'Times they are a-changin'. . . Dylan speaks', *St Louis Post-Dispatch Entertainment Section*, 7 April 1994.

Joe Dolen, 25 or 26 September 1995
'A midnight chat with Bob Dylan', *Fort-Lauderdale Sun Sentinel Today*, 29 September 1995.

Jon Pareles, w/c 21 September 1997
'A wiser voice blowin' in the autumn wind', *New York Times*, 27 September 1997.

Edna Gunderson, w/c 21 September 1997
'At the heart of Dylan', *USA Today*, 29 September 1997.

David Gates, w/c 21 September 1997
'Dylan revisited', *Newsweek*, 6 October 1997.

Robert Hilburn, December 1997
'Reborn again', *Los Angeles Times*, 14 December 1997.

Murray Englehart, 1999
'Maximum Bob', *Guitar World*, March 1999.

Mikal Gilmore, 2001
'Bob Dylan: an interview', *Rolling Stone*, 22 November 2001.

Robert Hilburn, 2004
'Rock's enigmatic poet opens a long-private door', *Los Angeles Times*, 4 April 2004.

Ed Bradley, late 2004
Broadcast on *60 Minutes*, CBS Television, 5 December 2004.

Edna Gunderson, 2004
'Dylan chronicles his journey', *USA Today*, 5 October 2004.

Jonathon Lethem, 2006
'The genius of Bob Dylan', *Rolling Stone*, 7 September 2006.

Copyright
Acknowledgements

INDEX